"Through powerful personal accounts, *Under Fire* gives an inside look at how this war was a watershed for journalism in more ways than one as spin-doctors and propagandists, on all sides, raised their art to new levels. It is filled with lessons for coverage of future conflicts. This is a tough-minded look inside the war as it really was and is superb war reporting by one of the world's premier news organizations."

—Dan Rather,
CBS Evening News

"Reuters has produced a marvelous book on the Iraq campaign filled with gripping front-line reportage as well as sharp discussion of what it was like to cover the fighting both as a reporter 'embedded' with the U.S. military and as a 'unilateral' operating alone. The book also gives a riveting analysis of reaction to the conflict in the Arab world."

—Peter Bergen, author of
*Holy War, Inc.: Inside the Secret
World of Osama bin Laden*

"As an embedded journalist, I saw only one tiny sliver of the war.
"Reuters fills in the blanks with insight, emotion, and even drama. One war from more than a dozen distinct and fascinating perspectives. *Under Fire* lets readers experience parts of the war that many may have missed, or misunderstood."

—John Berman,
Correspondent, ABC News

"First class reporting and analysis from the unsung heroes of Reuters."

—Martin Bell,
OBE, BBC reporter
and author of
*Through Gates of Fire:
A Journey into World Disorder*

Under Fire

Untold Stories from the Front Line of the Iraq War

Library of Congress Cataloging-in-Publication Data

A CIP catalog record for this book can be obtained from the Library of Congress

Publisher: Tim Moore
Executive editor: Jim Boyd
Director of production: Sophie Papanikolaou
Production supervisor: Nicholas Radhuber
Marketing manager: John Pierce

Manufacturing manager: Alexis Heydt-Long
Editorial assistant: Linda Ramagnano
Cover design director: Jerry Votta
Cover designer: Anthony Gemmellaro
Art director: Gail Cocker-Bogusz

Reuters
Executive editor: Stephen Jukes
Coordinating editor: Peter Millership
Commercial manager: Alisa Bowen
Front cover art photographer: Jerry Lampen
Cover photo copyright © 2003 Reuters

In compiling this book, thanks go to many people at Reuters including Doina Chiacu, David Cutler, Giles Elgood, Chris Helgren, Nicola MacPherson, Ingrid Montbazet, Barry Moody, Mair Salts and Alexia Singh.

Prentice Hall offers excellent discounts on this book when ordered in quantity for bulk purchases or special sales.

For information please contact: Corporate and Government Sales (800) 382-3419, or corpsales@pearsontechgroup.com

For sales outside of the U.S., please contact: International Sales (317) 581-3793, or international@pearsontechgroup.com

Printed in the United States of America

First Printing

ISBN 0-13-142397-5

Pearson Education LTD.
Pearson Education Australia PTY, Limited
Pearson Education Singapore, Pte. Ltd.
Pearson Education North Asia Ltd.
Pearson Education Canada, Ltd.
Pearson Educación de Mexico, S.A. de C.V.
Pearson Education—Japan
Pearson Education Malaysia, Pte. Ltd.

CONTENTS

FOREWORD

Propaganda, spin and half truths. Throughout the history of warfare, generals and political leaders have sought to influence and win over public opinion, trying to control the flow of information and ensure that their version of events is written into history.

It is equally the role of the war correspondent to cut through the propaganda, spot the spin and uncover the truth.

There is one tried and tested means of doing this—eyewitness reporting, covering a war as it unfolds from the front line and not being afraid to ask the awkward question.

And that is what this book is about: reporting the war in Iraq at first hand, not just from the U.S. and British perspectives on the battlefield, but also from the hospitals and the streets of Baghdad and throughout the rest of the country. In short, from as many angles as possible.

During the war, Reuters had more than 70 reporters, photographers and television news staff inside Iraq, some 30 of them "embedded" with U.S. and British forces; around 20 in Baghdad, subject to "minders," courtesy of the Iraqi Information Ministry; and others dubbed "unilaterals," working independently.

In this fashion, Reuters was able to piece together the complex mosaic of the 21 days it took to topple Saddam Hussein. The goal was to cover the war from all sides, in as balanced, factual and objective fashion as was possible. In the following pages, 15 Reuters correspondents tell their stories of the campaign.

Luke Baker, Adrian Croft, Andrew Gray, Matthew Green and Sean Maguire all rode with the U.S. forces and recount uneasy tales of the race to Baghdad as the troops' emotions seesawed between heady elation and raw fear; John Chalmers tells the story of U.S. Central Command headquarters in Doha, widely criticized by the media for its attempts to control the flow of information.

Nadim Ladki and Samia Nakhoul describe life under bombardment in Baghdad, slipping their minders whenever possible to check on the damage caused by air strikes and capturing the mood on the street. Their accounts include the death of Reuters cameraman Taras Protsyuk when a U.S tank shelled the Palestine Hotel. Samia Nakhoul, seriously injured in the same attack, tells of the operation by Baghdad neurosurgeons that saved her life while the battle for the city was still being waged. Tragically, a second Reuters cameraman, Mazen Dana, was to die on the outskirts of Baghdad in August. The death toll of journalists in this conflict has been unacceptably high.

By the time Reuters correspondent Rosalind Russell arrived in Baghdad a little after the attack on the Palestine Hotel, the statue of Saddam had been pulled down and looting was in full swing. Tigers in the city's zoo were crazed after weeks without food, and a patient at the al-Rashad psychiatric hospital appeared to be the sanest person in town.

Mike Collett-White, David Fox, Michael Georgy, Christine Hauser and Saul Hudson all spent the war and its immediate aftermath among the people of Iraq. They tell how ordinary Iraqis reacted to life after Saddam and after the demise of the all-powerful, all-seeing Baath Party. The mixed emotions felt by Iraqis toward the U.S. and British troops—liberators or occupiers?—run throughout their accounts.

Their reports include how thousands of Shi'ites from all over Iraq converged on Kerbala to mark one of the holiest events in their calendar, a gathering banned under Saddam since 1977; how an incongruous group of Iranian rebels in northeastern Iraq reached an uneasy peace with the Americans; and of life in the north with Kurdish fighters, the enclave wrested from Saddam's control after the 1991 Gulf War.

From Cairo, Caroline Drees captures the mood of the Arab world, united in anger and frustration at the United States and Britain.

Day by day during the war, each of these journalists and their colleagues provided a snapshot or tiny sliver of what was going on. The 15 authors in this book were part of a much bigger team effort. By pulling together all the strands of our news-gathering on editing desks in Dubai, London, Washington and Singapore, Reuters was able to cut through some of the fog of war.

But fog, of course, there was. This was arguably the most reported war in history—nearly 1,000 journalists were embedded with U.S. and British forces—and yet at times it seemed as though confusion reigned. Rumors quickly became fact. It is now a cliché, but as U.S. Sen. Hiram Johnson said, "The first casualty when war comes, is truth."

The port of Umm Qasr fell, by one count, 11 times before Iraqi resistance actually petered out; a popular uprising said to have broken out in Basra turned out to be wishful thinking on the part of the Americans and British; barrels of chemicals were found in the desert and hailed as weapons of mass destruction. But they turned out not to be.

In fact, the war marked a watershed for modern journalism in more ways than one.

The concept of embedding was historically far from new. Indeed, William Howard Russell was probably the first embedded journalist when he reported in 1854 on the Crimean War for *The Times* of London. Winston Churchill was also embedded as a 25-year-old correspondent in the Boer War (1899–1902) and famously mixed the roles of objective journalist and combatant by directing military action against the Boers when a British armored train was ambushed.

But all this was in stark contrast to the 1991 Gulf War, when the closest many journalists came to battlefield action was the video game-style film shown in the daily briefings by Central Command. For a generation of reporters covering the Iraq war 12 years later, embedding was new.

But did embedded mean being "in bed" with the troops?

Reuters decided it was essential to have this front-line perspective *but only* if it could be balanced with views from outside. In his account of the war, Andrew Gray—embedded with the U.S. 2nd Battalion 70th Armored Regiment—tells of daily frustrations. There was no hopping out of the Humvee to check out more closely what was going on. Where the soldiers went, you went too. They dictated the timetable.

Then there was the insidious danger of living, traveling and eating, day in, day out, with soldiers you were supposed to be reporting on. Many of the journalists who flocked to the conflict from around the world dressed and looked like soldiers. Some of the more gung-ho journalists even acted like them. One newspaper reporter began a story with the words, "We rode at dawn, the men of the 1st Royal Irish."

In truth, even the most hard-bitten reporter is likely to form some kind of bond with the soldiers he or she is covering.

This, then, was unique for the vast majority of journalists in Iraq, and the media had little by way of recent experience to guide them. How did you report objectively about men on whom you depended for your transport, food and for your very life? What did you do when those men made tragic mistakes and, as indeed happened, killed families driving toward a checkpoint?

Sean Maguire witnessed one Iraqi family torn apart in crossfire, a young girl suffering gunshot wounds and hideous eye injuries. Maguire was embedded with U.S. Marines, his unit moved on and he was frustrated. He couldn't carry through on the journalist's instinct to follow up on the story. It was six weeks later that he learned the name of the girl, Tghreed, and that she had survived but lost her right eye.

And so media guidelines for "embeds" evolved as the war advanced toward Baghdad, and valuable lessons were learned for covering future conflicts.

Embedded journalists actually signed up to military rules, the most important one being, understandably, that the exact location of a unit should not be revealed. But few of the reporters suffered from overt censorship by the Americans or British. In what seems to be a rare incident, one journalist, not working for Reuters, told of how her description of British soldiers "running for cover" was changed to "dashing for cover" because "running" sounded cowardly.

Embedding, coupled with the instant communications technology available to the press, clearly offered a new insight into the war. It delivered compelling television images in a way never seen before. But it is essential that the danger and temptation of self-censorship are recognized and countered.

Did Western news organizations then sanitize the war themselves? Certainly there were few images of dead Iraqis shown on U.S. television and only a few more in Europe, and those very late at night.

The Al Jazeera television network and other Arabic broadcasters rewrote the rules of the game and went to the other extreme, showing harrowing images of dead Iraqis and infuriating Washington and London by broadcasting images of dead U.S. and British prisoners and servicemen. Was this Iraqi propaganda or war in all its graphic horror? Was it factual reporting that simply breached the bounds of Western taste? Or was it gratuitous depiction of violence? Whichever of the above, Al Jazeera's cover prompted some Western media organizations to suggest it is time to re-evaluate their own policies.

Samia Nakhoul's brave reporting in Baghdad led her to the hospital bed of 12-year-old Ali Abbas Ismaeel, his arms torn off and reduced to stumps by a bomb blast, his body blackened and charred. The story and pictures taken by Reuters photographer Faleh Kheiber, also wounded at the Palestine Hotel a few days later, resonated around the world. Ali became the symbol of the suffering of Iraqi children, and campaigns were launched to raise money for him and others. Those were incredibly difficult pictures to look at, but they told the story so powerfully.

Of course, the spin-doctors, on all sides, raised their art to new levels.

Doha briefings, hailed by war commander Tommy Franks as a "platform for truth," were delivered from a Hollywood-style film set and caused an uproar among journalists—there was very little hard news offered, and what there was often came out first from the embedded reporters or from those back in Washington or London. But journalists who publicly criticized the Doha set-up were sometimes accused of being unpatriotic.

In London, the BBC became embroiled in a bitter dispute with the government, and Prime Minister Tony Blair's director of communications, Alastair Campbell, over whether the case for war had been "sexed up." It ended up with the apparent suicide of weapons expert David Kelly and a full blown independent judicial inquiry that dominated the British press throughout the summer.

From Baghdad, Iraqi Information Minister Mohammed Saeed al-Sahaf's confident pronouncements about Iraqi successes first enthralled Western television audiences, but he quickly turned into "Comical Ali" as his assertions provoked disbelief and then ridicule. But for Iraqis, he was anything but that. He was a figure who inspired fear, and many Iraqis appeared to have believed his confident daily accounts of impending American defeat.

And how much did journalists themselves provide the spin? The now famous toppling of Saddam's statute, so neatly symbolizing his downfall and echoing the fall of the Berlin Wall, appears to have been spontaneous enough. But it was hardly a mass popular uprising on the streets of Baghdad. When the cameras panned out, it quickly became evident that there were very few Iraqis around, and the statue was actually toppled with help from an American armored vehicle.

Although many journalists had actually pulled out of Baghdad before the war started, this was one of the most deadly wars on record for journalists—18 journalists or their colleagues had died in Iraq by mid-September—12 up to the time Saddam's government fell on April 9.

Then there were the casualties suffered by the U.S., British and Iraqi militaries and amongst the Iraqi civilian population. The overall Iraqi death toll will probably never be known, but academics and peace activists have estimated that up to 9,650 civilians died during the conflict and its aftermath.

The loss of life among journalists is nonetheless unacceptable and all the more disturbing, since it comes at a time when the media are better trained and better equipped to work in war zones than ever before.

An investigation by U.S. Central Command into the shelling of the Palestine Hotel concluded that U.S. forces acted appropriately and in self-defense. By mid-September, only a summary of the investigation had been released but on the face of it there are several unanswered questions. The hotel was home to the international media community in Baghdad and it had seemed to be the safest place in town, the scene of countless live television broadcasts. The highest levels of the U.S. military command were aware of this, but why were soldiers fighting on the streets of Baghdad not informed?

The media needs to know why Taras Protsyuk and Telecinco's Spanish cameraman, José Couso, were killed at the Palestine Hotel. We need to know why Mazen Dana, also killed by U.S. fire when he was filming outside a Baghdad jail, and other journalists died. We need to know for their colleagues and families and to learn lessons for the future.

Journalists have a right to report, without fear of attack or intimidation, whether embedded or working independently as free agents.

For only by covering all sides of a conflict do journalists have a hope of being able to distinguish truth from propaganda.

Stephen Jukes
Reuters Global Head of News
May 2000–October 2003

Iraq War Chronology

- **March 20** - President Bush announces start of campaign to oust Saddam, saying selected targets were hit by air raids in bid to "decapitate" the Iraqi leadership.

  Saddam appears on TV, three hours after raids began, urging Iraqis to defend their country. It was impossible to determine when broadcast was recorded.

  Iraq fires missiles at Kuwait, sending U.S. troops scrambling into chemical protective suits and setting off air raid sirens in Kuwait City.

- **March 21** - Invasion forces sweep into southern Iraq. Marines attack port of Umm Qasr. British troops capture Faw peninsula and take control of oil installations.

  Eight British soldiers and four U.S. airmen killed in helicopter crash on Iraqi border.

  U.S.-led forces unleash devastating blitz on Baghdad. Missiles slam into Saddam's palaces and key government buildings.

- **March 22** - Seven killed—six Britons and one American—when two Royal Navy Sea King helicopters collide.

- **March 23** - Royal Air Force Tornado jet shot down by U.S. Patriot missile near Kuwait border in first known "friendly fire" incident of war.

  Two U.S. soldiers are killed and 14 wounded in grenade attack at tented command center in Kuwait. A U.S. serviceman was arrested.

- **April 3** - Power goes off in most of Baghdad for first time since war began.

- **April 4** - U.S. forces seize control of Baghdad's Saddam International airport and rename it Baghdad International.

  Iraqi television shows footage of what it says is Saddam visiting residential areas of Baghdad.

- **April 5** - U.S. forces enter Baghdad for first time and take headquarters of Medina division of Saddam's Republican Guard.

- **April 7** - U.S. forces storm Baghdad, seizing two of Saddam's palace complexes.

  U.S. aircraft drop four 2,000-pound bombs on building after U.S. intelligence reports say Saddam and his sons Uday and Qusay might have been inside.

- **April 8** - U.S. tank fires a shell at Palestine Hotel in Baghdad packed with foreign journalists, killing cameraman from Reuters and another from Spain's Tele 5, just hours after Al Jazeera says one of its correspondents was killed by American fire.

- **April 9** - Saddam's rule collapses as U.S. forces sweep into Baghdad, taking control of capital and toppling statue of the Iraqi leader.

- **April 10** - Kurdish fighters take the northern oil city of Kirkuk as U.S. troops mop up die-hard Saddam supporters in Baghdad.

  Senior Iraqi Shi'ite leader Abdul Majid al-Khoei killed by mob at mosque in holy city of Najaf.

- **March 25** - Umm Qasr, where U.S. and British forces faced Iraqi resistance, is declared "safe and open."

  Convoy of Marines crosses Euphrates River and Saddam Canal at Nassiriya, resuming advance to Baghdad.

  Sandstorm descends on U.S. armored column slowing its advance on Baghdad.

- **March 26** - At least 15 people die in explosion in residential and commercial street in Baghdad's Shaab district. U.S. officials say

blast could have been caused by errant missile or anti-aircraft artillery or missiles fired by Iraqi military.

About 1,000 U.S. troops parachute into Kurdish-held northern Iraq and take control of an airfield.

- **March 28** - B-2 bomber drops two "bunker-buster" bombs on downtown Baghdad communications tower.

  At least 62 people are killed in air strike that hit Baghdad market.

- **March 29** - Car bomb explodes at U.S. checkpoint near city of Najaf, about 100 miles south of Baghdad, killing four U.S. soldiers.

- **April 2** - Marines seize bridge over Tigris River in central Iraq and take control of main highway from Kut to Baghdad.

  U.S. forces encircle Kerbala.

  U.S. Brig. Gen. Vincent Brooks says U.S. troops have destroyed one of six Republican Guard divisions defending Baghdad.

- **April 11** - U.S. and Kurdish forces take Iraq's third city of Mosul without a fight, sealing victory in the north.

  U.S. military issues deck of cards depicting 55 most-wanted Iraqi leaders.

- **April 12** - Amid widespread looting in Baghdad, priceless antiquities disappear from the National Museum.

- **April 14** - Marines enter Tikrit, Saddam's home town, taking control of Saddam's power base.

- **April 15** - Iraqi political and religious leaders hold first talks on their country's future with U.S. and British officials and pledge to work for democratic, federal Iraq.

- **April 22** - Thousands of U.S. soldiers pour into Mosul in tanks and armored trucks in show of force aimed at intimidating heavily armed rival factions.

  Hundreds of thousands of Shi'ite Muslims swarm through Iraq's holy city of Kerbala in pilgrimage marked by religious

fervor and slogans demanding U.S. troops leave.

- **April 28** - About 250 leading Iraqis from across political and ethnic spectrum hold meeting, convened by United States to launch new democracy in Iraq.

  U.S. troops shoot dead at least 13 Iraqis staging anti-American protest in town of Falluja.

- **May 1** - Bush says major combat operations in Iraq over

Routes the writers took during the Iraq war

 ①

Luke Baker
Advanced with U.S. 3rd Infantry, reached Baghdad airport

 ②

John Chalmers
In Doha with U.S. Central Command until April 19

 ③

Mike Collett-White
In northern Iraq, covered fall of Kirkuk and Mosul

 ④

Adrian Croft
With U.S. forces in Umm Qasr and Nassiriya

 ⑤

Caroline Drees
Reported from Cairo

 ⑥

David Fox
In southern Iraq, then headed for Baghdad and Tikrit

 ⑦

Michael Georgy
Mostly based in south, around Umm Qasr and Nassiriya

 ⑧

Andrew Gray
Advanced with U.S. 3rd Infantry to southern Baghdad

 ⑨

Matthew Green
Advanced with U.S. Marines, reached Baghdad on April 9

 ⑩

Christine Hauser
Covered Shi'ite pilgrimage to holy city of Kerbala

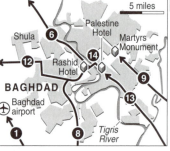

→ Main routes of correspondents

/// Kurdish-held area at start of war

Correspondents used satphones and laptops to transmit stories from cities and remote battlefields to Dubai

⑪

Saul Hudson
Trips included travels with Iranian Mujahideen rebels

⑫

Nadim Ladki
In Baghdad for most of war, expelled just before fall of city

⑬

Sean Maguire
Advanced with U.S. Marines, reached Baghdad on April 9

⑭

Samia Nakhoul
Wounded by U.S. tank fire on Baghdad Palestine Hotel

⑮

Rosalind Russell
Covered fall of Basra and looting in Baghdad after war

Chapter 1

Heavy Metal Warriors

By Luke Baker

Lost in the Desert

You know a sandstorm's bad when you can no longer see because your eyes are glued shut by a cement of sand and tears. You can't breathe because your nose is rigid with dirt, and every time you open your mouth to suck in air, another fistful of Iraqi desert is rammed down your throat. Like a swarm of tiny locusts armed with needles, the sand swirls and whips ferociously, probing into every nook and crevice, stinging and jabbing the flesh of your face and hands, and you cower in abject misery.

Curled up in balls in sleeping bags on the desert floor, or huddled against the sides of armored trucks, soldiers of the 3rd Infantry Division's 535 Engineer Company waited out the onslaught, hour by hour. But the storm was relentless. For 2-1/2 days it kept up its battering, cramming sand into fuel tanks, gun barrels, engines and supplies of every company and battalion, forcing the mighty U.S. Army to an unexpected halt.

Fearsome Abrams tanks stood still; Bradley fighting vehicles cut their engines, their crews holed up inside the armored shells. The wind blew so hard it threatened to topple a five-ton earth-mover from a transport truck. With visibility just inches, a lieutenant, weeks out of West Point, became lost when she wandered off to go the bathroom. She was found, hours later, nearly two miles from the camp in enemy territory south of the Shi'ite holy city of Najaf. Even something as basic as eating was a chore. Military rations MREs—meals ready-to-eat—don't taste great at the best of times and they are worse with a condiment of sand. In the time it took to shovel a plastic spoonful of Teriyaki-style beef from the tinfoil pouch to one's mouth, the food turned from its already unnatural brown to a glistening khaki and tasted crunchy.

It was less than five days into the war and things weren't supposed to be going like this. U.S. soldiers can take dirt, pain and exhaustion. But sandstorms brought their own particular torture, and the most immediate impact was on morale. When wind and sand blow, troops can't do what they're trained to do. They can't fight, they can't shoot—they can't even see. They can barely eat or sleep. Work becomes impossible—boredom and frustration set in, enthusiasm is drained and adrenaline sapped.

Sleeping outside in foxholes or on cots on a desert plain in the middle of a sandstorm, the mood darkened, soldiers of the 535th passed hours and days in stony despair, badgering journalists for weather reports and war updates. Many sat listening to Walkmans under makeshift tarpaulin shelters; others watched movies on DVDs in their truck cabins over and over. Those on watch strapped ski goggles to their faces and manned their weapons from lookout points, staring blindly into the dirt-brown haze, barely able to see to the end of their rifles. More than one mumbled, "Why did we want to take this country over, anyways?"

The storm also had deadly potential.

On the first day of the squall, four days into Operation Iraqi Freedom, the commanding colonel of the 937th Engineers agreed to take a photographer and me up to the front line, a few miles south of Kerbala, about 50 miles southwest of Baghdad. It was mid-morning, the skies were clear and Col. Mark Hildenbrand—loud-talking and confident, proud of himself and his men—was due to meet his commanding officer at an operations post of the 3rd Infantry Division.

He had a 10-digit global positioning satellite (GPS) coordinate—accurate to one hundred square yards—to tell him where to go and, even though bands of Baath Party militia were roaming, there weren't expected to be any problems. We headed north from near Najaf in a convoy of three Humvees, one armed with a .50-caliber machine gun, the others soft-skinned and with limited protection, just privates pointing their "locked and loaded" M-16s out of the windows. U.S. tanks had pushed through the area hours before and we passed burned-out Japanese pick-up trucks—the Iraqi militia's favored but ineffective assault vehicle—and off to the sides of the road charred corpses.

A few miles short of the meeting point, the road rose up from the plain through a steep escarpment with high banks on either side, a natural defensive position that the Iraqis had tried to use to repel the American advance, to little effect. Dead Iraqi soldiers lay around and the skeletons of vehicles mounted with anti-aircraft guns sat burning at the crest of the rise. At the top, the vast desert plain resumed, with flat dry bush and sand, relieved by the occasional patch of green, stretching northwest and away from the Euphrates valley for miles. And there in the distance, just short of the horizon, monstrous gray-brown clouds were gathering, growing dark and intense. The sandstorm was on its way.

"I think we can make it in time," said the colonel, gruffly telling his captain to ensure the coordinates of the command post were in the GPS. We headed off the road into the desert, visibility falling by the second as the storm drew nearer, wind buffeting the thin canvas doors of the Humvee and driving sand through the air vents and the gaps in the door frames.

Within minutes we were unable to see anything through the sand, and the midday sun darkened to a dull gray and the sky became an eerie, intense orange. So much sand was soon churning inside the Humvee that we could hardly see one another, let alone the vehicle a few feet in front. For half an hour we crawled on, heading north toward where we thought the front line stood, a fretful convoy of the blind, staring into the sandy abyss. As we inched ahead, the Humvee engine straining against the driving sand and threatening to quit, we became edgier. I strained my eyes to make out the road ahead, and silence and fear invaded the vehicle. How close were we to the front line, I wondered? Where was the command post? And more importantly, where the hell was the enemy? First a sergeant, then a major politely asked if they could use my satellite phone to call home.

Eventually, hideously lost, the colonel stopped and jumped out into the howling storm, a barely visible outline against the dark orange of the whipping sand. He shouldered his way over to our vehicle. "The GPS doesn't work," he screamed against the wind. "We'll have to sit it out." He retreated like a stumbling drunk to his Humvee and we prepared to hunker down, trying not to think about what it meant to "sit it out" somewhere so close to enemy lines.

Then the firing began. A powerful thud followed by a sharp whistling, loud even against the roaring wind, and then several more blasts, all seeming to come from a few hundred yards to our right. "That's an Abrams round!" screamed the sergeant major in panic. This was the math: if U.S. tanks were firing from one side, and the enemy was on the other, then our Humvee was right in the middle.

With no GPS, we took a basic compass reading and headed straight west, back toward the main road. Tanks were booming intermittently behind us as our vehicle inched away, crawling through the orange murk, following a compass reading off someone's $20 watch, until nearly an hour later, when we reached the relative safety of the road between Najaf and Kerbala.

It was a lesson in the shortcomings of technology and how nature can reduce even the most advanced army to dependence on any schoolboy's favorite gadget—a compass.

And it wasn't an isolated incident.

Col. John Peabody, the commanding officer of the 3rd Infantry's Engineer Brigade, and the man we were supposed to meet that day, also got lost. Peabody is a precise man, with steel-rimmed glasses and a no-nonsense demeanor. In his early 40s and a rising star—he was due to make one-star general right after the conflict—he hadn't had much experience of war. In fact, Iraq was his first major conflict and he wanted to come out of it having experienced the full scope of a soldier's life. He almost got more than he bargained for.

In the confusion of the slowly building storm, the leader of Peabody's small convoy took a wrong turn and ended up heading east toward the Euphrates, where pockets of Fedayeen were hiding out. Coming to a junction in the dirt road, the first car turned left, and the other two followed, slowly turning the right-angle bend. As they went, Peabody looked across to his right and saw three Iraqis crouched down on one knee about 50 yards away, one with a rocket propelled grenade launcher perched on his shoulder. He fired, and the rocket shot across the road, streaming fire behind it, hitting Peabody's vehicle on the rear panel, just above the tire. On impact, the rocket split in two, half shooting down and into the ground, half up through the roof. Bits of burning hot shrapnel flew and a captain sitting in the back-left seat was thrown clean out of the car by the blast. Unaware that they were a man down, Peabody screamed at his driver to put pedal to metal and the convoy raced off, kicking up clouds of dust and exhaust to add to the blowing storm.

Capt. Kevin Jackson, 28, was in a panic. Tall and athletic—a former guard on the West Point basketball team—he found himself crouching behind a low mound of sand and earth, trying to keep out of sight of the group of Iraqi militia just a few yards away. Taking advantage of the storm cover and the confusion, he began to run, crouching behind the earth berm as he went, following the road that Peabody and the others had taken. The Iraqis weren't sure whether they had a U.S. soldier on the run or not, but just in case shot off rounds, firing at the earth mound with their assault rifles and firing rocket-propelled grenades with no clear target. By chance, Jackson had been thrown out with his M-16 in hand, but he didn't return fire for fear of giving away his position. He kept up his back-bending dash, regretting having taken up smoking, until after more than a mile he came across a shallow hole. Diving down in the dirt, he folded himself up inside and took cover. For an hour he remained hidden as the Iraqis fired RPGs and mortar rounds in his direction. Eventually he heard U.S. vehicles heading up the road from the junction. When they were almost alongside, he leaped over the berm, waving his arms desperately. The first Humvee slowed, Jackson threw himself on the hood screaming "go, go, go," and the convoy made a mad dash for safety.

I met him two days later, still pulling bits of shrapnel from his face and arms, but otherwise looking fine. He and the colonel had had a heart-to-heart, and it was understood that no one had meant to abandon him to his fate, just that in the confusion no one even knew he was missing. His story was doing the rounds of the brigade and, despite always playing the episode down, Jackson became something of a minor celebrity—the guy who was blown out the back of a Humvee by an RPG and ducked enemy fire for more than an hour. He good-naturedly recounted the yarn to wide-eyed fellow officers, and told it to two reporters traveling with his unit, but underneath his easy-going bravado, there was a shaken man. "In a way, I'm almost glad it happened," he confessed one night. "I now know what it means to risk your life in war, and that's probably enough war for me for now."

The storm hit at the start of what became a six-day pause—a break that seemed interminably long given that Pentagon planners and commanders in the field had talked up the possibility that the war would last only days—not much longer than the 100 hours it took to prosecute the ground attack of the first Gulf War.

There were various explanations for the sudden halt: overstretched supply lines, the enemy resistance and the unpredictable, hostile terrain. But given that we'd already covered almost 280 miles in less than five days, it was the overstretched supply lines that made the most sense. Never before, stated one colonel, had a U.S. Army division extended itself over such a long front in such a short space of time. The logistics were mind-blowing. To get fuel for front-line units, tankers had to race back across the desert, skirting fighting as they went, and pick up supplies in Kuwait before heading back—a 560-mile round trip. Communications lines were at their limits, with elements of the same battalion unable to talk simply because they were too far apart for radio contact. Soldiers at the front were running low on "beans and bullets"—food and ammunition—not to mention fuel and fresh water in the heat.

At the same time, it was true the enemy was fighting differently than the U.S. Army had expected. Gen. William Wallace, the commander of V Corps and the man responsible for all land-based operations, admitted the U.S. Army had not war-gamed for a fight against non-conventional forces. Col. David Perkins, the commander of the 2nd brigade, had proudly waved Articles of Capitulation on the eve of the war, expecting that Iraqi commanders would line up to sign them, but it wasn't the case and it now seemed a naïve gesture.

In the event, U.S. forces were instead confronted by militias operating in small groups and prepared to carry out suicidal missions. Roving bands of fighters, often dressed in civilian clothes or in the baggy black uniforms of the Fedayeen, would stage guerrilla-style ambushes in the dark or the sandstorm—which they knew how to handle. Commanders said that smiling, waving civilians one second could turn lethal killers the next, pulling AK-47s from under their robes and opening fire. Gunmen would hide in man-sized holes to the sides of roads then jump out and fire their weapons at the sound of approaching vehicles, knowing for sure that they would be blasted to bits, but still hoping to kill a U.S. soldier in the process. With the militias using civilian vehicles to move around, U.S. forces could never be sure if an approaching car was a hapless Iraqi civilian or a

Fedayeen assassin. One colonel took to hailing every car that went by his vehicle, waving one hand far out the window in an excessively jovial greeting, while keeping the other tightly gripped on his pistol. "Look!" he once exclaimed with relief. "Those Iraqis are driving an American car!"

At night, the fear of attack surged. Our camp just south of Najaf was in a sensitive spot where the 535 Engineers were building a secret airstrip for Unmanned Aerial Vehicles (UAVs), the hi-tech remote-controlled spy planes used to get "eyes on" the enemy ahead of the assault on Baghdad. With groups of Iraqi militia roaming the area armed with mortars and RPGs, the camp was on constant alert, unsure whether the Iraqis knew what we were up to. Reports would come in over the radio that a group of 15 armed Iraqis was "on your perimeter" and there would be panic, with security levels raised so that every soldier had to be on guard, not just the one in four who were normally on duty. One night, mortars landed close to the emerging airstrip. But most of the time the reports were false, which in itself was a small success for the Iraqis, because it kept troops awake all night, eyes peeled for danger, hearts racing and adrenaline pumping. The morning would reveal a land of dark-eyed zombies who would then have to do a punishing day's work on the urgently needed airstrip. The hair-trigger alarmism put everyone on edge, greenhorn 19-year-olds and experienced officers alike. Every shadow was a threat, and more than once I was roughly shaken awake in the middle of the night by an aggressive grunt demanding to know "why the hell the sleeping dumb ass" wasn't on guard too.

The Iraqi guerrilla techniques were deemed to be having an effect, by unsettling the enemy. Senior officers openly fretted about how the U.S. Army would combat a determined guerrilla force. Pockets of resistance could hold out for months if not years, some speculated. Only days into the conflict, soldiers and officers were beginning to wonder if the war might not end up dragging on much longer than planned. Lt. Col. Paul Grosskruger, the square-jawed, blue-eyed commander of the 94th Battalion, turned to his officers at a briefing the morning after one nerve-fraying false alarm and solemnly declared: "This isn't just any Gulf War II. This could turn into a Danang."

It was all a long way from the confident, buoyant spirit that accompanied the lightning surge across Iraq's vast emptiness just days before. In fact, the desert thunder-run seemed almost to belong to a different war, one where the enemy played no part and the ground was there for the taking. As invasions go, the 3rd Infantry's race over the border and through the desert was a cakewalk.

Desert Thunder Run

Thursday, March 20 was a hot, hazy day that turned muggy during the afternoon. We knew it was the day the war would begin, but we weren't allowed to say. (The army's restrictions on what "embedded journalists" could report were strictest when it came to the launch of the attack. A radio correspondent, whose station wanted him to go live with the invasion, dismissively told his editors: "And what, go on air and say, 'I'm with an undisclosed unit in an undisclosed location conducting an undisclosed operation into an undisclosed country?'") We'd even been told what time we were set to "LD"—cross the line of departure and surge into Iraq: 2200 Zulu or 0100 Kuwait time, an hour into March 21. It was a long, slow and draining wait, half filled with back-slapping, brothers-in-arms camaraderie, half with stomach-hollowing tension. The soldiers had used their ritualistic head-shaving and equipment-checking to steady their minds and prepare for war. One young sergeant shaved every hair on his body apart from his eyebrows, which grew together in the middle. Prayers had been said and letters from wives and husbands read. Photos of family and friends had been pored over and tucked back into the lining of Kevlar helmets. Lucky charms were touched, kissed, or otherwise implored for whatever protection they might impart. Endless cigarettes had been smoked, youthful indiscretions revealed and an uneasy confidence seemed to prevail.

The biochemical attack warning was strange in its ordinariness. A message happened to come over the radio from the battalion commander. "A missile is incoming, projected to impact near our location. Everyone into MOPP 4." I was standing next to Capt. Alex Deraney, the commander of the 535th, at the time. The moment the order came I ran like a man possessed, realizing that, while I might have my nuclear, biological and chemical suit on and a gas mask at my side, I didn't have the rubber boots or gloves to hand. I sprinted down the long rows of vehicles already arranged in convoy for departure, their engines running, screaming "Gas! Gas! Gas!" as I pulled the mask on in fumbling desperation, sending chemical injectors tumbling into the sand. MOPP 4 is the highest level of chemical warfare protection.

Once we were all decked out in our kit, we waited with a strange quiet, some standing staring at the sky, others crouched under vehicles, all a little nonplussed, wondering quite when and where this missile was going to hit and what chemical or biological agents would look like when they came our way. It was insanely hot.

As we waited, half expectantly, to find out what it might be like to be "slimed," one soldier keeled over, falling to her knees, writhing and clawing at her mask. Colleagues rushed to her aid, but weren't quite sure what to do—rip off her mask and potentially expose her to chemicals, or try to treat her as she was? Someone tore off her mask. She was hyperventilating, her eyes rolled back in her head and spit foaming at her mouth. A medic pulled out an automatic injector, pushed it up against her thigh and gave her a shot. It calmed her briefly, but she was soon thrashing around again. Seconds later the 'all clear' was given and we were told to drop down to MOPP 2, removing our gloves and masks—the missile had hit three miles from our position but apparently hadn't brought any biological or chemical agents with it. Ripping off their masks and gloves, the medics attended to the panicked private, who was given another shot and seemed to stabilize.

An hour or so after that, as night came, three Cruise missiles flashed overhead, streaming flame behind them, seeming no more than a few hundred yards above the ground.

"The fireworks have started boys, it's time to hit the road," declared the tough-as-boots, tobacco-chewing Deraney. Driving from Kuwait through the U.N. demilitarized zone and into Iraq was peculiar and at times surreal. It started ordinarily enough, with our convoy pulling away more or less on cue. Deraney's 535 is known as the Heavy Metal Warriors—a company of mechanics and engineers who use impossibly large, 48-wheeler transport trucks to lug oversized pieces of industrial equipment onto the battlefield in order to clear the pathway for an advancing army. With huge insect-like graders and earth-scrapers, steel-clawed wreckers, armored bulldozers that weigh more than an Abrams tank, and steamrollers the size of small ships, Deraney's team was ready to tear down, flatten, roll and tarmac every square inch from the border to downtown Baghdad. It was the Heavy Metal Warriors who were tasked with going in and pulling down the razor wire on the Iraqi border to make way for the tanks and Bradleys.

While those operations were under way, the rest of the 2,000-vehicle convoy, virtually the whole of the 2nd Brigade of the 3rd Infantry Division, was inching its way towards the border. The convoy began shortly after midnight just over a mile from the DMZ, but it wasn't until 5:30 the next morning, in the dim dawn light, that we finally passed a small sign reading "Welcome to Iraq." At the side of the road, in front of a bland administrative building, a few old men in traditional robes, *kaffiyahs*, and sandals were sitting drinking tea and watching the never-ending convoy go by, a mixture of surprise and curiosity etched on their weather-beaten faces. One stood up and snapped a photograph, smiling as he sat back down as if pleased to have been witness to a small piece of history.

As we steadily made our way into Iraq, the sun rose and we had a view of the land ahead—a vast desert plain of sand and scrub stretching out across the horizon, not a human, an animal or the vaguest sign of life in sight. Ahead, to the sides and behind, for hundreds of yards if not miles, stretched the assembled military muscle of the U.S. 3rd Infantry. Tanks, Bradleys, APCs, five-ton trucks, fuelers, Humvees, mechanics' vehicles, mobile kitchens, signals and transmission equipment, bridging teams, decontamination units and the 535's assortment of heavy, armored steel, all kicking up a sea of dust as they charged across the sand, following the goat trails that crisscross Iraq's empty quarter. Clattering nearby were small Kiowa helicopters, skimming not more than 50 feet above the ground, nimbly scouting the route ahead and ready to call in the Apaches at any sign of danger. Every now and then we would pass the rusted wreckage of an Iraqi tank or artillery gun destroyed in the previous Gulf War. But mostly there was nothing.

And with nothing to hinder its advance, the convoy began to resemble charging cavalry, covering the desert emptiness in record time, sometimes gobbling up more than 18 miles an hour. After a while, herds of goats became visible on the horizon, driven on by small boys aimlessly thwacking sticks, and then camel trains emerged through the heat haze. Off to the sides of the route, Bedouin tents were scattered, old men and women sitting under their flat, low canopies sheltering from the heat and dust. They hardly looked up as the convoy rumbled past but their children came running to get a closer look, shielding their eyes with their hands as they stared up at the huge, unfamiliar sight.

Squashed into the back of the 48-wheel transporter, ammunition boxes under my feet and a nervous private fiddling with the trigger of his SAW machine gun alongside, it felt peculiarly intrusive and even an affront to be charging across this people's land— through their backyards—uninvited. The soldiers felt strange about it too. They knew these Bedouin weren't the enemy and weren't about to launch an attack, but at the same time the Bedouin were the first Iraqis they had seen and there was always the risk that one of them would fire off a round. There were also fears, sewn by intelligence reports, that innocent-looking Iraqis might actually be shielding chemical or biological agents that they would unleash on unsuspecting American soldiers the moment they got close enough.

The convoy drove on for hours, the sun slowly and steadily arcing over the heads of me, the nervous private and the two up front. They were a teenager from Idaho who grew up driving trucks and joined the army to do more of the same and her co-driver, a mechanic from Louisiana who was never happier than when she had something to fix. When it became dark and they became tired, they plugged CD headphones into their ears and wired themselves to the road with booming gangster rap or thrashing rock—the modern soldier's equivalent of Vietnam's Dexedrine.

In the past-midnight darkness, the convoy turned chaotic as vehicles moved without lights to avoid being seen and huge clouds of dust were kicked up. Often the convoy would grind to a halt because of a bottleneck and drivers would fall asleep as they waited to move on. When the vehicle in front had moved away, someone would have to run from behind to wake up the sleeping driver, who would then move nervously into the darkness, unsure where those in front had disappeared to. Fuel trucks, tanks and Humvees ran off the road in confusion. There were shunting crashes, trucks jack-knifed and any number of vehicles ended up pitched down into roadside gullies. And all around, long trains of vehicles would try to snake past the mayhem, pushing on determinedly towards Baghdad.

Sometimes, in the back of the truck, we would catch a moment's sleep only to have it interrupted a second later by a jarring shudder as the driver, staring through the green haze of night-vision goggles, would have to slam on the brakes to avoid a crash.

Nearly 48 hours into the cannonball run, things were largely going to plan, but the logistics of moving thousands of vehicles across vast, unfamiliar terrain had put us behind schedule. The pre-war time frame had us covering three-quarters of the 370-mile route from the border to Baghdad in a little over 24 hours. Perkins had confidently declared before we crossed into Iraq, "We'll take more ground in 24 hours than Allied forces took in six months of World War II."

While we weren't hugely behind that timeline, every extra hour of driving meant another hour of exhaustion for the drivers. Accidents happened and equipment was failing. In a nearby unit, a soldier was killed and another badly hurt when their supply truck ran off the road. Four people in the unit I was traveling with were injured in crashes and one 48-wheel transporter was abandoned. In the company, a 23-year-old private lost his hand when a loaded fueler rammed into his stationary vehicle. The private had his hand hanging out the window at the time and it was taken nearly clean off. He was evacuated and they asked me to sit in his place alongside his distraught partner.

Clambering aboard the small Chevrolet—a vehicle loaded with power supply and mechanics' equipment—I could see Sgt. Johnny Montoya was deathly tired and horribly disturbed. He was cold and silent as we set off into the third night of the drive, staring ahead through the one lens of his night-vision goggles, music blaring in his ears to keep him awake.

Around midnight, I woke with a start to see us drifting off the road, Montoya asleep. I lunged at the steering wheel and he jolted awake, slamming the brakes in alarm. He had been driving for nearly 60 hours and was a physical wreck, on the point of collapse. His hollowed, bloodshot eyes seemed to stare blankly—not at me, but at a point just beyond his nose. "You've got to drive, man," he mumbled, "otherwise we're both gonna end up dead."

This was an issue I'd struggled with endlessly in my mind, even before taking the embed assignment. What happens if you're asked to get involved? You're eating the U.S. Army's food, sleeping on its cots, driving around in its vehicles and being protected by its troops. So what do you do if they suddenly ask you to help out? A small favor to make their lives easier? A little helping hand for a soldier comrade? It may seem like a minor thing, but wouldn't it mean crossing the line between objective observer and engaged participant, no matter how minimal the participation or how reluctant?

In the weeks in the desert before the invasion, soldiers had wanted to show me how to handle an M-16 and feel the weight of a SAW machine gun, but I'd demurred. I did not want to be seen as crossing the line. Now, just hours into the war, I was being asked to assist the U.S. Army by driving one of its vehicles.

It was pitch-black and freezing cold in the desert west of Samawa. I looked at the exhausted Montoya, thought about the others who had already crashed, and decided that if I didn't take the wheel there was a high chance we were going to end up in a ditch by the side of the road. The survival instinct kicked in: I had a better chance of staying alive if I took over the driving. It seemed at odds with the goal of detached journalism, but I decided that if all the Army needed at that point was someone capable of staying awake behind a wheel, I was willing.

I got out and Montoya slid over.

Once I was in the driver's seat, he passed me his CD player. "Put this on and make sure it's loud," he said. And so, with the head-slamming aggression of the "Linkin Park" rock group turned up to maximum volume 10 and shaking in my brain, we set off again, trundling north into the darkness. It was to be the last stage of that first convoy—at 5 a.m., with the sun creeping into the sky, we stopped just south of Najaf, where 535 was to build the UAV and C-130 landing strips.

Both strips were crucial to the war plan because without UAV flights the commanding general couldn't see enemy positions up ahead and without C-130s he couldn't get vital supplies to front-line troops, a big concern given the stretched logistics. But there were problems. Being close to the Euphrates, there was water not far under the soil and when the rollers and scrapers hammered down the dirt to make it flat, puddles formed on the surface. Deraney needed something to soak up the water, and the search for it produced one of the more surreal episodes of the war. The U.S. Army needed to go shopping in the desert.

Deraney, Sgt. James Osborne—the company's Arabic speaker—I and a team of well-armed troops set off with $10,000 in cash and a booklet of U.S. government IOUs to buy some rocks and clay. The first port of call was a semi-abandoned quarry just down the road from our makeshift camp that turned out to be owned by a young man named Hussan. He was a little surprised to find three U.S. Army Humvees loaded with armed men pulling up to his doorstep. His pack of mangy dogs was caught between alarm and exhaustion but ultimately couldn't be bothered to bark. As Hussan stood frozen in fear on his front step of his rundown gray-brick home, Osborne leapt out and walked over to introduce himself.

"Hello, we're from the U.S. Army," he said in his politest Arabic. "We were wondering if we could have some of your rock?" "Sure, take all you want," replied Hussan, eyes nervously darting over the visitors. "Well, we won't just take it; we'll compensate you for whatever we take." "Oh no, you don't need to do that," the Iraqi replied, waving his hands urgently, perhaps feeling overly generous due to the presence of a half-dozen U.S. soldiers armed with M-16s. The rock was taken and Hussan was paid, his face switching from terror to joy as he received the American windfall, several hundred dollars. The transaction fell under the U.S. Army's rules of war. An invading army can take whatever it wants when it comes to government or public property, but private property has to be paid for, or the owner recompensed. Each unit travels with $10,000 in numbered $50 bills for any unforeseen expenses as well as a book of government-issue IOUs promising that whoever is owed can make a claim or have their property redeemed.

While Hussan got his cash, there was no one around at the clay pits when we went to pick up earth later in the day. The soldiers took several hundred tons of the damp red stuff, transported it in seized Iraqi dump trucks, and left a scrawled white receipt on a gate-post in exchange, blowing in the wind.

Saddam International

UAV flights were soon departing from the abandoned airfield but the C-130 strip was way behind schedule. Fearing that we would end up stuck with frustrated engineers while the rest of the 3rd Division moved on the capital, I left with Peabody in a convoy of tracked, armored vehicles, pushing past Najaf and on through the desert until just south of Kerbala, where the front line stood.

The desert thunder-run was long behind us, the sandstorms were almost a memory and U.S. commanders had made it clear that the next phase of the war was about to begin. The plan was to surge to the west of Kerbala, site of one of Shi'ite Islam's holiest shrines, and push through a three-mile-wide area between the city and nearby lake Milh, dubbed the "Kerbala Gap." Once to the north, we would swing right and head beyond Kerbala toward the Euphrates and Baghdad.

It was a slow, steady, tense convoy. The enemy was nowhere to be seen, and that added to the fear. U.S. strategists had predicted that if Saddam decided to use chemical weapons anywhere, one of the best places to do it would be the Kerbala Gap—a space only a few miles wide through which 6,000 men and their vehicles would have to push. The constriction would create a bottleneck, turning the 2nd brigade into a big sitting duck. The absence of Iraqis only made it seem more likely that it would happen. We were checking the wind to see if it was possible that a chemical cloud could blow our way.

But the attack never came and we rolled on unopposed. The surge became absurdly easy.

What had happened to the enemy? Where were the legions of Republican Guards? The feared Nebuchadnezzar, Medina and Hamarabi divisions? Where were Saddam's Baath party militia and the Fedayeen faithful?

The questions were on soldiers' lips, but the fear was largely out of their minds, which remained focused on the road ahead. There was a definite sense of brio and self-confidence in the air—more joking and storytelling. Some took wagers on who would be the first to open up in Baghdad—McDonald's, 7-Eleven or Starbucks.

The 3rd Infantry Division had built up an irrepressible momentum and, feeling on a roll, was hyped to charge toward the prize—Baghdad. The only military obstacle between it and the capital at that point was the Euphrates.

On the far side of the river, a team of Iraqi soldiers had wired the bridge with explosives, burying the charges into the huge bridge supports. They waited until U.S. tanks were on the span before detonating, hoping to maximize the impact, and as the tanks rolled forward, a huge blast went up, smoke and dust surging into the sky and an echoing boom shaking the humid air. For all the fireworks, though, there was little result. The Iraqis had screwed up the wiring, attaching only half the explosives to the detonator and blowing up only one side of the bridge. The 1st Brigade was free to press its no-turning-back drive toward Saddam International Airport.

I was held back with Peabody and the engineer brigade, which had to coordinate the passage of the rest of the 3rd Infantry over the river. But two days later, on April 6, the order came to move up.

A small convoy of Humvees, APCs and two-ton trucks escorted by Bradleys hit the road. Fighting was still going on and pools of blood were drying on the roadside next to destroyed Iraqi tanks and abandoned bits of weaponry. Occasionally, there would be a putrid stench as we passed a dead body left rotting in the heat, and in fields dead cattle and sheep lay scattered—shot up in the darkness after their bodies set off a soldier's heat-sensitive sights.

As we got closer to the outskirts of the capital, with villages slowly turning to towns, local men, women and children wandered freely along the roadside, waving tentatively. Some smiled as we approached, but their expressions often turned disdainful once we'd passed. Steely-eyed old men drinking tea under reed canopies watched expressionless. One soldier threw some food out of the window into a crowd of boys and they scattered like skittish cats, fearing it might be a grenade. Outside every settlement, whether hovel or proper home, hung some piece of white cloth—from handkerchiefs to underwear—and civilian cars coming down the road slowed so occupants could wave makeshift flags of surrender out the window.

The airport, when we finally got there, was a testament to hard-fought victory. The scene was like the set of a disaster movie. The burned-out shells of Iraqi Airways 737s lay in heaps on the bomb-scarred runway. Half a dozen aircraft were parked at awkward angles around the airport, either riddled with bullets or hit by tank shelling. Incinerated airport buses lay like skeletons on the service roads criss-crossing the complex, blasted to smithereens by uranium-tipped Sabot rounds from U.S. tanks. The charred bodies of their occupants lay piled in the aisles, the only thing marking the dead as soldiers were the AK-47s held rigidly in their burned hands. The bodies of those who jumped free ahead of the inferno lay bloating in the sun. Nobody wanted to cart them away. Every building on the site had been searched and cleared by U.S. troops, leaving behind a maelstrom of smashed glass, busted-down doors, cracked marble and shot-up furnishings. There was no power, no sanitation and no running water. The hundreds of Iraqis previously employed in airport services had fled, leaving the keys to the fleets of mobile airplane stairs, maintenance buggies and fuel trucks still in the ignition.

The portraits and photographs of Saddam that had adorned the walls were torn down and piled in a jumbled heap outside, their glass frames smashed and canvases slashed. In the grime of abandoned aircraft fuselages, soldiers had scrawled graffiti: "Go Blue," "Don't mess with us" and more vividly, "Saddam blows goats." Dozens of Saddam statues and mosaics that decorated the airport grounds were defaced with bullet holes or had their heads knocked off. Wherever 'Iraq' or 'Iraqi' was written, the nationality was scratched out or covered up. Soldiers took to wearing Iraqi Airways stewardess name tags and reveled in driving the airport buggies.

Within days, 7,000 troops were on base and the number was expected to swell to more than 12,000 as reinforcements from the 101st Airborne and other divisions arrived. Someone was needed to decide where such a crush of people was going to stay, how buildings would be distributed among units, how sanitation would be handled and who was going to gather up and bury the Iraqi dead littering the airport grounds. Capt. Jackson, the man blown out the back of his Humvee 10 days earlier, was given the job. "We've got an entire army and air force operations base sitting right here on Saddam's doorstep," he declared with a growing sense of victory just the day before Saddam was toppled.

But in the end, the airport was as close as some soldiers ever got to downtown Baghdad. While the second brigade had taskforces parading through the middle of town, overrunning Saddam's palaces, much of the rest of the 3rd Division's military muscle was back at Baghdad International. When the statue of Saddam was pulled down on April 9, airport-bound troops watched the scene on CNN and Fox from the comforts of the Iraqi Airways offices. In this first-of-a-kind media war, in which journalists lived and worked cheek-by-jowl with soldiers, it was the world's media that ultimately allowed U.S. troops to experience the defining moment of their own victory.

The toppling of Saddam's statue marked the end of the campaign for many, and for the dozen or so journalists who by that stage had made it to the airport, it was time to think about leaving. Gen. Buford Blount, the two-star commanding general of the 3rd Infantry Division, declared the end of combat operations to be days away, although he added wisely, "It's not clear when we'll be able to declare final victory." With Special Forces flights landing on the military runway each night without incident, despite the occasional rattle of anti-aircraft fire, the army deemed it okay to fly a few people out. And so it was that almost exactly three weeks after we had rolled uncertainly into Iraq, we rumbled after midnight down the runway of Baghdad International, strapped into the jump-seats of a Special Forces C-17, on what was dubbed the first flight out of "Free Iraq."

Chapter 2

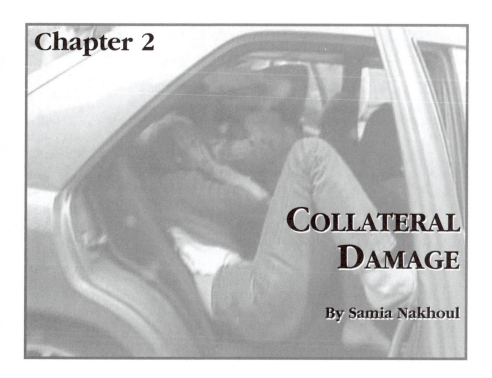

COLLATERAL DAMAGE

By Samia Nakhoul

Comatose, he lay on a makeshift bed, almost mummified in bandages meant to staunch his terrible head wounds. From time to time his little naked body twitched from the shocks going through his fast-failing brain. Nobody at the hospital knew his name and no one from his family sat by his bedside. Instead, I was lying next to him, with wounds to my own head from an American tank shell, waiting for surgeons to remove shrapnel and bone fragments from my brain.

That was April 8, the first and final day of the long-awaited "Battle for Baghdad." I was lying there in the hospital like scores of Iraqis wounded on the day Baghdad fell into the hands of U.S. troops.

Unlike the little boy, I was conscious. I asked the nurse why he was alone, with no relatives to look after him. She told me that 17 members of his family had died in the shelling and bombing. "Don't be shocked," she added gently, "he is going to die."

I drifted in and out of sleep, waking up and staring at him to see if he was still breathing.

Outside, the Iraqi capital was falling, almost without resistance. Yet the U.S. bombardment was still thundering, and I was waiting to be operated on in this chaos, with the sounds of battle around me.

An Iraqi friend who stayed by my bedside read Koranic prayers for the boy all night. The following day he died. I was asleep when he passed away. I woke up and saw that his cot was empty. I did not need to ask. For the first time in my life I felt relief about death. I thought: why would this boy want to wake up to such a cruel future, with no family and a life shut in by brain damage? At least, I felt, he would be reunited with his family.

This boy—he was about 9 when he died—brought back haunting images of all the horribly wounded children I had seen during the three weeks of the war. I realized that I had never seen so many children hurt as I had in this war—not even during the long Lebanese civil war I had lived through and covered.

His was just one example of the terrible suffering children in Baghdad endured during the bombing. The Red Cross had told me three days earlier—when American troops first pushed into the capital—that hospitals were admitting more than 100 casualties an hour. Most of them were civilians—a lot of them children—and many had the terrible wounds that modern weapons inflict—injuries that are almost impossible to survive. Those who could get to a hospital in the anarchy of Baghdad were the lucky ones.

Praying for Survival

When I headed to Iraq in February 2003 to cover what by then looked certain to be an American-led invasion, I was steeled for what I thought would be a nasty war. But I never imagined it would turn out like this for me.

I was taken on a stretcher to the operating room. The pre-op drugs being dripped into my arm were beginning to take hold. Almost everything that had happened since I arrived was racing through my mind. I had come to cover a war and now I was praying for my own survival. I started slipping into unconsciousness. I didn't know in what shape I would come out of this, and had little idea of what sort of war I would wake up to, now that the Americans had entered Baghdad in force.

I was lucky to have by my side Iraqi colleagues, as well as a close friend and former Reuters boss, Paul Eedle, working for Britain's Channel 4 television. He arranged for the operation and, crucially, had established the urgent need for it by carefully questioning the neurosurgeon at the Iraqi hospital and checking with doctors of the International Red Cross. I was equally fortunate in the skill and dedication of the Iraqi surgeon—who had been working day and night in appalling conditions, with limited supplies and equipment. It turned out, too, that he was extraordinarily prescient.

He had told Paul and me before midnight on the day I was wounded that while he had a team ready to operate on me that night, this might not be the case the next day. And so it proved. The flood of casualties was such that the surgeons were overwhelmed, operating in the hall in front of us. At the same time, the chaos in the streets had already started to spill into the city's clinics and hospitals. My doctor took what seemed to be a radical decision. He arranged for an ambulance to take me back to the Palestine Hotel, just 16 hours after the surgery. At least you will be safer there, he said. He was right again.

As I was being ferried across town, the looters were going to work and had already raided most of the city's hospitals—including the one that had just saved my life.

Arriving at the Palestine, I caught a glimpse of what would become one of the most memorable scenes of the war—Iraqis and U.S. Marines pulling down a huge statue of Saddam Hussein in the square opposite the hotel.

By then, however, more powerful images of the war had been burned into my mind.

Fatalism and Defiance

When I arrived in Baghdad I was uncertain what mood I would find on the streets. Exhausted by years of war and sanctions, Iraqis displayed a mixture of fatalism and defiance. They went on with their lives: working, sending their children to school, shopping in the markets and visiting their families.

They were living in denial, refusing to face up to what was coming their way. Who could blame them? They knew the cost of expressing their feelings under the dictatorship of Saddam Hussein.

Helpless, and with no voice in how their country was governed, they usually just said they had only God to rely on.

The isolation Iraqis lived in was staggering. Under Saddam, there was a near total blackout on foreign news, to the point that most Iraqis had no idea of the U.S. military build-up taking place around them. They had no access to international newspapers or television—except through occasional contacts with visiting journalists. Foreign short-wave radio broadcasts were routinely jammed. Yet I could scarcely believe what I was hearing when an Iraqi woman friend whispered in my ear: "Is it true that the Americans have sent a lot of troops to Kuwait?"

That was a week before the war started.

When I told her what was about to happen she was terrified. Saddam would be an Iraqi Nero, and like Rome, Baghdad would go up in flames. "He will never surrender. He will destroy the country over our heads," she said. It became clear then that, while she was oblivious to events beyond Iraq's borders, she was well aware of what had gone on inside them. A Sunni Muslim from the minority sect that ruled Iraq, she knew how Saddam had used chemical weapons against the Kurds and how he had massacred the Shi'ites.

Nevertheless, many Iraqis then still had hopes that the United Nations—whose weapons inspectors were in the country—could prevent a conflagration. After all, during the stand-offs between Saddam and the international community in 1997 and 1998, the United Nations had managed to stave off conflict at the last minute. And when its efforts failed, as they had when American and British warplanes attacked for four days in December 1998, the consequence had been only slightly worse bombing than Iraqis had become used to since the end of the last Gulf War in 1991.

As far as ordinary Iraqis could gather, the return of the weapons inspectors was now bringing about disarmament. Day after day, journalists trooped out to sites where the inspectors, with Iraqi help, were destroying al-Samoud missiles deemed illegal by the United Nations. As the search went on for weapons of mass destruction—the ostensible reason for the crisis—people still had flickers of hope that, maybe, things would get better. Iraq was after all seen to be cooperating with the inspectors. As journalists, however, we were feeling increasingly uncomfortable, because by now war seemed inevitable.

The public mood turned once Saddam, who had increased the frequency of his appearances on Iraqi television, suddenly announced to his people that war was imminent. The Iraqi dictator had been shown conferring with party chiefs and military commanders, and receiving the ritual obeisance of tribal leaders and regional governors. Now, he was giving pep talks to soldiers and lower-ranking officers, and urging ordinary Iraqis to start digging trenches.

The effect of this was to electrify the capital. Iraqis were no longer in any doubt about what awaited them. The countdown to war began once the United Nations weapons inspectors were withdrawn.

Immediately, jittery Baghdadis poured into markets to stock up on food and provisions as if they knew they would have to resist a siege. Gasoline to run standby generators was especially prized after the experience of previous wars when electric power was cut. Many prepared sandbagged rooms to shelter in. Those who could packed up and fled to the countryside, or to Syria and Jordan.

I found alarming evidence of the spreading panic in the capital's maternity hospitals. Many pregnant women opted to have Cesarean sections rather than risk having their babies during war, even though they were well short of their natural due date.

Three days before the invasion, a clammy sense of foreboding hung over the maternity wards of Baghdad's Elwiyah hospital.

"This life is horrible," said Maysadoun Kazem, a 35-year-old woman with two children, as tears streamed down her face. "I am terrified that war will break out and I won't have my baby on time.

"I just want to have my baby. I want to have him next to me. I don't want anything else," she said.

Women who had reached their natural term were taking longer to give birth because of fear and stress. With no anesthetic for epidural injections, women endured agonizing deliveries.

Tiny, premature infants were placed in incubators that didn't work properly and nurses struggled to convince overwrought mothers not to take their newborns home too soon.

One group of older children didn't have it much better.

They had been orphaned by the first Gulf War and now they were afraid that was not the worst that could happen to them. They sensed that war could soon separate them from each other—breaking the only real bonds in their already shattered lives.

Orphans who had found precarious comfort with each other were terrified that their lives would be torn apart again by the deaths of brothers, sisters or friends. Fearful of being alone once more, they lived in horror of the coming conflict.

One young woman, 17-year-old Hind Ziad, was 5 when the first Gulf War killed her father and broke the health of her mother, who died soon after. "My father left for the war and never came back. He was declared missing in action," she explained.

"My mother went into shock, she was grieving all the time. She got very sick and died eight months later."

Hind and her two younger brothers ended up in separate government orphanages. "War is a tragedy," she said, trembling at her memories of the last Gulf conflict.

"It was terrifying. Everything was frightening, the sound of the planes . . . the bombing. We were crying with fear. My mother used to hug us and cuddle us all night until the bombing stopped."

The frail-looking Hind was seeing her brothers once a week, and she was desperate that the war should not thwart her plans to reunite the family.

"All I want is to become a family once again", she said, sitting on a plain iron bed in Baghdad's al-Riya'a orphanage. "When I am 18 I can leave here. I will get a job and my brothers can come and live with me."

Chronicle of a War Foretold

By now, journalists were becoming distinctly uneasy. Trying to distinguish snippets of real information in the swirl of rumor became a full-time job as the war drew nearer. There were elements of a sort of Chronicle of a War Foretold in the briefings and leaks— much talk of what the Americans were apparently billing as a "shock and awe" blitz, of new bombs of almost nuclear power, of more than 10,000 missiles and smart munitions that would engulf Baghdad.

Seasoned diplomats still in the city—most countries had evacuated their staff long ago—were urging correspondents to leave. "Take this seriously," one ambassador said as he prepared to leave. "The Americans intend to use unprecedented force."

The bombing itself, several of us felt, was only one of the dangers. Some diplomats and military sources were predicting a 60-day siege of Baghdad as the denouement of the war—a prospect anticipated by some Arabic newspaper commentators as an "Arab Stalingrad."

In the end, about 500 journalists and media staff stayed, while around 1,000 pulled out or were withdrawn by their editors. Among those who left were U.S. television networks, some of their staffers saying they had received explicit warning from the Pentagon that no target was off-limits.

Some departing diplomats warned us about the risk of chaos once Baghdad fell. But we didn't pay them much heed at the time.

By now, any hopes that Saddam would seek exile, or that senior officers would stage a coup against him to avert war, had evaporated.

On the day the war began, an unofficial deadline circulated among the journalists. The Al Rasheed Hotel, headquarters of the international media, was deemed a target by the Pentagon and our editors asked us to move. The alternative was the Palestine Hotel, on the other side of the Tigris river. We moved there at midnight on March 19. A few hours later the bombardment of Baghdad began. We immediately realized that our new quarters were opposite one of Saddam's palaces, which would soon explode in flames before our eyes.

I am used to covering wars, but I can't pretend they don't terrify me. The bombardment on the first night was relatively light. In the early hours of the morning I went with our photographer, Faleh Kheiber, on a tour of the city to see what had been hit. I saw a group of militiamen and some people on the streets inspecting damage. I insisted on stopping to talk to them. It was a bad start.

A convoy of ostensibly civilian cars and taxis suddenly stopped. Bodyguards with guns jumped out and grabbed Faleh. The reason for their presence became clear when the interior minister emerged—and began cursing and threatening Faleh, an Iraqi. When I said we were journalists from Reuters I was pushed back into our car. In the end they let us go—but only after promising Faleh they would "crush his head" if he took any more pictures of bomb damage. They called him a traitor.

The following day we realized that a relatively light raid had announced the beginning of the war. It was an "opportunist" strike, aimed at "decapitating" the Iraqi leadership, and not part of the massive bombardment that had been promised, and which now materialized with all its terrifying force.

Baghdad was pounded with explosions of unbelievable ferocity, lighting the skies with fireballs and shaking the foundations of the ancient city. American armored columns raced north toward the capital, the main objective in the war to topple Saddam.

Every night, U.S. warplanes blitzed Iraqi ministries, government buildings, communication centers and Saddam's palaces—including the one opposite our hotel. And every morning, I would do the rounds, check the damage, and talk to anybody who had ventured out in the lull.

Baghdad by then became a city with two lives, determined by the rhythm of the air raids, which were heaviest after dark. At night, people would stay at home or in bomb shelters. By day, they would emerge to buy food and check on relatives.

Clouds of thick, black smoke from oil-filled trenches, set ablaze by Iraqi forces in a vain attempt to hinder the air strikes, blotted out the sun and added to the grim mood of a city facing invasion.

Shaken residents were angry at the terrifying scale of the air raids and bitter that their lives were, once again, being turned upside down by war. Having already endured two wars in two decades, the adults had learned to cope with fear. But that did not help them calm their terrified children.

On the streets, the talk was about how long the war would last, with some predicting that any battle for Baghdad would be slower and more painful than the United States expected. By then many Iraqis seemed more interested in surviving the conflict than in its outcome.

But when the telephones, electricity and water went off, Baghdad was gripped by a sense of despair and resignation. Mosques filled as the missiles and bombs fell. Living through their third war in 20 years, Iraqis sought spiritual reassurance. They placed their fate in the hands of God.

The reality of the war did not take long to hit home. As the bombing intensified, survivors in the worst-hit neighborhoods recounted tales of horror.

Nothing—not even the carnage in Lebanon—prepared me for what I saw at hospitals and at the big market bombings, which destroyed entire families.

At al-Shaab market, located in one of Baghdad's Shi'ite neighborhoods, which was hit on March 26, I found myself standing on human remains. Dark pools of dried blood stained the road, human body parts lay grotesquely in the rubble, and the stench of charred flesh hung in the dusty air.

Shoes scattered across the market testified to the panic of those who scrambled to escape when the missile struck.

Distraught Iraqis wandered through the carnage. No words could comfort a father grieving for his son. There was sorrow, fury and despair.

I was a journalist, but no longer just a witness. The grief of those around me cut deeply. There was no need to intrude or ask questions. I just had to listen to their mourning.

"My shop was burned, my car was demolished. I don't care about all this but why our families and children?" one grief-stricken father said.

In a ruined house, Hamdiya Ahmed, 35, wept for the loss of her mother while searching in the rubble for family papers.

"Yesterday was horror, horror itself. We were having breakfast when the missiles fell. People began running in circles; they were hysterical. Some had lost arms, others their legs. We were looking for each other in the rubble to see who died and who survived."

Dressed in black, Ahmed surveyed what was left of her home—splintered furniture, burned clothes and curtains, shards of metal and shreds of human flesh.

Two days later, at least 62 people were killed in an accidental strike on al-Shula, another poor and crowded Shi'ite area in west Baghdad. Whole families were wiped out. Almost every house had a horror story to tell.

A man stood outside his home sobbing uncontrollably for his 5-year-old son, killed near the market. Another man looked like he was in a trance, unable to speak. Friends said his wife, his child, and the wife of his son had been killed.

At the house of Sumaya Abed, the scene was one of devastation. She was delirious with grief. "Ali, Hussein and Mohammad are gone. My three boys are dead," she sobbed hysterically, sitting on the floor of her house amid dozens of black-clad women, striking her face in a traditional gesture of mourning. "Oh God, whom shall we turn to in our sorrow? Oh God, whom shall we tell of our grief?"

Mohammad, the youngest at 11, had been born in the first war, Abed, 53, said, only to be killed in the second. "What is left for me to live for?"

Nearby, Arouba Khodeir, 39, was wailing desperately and striking herself in the face and chest, as neighbors tried to comfort her for the loss of her son, 11-year-old Karar. "My son had his head blown off," she screamed. "Why are they hitting the people? Why are they killing the children?"

Blinding grief was mixed with fury at President Bush, who had promised to limit the loss of civilian life. But there was also deep anger at Saddam Hussein in these poor districts inhabited by members of Iraq's Shi'ite majority, kept so long under the thumb of the Sunni Muslim minority incarnated by the "regime" of Saddam. It was this regime, al-Shula residents explained, that had sited missile launchers and anti-aircraft guns in their teeming neighborhood.

It was one harrowing story after another. At the house of Hasna Shallum, women had gathered to mourn her 20-year-old daughter, Shaza, killed by a piece of shrapnel through her neck. She had been holding her 6-month-old daughter; little Fatima was found alive in her dead mother's arms, and brought to her grandmother's house, where the wails of mourning drowned out the cries of the infant.

The U.S. military said it was unclear who was responsible for these tragedies. But to the traumatized residents of al-Shula and al-Shaab, promises of an inquiry meant little. Such scenes rapidly become part of daily life as the blitz continued. The bombing not only obliterated ministries and military targets, palaces and communications facilities, as the Pentagon had promised; in a crowded city where military installations were located in residential districts, bombers hit homes too. Hospitals filled up—evidence that precision bombing was not always as precise as the military claimed.

Visiting hospitals was heartbreaking, above all because of the children.

The moaning of Aisha Ahmed, aged 8, filled one emergency ward. "Mummy, I want my mummy. Where is my mummy?" Aisha kept saying. Yet neither nurse nor neighbor trying to comfort her dared to answer.

Her 4-year-old brother, Mohammad, had died and her mother and other brother were in critical condition undergoing surgery for head and chest injuries. Her father and two sisters were all badly injured in another hospital.

The ward was a scene of pure misery: parents sobbing and praying and children crying. One father was telling his child he would be all right "because God is looking after you."

Mothers spoke of their children crying and trembling when they heard the bombs. They said their children refused to eat or sleep.

"Whenever he hears the explosions he grabs me, I hug him and caress him until the bombing stops," one mother, Madiha Mohsen Ali, 40, said.

"He does not sleep or eat. He just keeps asking: 'Mummy when will this banging stop?' I keep on telling him that nothing will happen to him anymore."

Streets became more and more deserted and hospitals more and more packed as the battle neared Baghdad. The strain of war was etched on people's faces.

Nowhere was safe any longer. Our reporting from the streets became increasingly dangerous. In one of the ritual morning tours, I found myself in the middle of a smoldering street and flattened buildings. Fifteen minutes before, one rescuer said, warplanes had struck the Baghdad Trade Fair complex and nearby buildings, also hitting the Red Crescent maternity hospital in the heart of the capital. Motorists who had come out during a lull in the bombing were caught under the falling missiles. Just in front of us I counted five wrecked cars with their drivers burned to death inside.

Fear had reached into our offices. With no communications around the city, my Iraqi colleagues were living through unbearable anguish, unable to get news about family or relatives. One afternoon, Hassan Hafidh, my Iraqi colleague, and I, heard sobs coming from the bathroom. It was our driver Mohammad.

He decided to risk a dash through the bombing to check on his wife and children at home, where he had not slept for many nights. When he arrived, he found an empty house. He raced back to the office, and now, quietly and away from our eyes, he lost control, thinking the worst must have happened.

We did all we could to calm him down. They must be fine, they must have fled to a safer place, we kept telling him. "Think positive," I kept saying. But in fact, we were just as worried as he was. We just did not know how to comfort him. The next day we learned that Mohammad's brother had taken the family and fled to the countryside.

With every military advance toward Baghdad, casualties were piling up. According to unofficial estimates from academics and peace activists, by the middle of November 2003, some 9,650 Iraqi civilians died in the conflict and its aftermath.

Visits to hospitals were torture for me. Yet I felt obliged to tell the story of what Iraqis were going through. But what I saw on April 6—a day after American forces penetrated Baghdad—will stay with me for a very long time.

It was supposed to be a normal visit to one of the big hospitals to check U.S. claims that casualties were more military than civilian.

When I put this question to the director of the hospital he looked at me and said: "Stand at the emergency gate and you will see for yourself." He was right.

Ambulance after ambulance raced in with casualties. Victims also arrived in civilian cars. When stretchers ran out they were carried in bed sheets. Doctors worked frantically and staff had no time even to clean blood from gurneys. Patients' screams and families' cries echoed across the wards. I turned my face from the horrific sights I was seeing. They were amputating legs in front of me.

I stood there numb. Two brothers wept loudly after the doctor announced that their two other brothers had died in the bombing. "What harm had they done? They were praying in the mosque when a rocket struck," they said. The preacher at the mosque also died at the hospital.

How many women cried, I cannot remember. How many patients screamed, I don't want to remember. I felt sick.

But the horror did not stop there. I asked a head nurse what was the worst case they had received. She said there was a 12-year-old boy who was badly burned but that I could not see him because he was in intensive care. I asked her to allow me a short visit. We needed the director's permission.

They gave me a gown and a mask and I stepped into his bare room. My heart froze at what I saw.

Ali Abbas Ismaeel was lying in his bed with his charred flesh salved in white ointment and a rudimentary protective cage to protect his burned torso. There were just bandaged stumps where his arms used to be. He looked at me with the expression of a broken and traumatized soul. He did not speak.

I did not know how to begin. I looked into his beautiful but pained eyes, sat by his bedside and gently touched his hair. I told him I was a journalist; I did not want him to think I was a relief worker or specialist who could help him out of his terrible condition. Yet when I asked him what had happened to him, I told him I wanted to help if I could.

He had been trying not to, but then he started crying. He poured his heart out and told me his story.

He was asleep when missiles shattered his home and most of his family, blowing off his arms and leaving him orphaned.

"It was midnight when the missiles hit us. My father, my mother and my brother died. My mother was five months pregnant," Ali said.

"Our neighbors pulled me out and brought me here. I was unconscious," he said.

On top of losing his parents, he would have to deal with his terrible disabilities. Thinking about his sad future, he timidly inquired whether he could get artificial arms.

"Can you help get my arms back? Do you think the doctors can get me another pair of hands?" Ali asked.

"If I don't get a pair of hands, I will commit suicide," he said with tears spilling down his cheeks.

His aunt, three cousins and three other relatives staying with them were also killed when the missiles hit their house in the Diala Bridge district east of Baghdad.

"We didn't want war. I was scared of this war," Ali said. "Our house was just a poor shack, why did they want to bomb us?" the boy asked, unaware that the area in which he lived was surrounded by military installations.

Now Ali spoke of the broken dreams of a childhood already lost. "I wanted to become an army officer when I grow up, but not any more. Now I want to become a doctor, but how can I? I don't have hands," he said, trying to hold back his tears.

His aunt, Jamila Abbas, looked after him; feeding him, washing him, comforting him with prayers and repeatedly telling him his parents had gone to heaven.

Watching him, I could no longer tolerate the pain and grief. I wanted to get out before I broke down.

Yet after I left I was in a daze, sobbing with grief as though I had just come from a funeral. His image would not leave me and I could not write the story. But the vision of him would not let me rest until I had written it.

Sorrow must have been so engrained on my face that people kept asking me if something was wrong.

The following day, there was an unusual buzz, with everybody trying to find out what had happened after a massive raid on a residential area in the Mansour district of Baghdad.

Something changed that night—changed drastically. I remember Iraqi television began airing old national songs with footage of Saddam from his younger days. The military spokesman who used to appear every 10 minutes with a list of fictitious Iraqi victories vanished. The news bulletins were unusually short and showed what were clearly old meetings between Saddam and sycophantic aides. That night a strange mood of foreboding overwhelmed Baghdad.

We did not know what was going on. But to me it felt like the obituary of a regime. There was an eerie silence that night and, for a change, no bombardment. I decided to check my e-mail.

My heart lifted, to the extent that it could amid such tragedy, when I found two e-mails—one from an individual and another from an organization—asking me for contact details for Ali. They wanted to adopt him, provide him with medical treatment and help him. I was delighted, and I replied that I would get in touch with his doctor so he could contact them.

Electric Day

Just before dawn the next morning, the Reuters news desk telephoned to tell me that the Pentagon was saying that the April 7 strike on the Mansour district had targeted Saddam, his sons and some top aides.

It was an electric start to a day that was to go in a very unexpected direction.

As dawn broke, the calm was shattered by a massive bombardment of central Baghdad. I began to file a report. But soon a new pattern emerged, which suggested to me this was the kind of bombing and shelling laid down to accompany a ground offensive.

American troops had already seized the presidential palace compound opposite us. In the light of day I could now see their tanks and Bradley armored vehicles moving toward the intersection that links the compound to the Information Ministry, the prime minister's office and the foreign ministry near the Jumhuriya bridge across the Tigris.

Iraqi television and radio went off the air. Government minders disappeared from the hotel. Artillery and warplanes were pounding Baghdad and tanks were pushing forward. I could no longer see from our fourth floor balcony in the Palestine Hotel, so I went up to our other office on the 15th floor for a better view.

From there I saw two American tanks advancing on the Jumhuriya bridge. Artillery was firing at the al-Rashid military camp to the east and tanks were shooting across the bridge. I called our desk in Dubai to report that Baghdad was crumbling, that American tanks were in the heart of the city, and that there was no apparent resistance.

I said I would call back with more details. I returned to the balcony. Suddenly our photographer Faleh Kheiber pointed to the left and said: "Samia—look, look." I turned and saw an orange glow—for maybe less than a second—because that was the tank shell that ploughed into our office and cut through us.

What do I remember? I remember my face burning and bleeding, and my head also bleeding. Panic, screams, and colleagues carrying us. The pain was overwhelming. Who else was hit, at that stage, I did not know. I knew both Faleh and I had been, and I recall people carrying us and shouting for someone to call the reception desk to turn on the generator for the lifts. In the lift, I thought I was going to pass out. In the car to the hospital I tried to open my eyes but saw nothing but blackness. I thought I had lost my sight. I could not imagine a life without my eyes. Then I thought how the news would affect my family. I had not told my mother I was in Baghdad, because of her health. I thought of my husband, David, in London. He did not want me to come here, but he respected my decision. The day before I had been telling him it was coming to an end and I would be with him soon.

I still thought that only Faleh and I were wounded.

At the first hospital they cleaned my wounds and wiped the blood from my eyes. I realized I could see. It was there that I heard somebody in the hall saying Taras Protsyuk, our television cameraman, had died. My heart dropped. He had been on the balcony, but I had no idea the tank shell had hit him too.

Then I heard that our TV technician, Paul Pasquale, had been wounded, and then about Jose Couso, a cameraman for Spain's Tele 5 television, who did not survive his head and body injuries.

At that moment, I felt things could never be the same again. I knew I might survive my wounds, but I would carry a wound deep inside. I had flashbacks of Taras from assignments together—how in the interminable waiting that makes up a lot of journalism he would try to talk to me in Arabic. A Ukrainian, he grew up partly in Syria where his father had worked. He had told me about his young son.

Taras had survived wars in the Congo, Afghanistan, and the Balkans. Why had this happened now, I kept on repeating in my mind. We were not on the streets but in our office, in a hotel known to the world as the Baghdad headquarters of the international media. It was from there, morning and night, that journalists broadcast their accounts of the war to millions of homes around the globe.

I thought about how we had all been waiting for the war to end, talking about going home and going on vacation. But the ending was not a happy one.

I could not bear to think of how Taras's death would affect a wife waiting to see her husband and a son longing for his father.

My wounded colleagues and I found ourselves among the victims we had been reporting on. There I was, being ferried from hospital to hospital under shelling and bombardment, thinking that I might be hit again.

I ended up at a neurological hospital where I was operated on while my editors organized our evacuation with the U.S. Marines. I never thought I would be leaving Baghdad this way—by stretcher, ambulance and military plane.

I had glimpses of colleagues and friends who came to say goodbye. It was a strange farewell.

And as I looked at the American troops fanned out over the city, I knew that a chapter in the troubled history of the Middle East had come to an end and a new, unknowable one had just started. All I hoped was that the suffering of the Iraqis would soon be over.

Over the years I had become fond of Baghdad and its people. I began covering Iraq in the 1990s, when it was already laid low by war and sanctions. But this ancient city on the Tigris, jewel of the land "between the rivers" and a beacon in the Arab world, shaded with its palm trees and cooled by its river, had a special appeal for visitors.

Like many, I came to know the Iraqis as decent, proud and cultured. And the Iraq I liked was not the Iraq of Saddam, but the home of 24 million people who are the inheritors of one of the Arab world's richest civilizations.

From Iraq came scholars, poets and writers of renown. Its philosophers were pioneers of Arab culture from Mesopotamia to Andalusia. Even though its once-wealthy middle classes have been forced into penury—forced, for example, to sell off their libraries book by book to feed their families—it is a culture that will endure.

As for me, I was evacuated back down the American line to Kuwait. While I waited I burned with fever, slipping in and out of delirium. After the ambulance came the helicopter. At the first American field hospital I was consumed by shivers and not even four woolen blankets could warm my shaking body. Then came the troop transport plane, to a field hospital near Kuwait City airport, where my husband found me. I was out.

Chapter 3

TOO CLOSE FOR COMFORT?

By Andrew Gray

$\mathbf{T}$oo many war stories glamorize the narrator, so let me be clear that this tale is not about the typical experience of an embedded reporter in Iraq. Much of that was uncomfortable but undramatic—long, bumpy rides through the fiercely hot desert, getting up in the dead of night and waiting for hours while plans were changed and changed again, living and sleeping in the same sweaty clothes for days. But the story illustrates one big disadvantage of being a journalist traveling among soldiers: If they're a target, then you're a target.

Early in the morning of March 31, the captain responsible for reporters came over as I was packing away my sleeping bag and camp bed after another night in the open. He asked if I could be ready in five minutes. Shortly afterwards, we headed north from the town of Kifl in two Humvees, myself in the back of one, two more journalists in another. The battalion I was with, the 2nd Battalion 70th Armored Regiment, was attached at that time to a brigade of the 101st Airborne

Division. The plan was to observe an attack by the two units on Iraqi positions on the eastern bank of the River Euphrates, near the city of Hilla, about 60 miles south of Baghdad. A sergeant major was not happy. He thought it was too dangerous. He turned out to be right.

Signs of combat were scattered along the road running through fields of palm trees. Blackened, burned-out hulks of vehicles and twisted metal fragments. At least one body lay prostrate in bad shape. Concertina wire, a crater. It was the aftermath of U.S. air strikes on Iraqi paramilitaries.

Twelve days into the war, the battalion was going to be directly involved in an attack for the first time. Some soldiers were visibly nervous. What made me nervous was how inexperienced some of them were. Yet their actions could determine my own fate. The Humvees themselves added to a feeling of vulnerability. Not only did these models not have any armor plating, they did not even have the metal body of a normal car. Doors were made from thin, rubberized canvas. You didn't wind the window down—you unzipped it. Soldiers with us reckoned we should at least have had a machine gun mounted on the roof. But we didn't. All we had was a couple of soldiers in each vehicle with automatic rifles, which they said had a tendency to jam because of the sand. The soldiers poked their rifles out of the Humvee as we traveled. "Hey, you gotta use it, use it," the battalion's sergeant major told one of them as we drove by.

Two Apache helicopters circled the area as we took our place behind tanks and armored vehicles in the column. Thumps and loud pops of artillery fire began at around 7 a.m. The first sign that the battalion was not having everything its own way came soon afterward. A voice came over the crackly radio, giving a grid reference and declaring, "We are taking fire." Soon there were reports of hostile fire from AK-47 automatic rifles and rocket-propelled grenades (RPGs). Someone was firing an AK at one of the helicopters.

We started to hear a lot more loud thumps and bangs around us as we drove forward. "Just hoping it's friendly," I wrote in my notebook at the time. Then it was clear we were far too close to the fighting. As an armored personnel carrier turned left into a field, an explosion went off just to its left, and black smoke began to rise. This was just a few hundred yards away. The Humvee in front started to reverse rapidly, and the lieutenant in charge of mine told his driver to do the same. We reversed at high speed with explosions going off around us. Every time I heard one, I was looking to see if something had ripped through the Humvee, almost expecting it. Some mortar rounds landed where we had just been.

We turned and started racing back up the highway as the radio brought news of more trouble. "Need medevac"—a call for a helicopter to evacuate a casualty to a military hospital. "Bounty's in the shit up there," the battalion commander reported over the radio, referring to one of his three tank companies. "Artillery, casualties—friendly casualties. Lots of dismounts"—a term for enemy fighters on foot.

Then we stopped and started to drive back toward the fighting. I couldn't believe it. I didn't want to be anywhere near that. "We're going back up there?" I wrote incredulously in the notebook. We stopped again as a tank approached, carrying a casualty. The captain told me to get into the other Humvee so he could get the soldier into his vehicle and take him back. Out of our sight, the captain took the casualty in his arms. He told me later he was pretty sure the soldier, just a few days away from his 21st birthday, was already dead at that point.

The captain's Humvee raced off, and we followed. After a few miles, our vehicle stalled and could not be restarted. We were stranded in the middle of the empty road. The Humvee did not have a radio, so there was no way to tell anyone what had happened. We could only hope that the captain had noticed we were no longer following him, that he would send help and that we would be safe until it arrived. Fortunately, we were now some distance from the fighting. The rumbles from the battle were still audible, but they didn't sound very close. If the car had stalled back there, things would have been much worse.

"You guys got your baptism of fire," a lieutenant in the front of the vehicle told us. "That's something to write home about." His remark was part joke and part jibe at reporters who had complained about not having seen enough of the war so far.

The captain came back and found us after about half an hour. More soldiers arrived and towed the Humvee back to the battalion's base. Soldiers there had been through an eventful morning too. Artillery (it may have been "friendly," but that doesn't help if it kills you) had landed within a few hundred yards of the base. An Apache had performed an emergency landing after the co-pilot received a facial wound, presumably as a result of the gunfire attack. After he received medical treatment, the chopper took off and unleashed some gunfire nearby at a possible target.

One soldier was exuberant. His vehicle had come under RPG attack—the crew had responded and killed four Iraqis. Another guy in his vehicle, a medic, was in a very different mood. He was obviously shaken up and had just been to see the chaplain. Medics don't normally shoot, but when the vehicle came under fire, he did, and, as he said quietly, "unfortunately killed someone."

"He's a medic. He didn't sign up for this," his comrade said.

On days like that, as an embedded journalist, it was easy to wonder what you had signed up for yourself. It was now very clear that we had agreed to be exposed to many of the same risks facing the soldiers we followed. At the same time, we had signed away many of the freedoms journalists have when they operate on their own and discarded some of the preferred practices of war reporters.

Safety in the Hands of Strangers

Day-to-day decisions about our safety were out of our hands. As a journalist working independently, you have the freedom to decide whether you go down a particular road or enter a particular village. Reuters reporters covering a conflict normally have to consult news editors daily about their movements and seek permission for any trip inside a dangerous area. That wasn't an option if you were embedded. Where the soldiers went, you went.

Many war reporters also try not to travel with troops, even if they end up following fairly closely behind them. Quite apart from the considerable ethical implications, being inside a military unit means you are generally indistinguishable from the troops as far as their enemies are concerned. This was particularly true in Iraq. We had no transport of our own, just small cramped seats in the back of the soldiers' Humvees. For the first 10 days, we wore the same desert-khaki chemical protection suits as the troops. Afterward we were allowed to wear civilian clothes but only in muted colors, very similar to the soldiers' combat fatigues. It's doubtful whether Iraqi forces were able to tell us apart at all and also doubtful whether it would have made much difference. Would they have appreciated the concept of the embedded reporter? Would they have considered us innocent neutrals when we had chosen to travel with their enemy? I can't imagine a member of the Fedayeen paramilitaries squinting through his binoculars and shouting: "Hold on, the guy in the back appears to be wearing a cream linen shirt rather than combat fatigues. He must be an embedded reporter. Aim your rifle to the left so you don't harm him and get the soldier in front.'

So why take the risks that were inherent in embedding? Why sacrifice control over your own movements and place yourself alongside soldiers in the line of fire?

In part, the answer is that being embedded actually seemed like one of the safer options for foreign reporters planning to cover the Iraq war. Traveling with the most powerful military in the world afforded a degree of protection no private security firm could provide. This was one of the greatest military mismatches, and we were with the overwhelming favorite. Many of us also chose to travel with commanders a little behind the front lines to have a better overview of what was going on. This also meant that, in theory at least, by the time we reached any location, the worst of the fighting should have been over.

The Iraq war was an exceptionally dangerous one for journalists, but embedded reporters did turn out to be safer than others. Two died as a clear result of combat: Christian Liebig of German news magazine *Focus* and Julio Anguita Parrado of Spanish newspaper *El Mundo*. Both were killed when a rocket struck the headquarters of the 2nd Brigade of the U.S. Army's 3rd Infantry Division south of Baghdad on April 7. Another journalist, *Washington Post* columnist and former *Atlantic Monthly* editor Michael Kelly, died in a Humvee accident. A fourth, NBC's David Bloom, died after suffering a blood clot on his lungs.

Regardless of the causes, four dead among the 600 embedded journalists in such a short period is a high casualty rate. A further eight journalists and their assistants were killed in Iraq during the period of major combat. Two more died from health related causes and two are still missing.

Since President Bush declared main combat operations over on May 1, four more have died to bring a total of 18 journalists dead from March 20 to the time of writing.

If you had to cover the war in Iraq as a foreign correspondent, where would you choose to be? In northern Iraq, with U.S. bombs falling from the sky and Kurdish guerrillas fighting Iraqi forces and Islamic militants? Australian cameraman Paul Moran was there. He was killed by a car bomb on March 22. A BBC cameraman and a BBC translator were also killed in the north in separate incidents. What about the south, moving in from Kuwait and operating on your own with the war only just begun? Terry Lloyd of Britain's Independent Television News was killed there on March 22, and two of his crew remain missing at the time of writing. Or how about Baghdad, first facing the risks of U.S. bombing with a "minder" at your shoulder from a ruler who had used foreigners as human shields, then later caught in the middle of ground combat between Iraqi and U.S. forces?

My colleague Taras Protsyuk, a Reuters cameraman, was killed by a shell from a U.S. tank that struck our office in the Palestine Hotel on April 8. Three other members of the Reuters team in Baghdad were wounded. A Spanish cameraman, Jose Couso, was also killed in that attack. The thought that Taras, who had always been so full of life, was suddenly dead was hard for many Reuters staff to deal with while also trying to keep covering the war. "You must grieve for your friend," the chaplain of the 2-70 Battalion told me. But that's especially hard when your friend has been killed by a U.S. tank shell and you are in the midst of a U.S. tank battalion—a particularly upbeat battalion that day. Its men had just come through fierce fighting unscathed and had camped next to some warehouses that gave them access to running water for the first time in weeks.

That day I wished I wasn't with the battalion, its cheerful soldiers oblivious to the death of my colleague. But in general, I was glad to have their protection, their knowledge of military matters, their experience from previous combat, their food rations, their water and their medical facilities all at my disposal. The commanders took great care with the safety of their 600 men and four accompanying journalists—myself, Reuters photographer Peter Andrews and two colleagues from the *Chicago Tribune*.

The Allure of Access

Of course, as that final day in March showed, no one gets safety assessments right 100 percent of the time. But the risks were considered worth taking because the embedding system offered reporters the chance to witness events for themselves. That was a big step forward from the 1991 Gulf War, when most journalists were kept far away from the fighting. Naturally, what we would see would not be the complete picture, but just a small piece of a big and complex mosaic. Responsible news organizations knew their embedded correspondents could not tell the whole story, and they deployed other reporters to try to fill in as many gaps as possible. It was not a perfect solution, but it was preferable to relying solely on the briefers at Central Command in Qatar.

When one of the first battles of the war took place, to gain control of Talil airfield near Nassiriya on the night of March 21, I was close enough to hear and see the massive explosions lighting up the dark sky. It looked like a huge fireworks display, but the sounds were much louder and deeper. My view was far from perfect, but I knew enough at least to report via a mobile satellite phone that a battle was going on. The next day, a senior officer who had monitored the fighting on his radio gave me more details for an updated report. It wasn't ideal, but it was better than waiting for a press release drafted by a public relations specialist.

Access to the military radio network was a big advantage for embedded reporters. We could hear raw, uncensored communication between soldiers, most of them unaware or unconcerned that journalists were listening. Sitting in the back of a Humvee on another hot, bright morning in the desert, I heard over the radio that a suicide bomber had killed at least four soldiers between Najaf and Kerbala. Of course, we had to be careful, as initial reports in the military, just like first police reports of a crime, often turn out to be wrong. But the radio was a valuable source of tip-offs, and that report turned out to be completely accurate.

The access granted by the embedding system allowed journalists not just to break news that was later confirmed in Qatar or at the Pentagon but also to add a more human angle or colorful descriptions. Sometimes it gave them the power to contradict the official line. In a case that became famous, *The Washington Post's* William Branigin filed a report of the killing of Iraqi civilians by U.S. soldiers at a checkpoint, which did not tally with the official version. Branigin said 10 people died; the Pentagon said seven. Branigin said a captain blamed a platoon commander for the deaths. "You just [expletive] killed a family because you didn't fire a warning shot soon enough," the captain yelled, according to the report. The Pentagon, in contrast, praised the soldiers involved, saying they had fired warning shots and acted with restraint. There were enough discrepancies to prompt widespread questioning of the Pentagon's account. Without an embedded reporter on the scene, that would probably never have happened.

For many of us, it was not just our free access to soldiers and operational information that came as a surprise. It was also our freedom to publish the material we gathered. Fears had arisen over the Ground Rules, a 50-point document setting out everything we could and could not report. Officers also had the right to read our material first and insist on elements being omitted if it was deemed they jeopardized security. The main restrictions were on specifying exact troop numbers and locations, but these proved not too onerous. Fairly general descriptions could still convey a good idea of how many soldiers were involved and where they were, and these restrictions became less and less relevant as the conflict progressed. Iraqi forces soon had a good idea from the fighting itself of exactly where their enemy was and in what strength. Not once did a military officer ask to review a story of mine before it was sent.

Nevertheless, the nature of the access we had—a lot of time with U.S. military personnel, a lot less with ordinary Iraqis—and our lack of free movement meant that our stories sometimes lacked all the facts we would have wanted to uncover. Journalists write the first draft of history, the cliché goes. Maybe, but this one was still fairly heavily ghostwritten by the U.S. military.

When embedded reporters arrived in Kifl after the fighting there ended Saturday, March 29, local people had fled and the U.S. Army units involved were pulling out. Dozens of bodies were still lying in the streets. U.S. officers told of swarms of Iraqi forces setting up sniper nests in the main street, firing from doorways, windows and market stalls, even taking to canoes to try to fix explosives to the town's strategically important bridge over the Euphrates. Soldiers from the 3rd Infantry Division fired two depleted uranium tank shells right down the main street, the vacuum effect of the explosions literally sucking the insurgents out of their hideaways into the street, and the guerrillas were defeated, they said. There were no local people around to interview, so that was the story the world first heard of the fighting in Kifl.

In the following days, residents began to return to the town. Some of them had very different accounts of what had happened. Few, if any, Iraqi fighters or none at all had been in the town when the U.S. Army arrived, they said. The Americans had fired at anything that moved and killed innocent people, they said. The people of Kifl are

Shi'ite Muslims, generally no friends of Saddam Hussein and his mainly Sunni Muslim ruling circle, so they had no obvious reason to help him in a propaganda battle against the Americans. They were also disgruntled that U.S. forces had been in the area for around a week but they had received none of the food and medicine the United States promised to provide as it dismantled Saddam's regime. I noted all of this in a story on April 3. But the war had moved on by then, and few people are interested in second drafts of history.

In truth, the situation in Kifl was extremely confused. Local people could give differing versions of just about anything, even the size of the town's population. The U.S. military's account of what had happened may have been largely or entirely true. But as embedded reporters, we were not well equipped to check. If we had been traveling independently, we would have driven into Kifl in our own armored car, accompanied by an Arabic-speaking interpreter. We could have spent a few days in the town, interviewing local people separately and building up a picture of what happened based on details common to all their accounts. We would have been free to enter their homes and to follow them to places they wanted to show us.

As it was, we were tied to the U.S. military. We could go out of the battalion's temporary base, the courtyard of a vehicle workshop on the edge of town, only when soldiers had time and transport for us. In what was still a sometimes-hostile environment, we were not going to be taken to homes or other locations where an ambush could lie in wait. Most of the time, we could talk only to local people we came across in the course of the military's work. The battalion had no interpreter, so we could talk only to those who spoke English, and it was broken English at best. We moved on from the town when the battalion got orders to move, not when it suited us.

That we could not be sure of what had happened in Kifl was not the fault of the battalion. In fact, its soldiers often went out of their way to help us visit the scenes of fighting and meet local people. But its primary job was to wage a war and take care of its own soldiers, not to operate as a support team for a few journalists. Our job was to follow it and report on what it did. By its very nature, the embedding system was bound to make covering one side of the story much easier than covering the other. Not even its creators could argue it was ideal for reporting on the fate of Iraqi civilians.

Ethics and Embedding

The Pentagon's choice of the word "embedding" suggested to some that the system was about more than just giving reporters access to military units—it indicated we were expected to become an integral part of them. Where would that leave journalistic impartiality? Inevitably, the word gave rise to a lot of talk about reporters being in bed with the military, and there were plenty of examples of journalists using the term "we" to describe the units with which they were traveling, implying that there was no difference between them. One female writer began a piece with the words, "We rode at dawn, the men of the 1st Royal Irish." A television reporter told his viewers as he flew with a group of soldiers that "we" were only 10 minutes away from "our" target.

There are many journalists who are smart enough to remember that they are not really soldiers even if they are spending all their time with a military unit. But even those of us determined to preserve the distinction worried that, subconsciously at least, we could become too close to the men who were, after all, protecting us, transporting us, feeding us and living with us for weeks on end through highly stressful times. Would we end up being too soft on them? Some "embeds" probably were. But that was often their choice, not an inevitable consequence of the embedding system. I reported on several incidents and issues I'm sure many in the military would rather I had avoided, as did other embedded journalists.

Once I wondered if I had erred on the side of too much generosity. An officer told me he had been admonished by a general who had seen a tank from the battalion trundling through the site of the ruins of ancient Babylon. I reported the incident, and it's very unlikely it would ever have been made public if an embedded reporter had not been present. It's not the sort of thing the briefers in Qatar were mentioning. But I left out the name of the battalion in my report. Afterward I wondered if this had been a subliminal attempt to spare the soldiers bad publicity. Later it emerged that the vehicle had not been from the battalion, and I was glad not to have been too specific.

It was certainly not always easy to maintain journalistic distance. The commander of the 2-70 Battalion, Lt. Col. Jeff Ingram, had set the tone for how we would be treated throughout his unit by welcoming us warmly and encouraging everyone to be open with us.

"We're gonna treat them like we would treat anyone else in the battalion—we're gonna treat them like shit," he joked at a meeting of his key staff in the Kuwaiti desert soon after we joined them. He presented me with a golden pin badge depicting the battalion's crest— a green shield bearing five yellow arrowheads for five invasions dating back to World War II, with the motto "Strike Swiftly" underneath. "You're one of us now," he said.

That was the problem. We weren't one of them. We were journalists along to report on what they did. But if we shunned offers of friendship and help, we risked being seen as aloof and untrustworthy. That would make it much more difficult to get information and report accurately on both events and the feelings and thoughts of the soldiers involved.

This was a new experience for reporters, with no predefined, clear-cut rules from journalism professors or editors on how to deal with every situation that may or may not equate to getting too close to the troops. Should we let them use our satellite phones to call home? Should we allow them to e-mail from our laptops? Should we accept their battalion souvenirs and military clothing? Often, we made the rules up as we went along, based on little more than gut feeling. It was difficult sometimes to know what constituted simply being decent to another human being, who happened to be a soldier, and what constituted helping a warfighting machine. I didn't like the idea of displaying the souvenirs or wearing the uniform, but others felt differently. Most of us allowed the occasional e-mail or phone call to a loved one.

To close, here is another war story. It's shorter than the first, but it also says something about the embedding system. It takes place on a tense journey into the Shi'ite holy city of Kerbala, about 70 miles south of Baghdad, on April 5 with U.S. forces aiming to destroy Iraqi fighters there.

Gunfire broke out alarmingly close to the convoy we were traveling in at around 8 a.m. The vehicles pulled into the side of the road shortly afterward, and infantry soldiers from the 101st Airborne Division, carrying rifles, ran toward a building on the other side, the pouches with their gas masks bouncing off their thighs. They stopped and crouched behind trucks for cover as they went. A pile of bodies lay beside a tractor with its engine still running. Several bursts of automatic gunfire went off. The driver of the vehicle I was in took aim several times during that anxious hour when he saw figures moving behind a wall on the other side of the road. But he did not have a clear enough view to shoot. The convoy moved on shortly before 9 a.m. U.S. officers later said the bodies piled by the tractor had been Iraqi insurgents, either armed or reaching for weapons, and U.S. soldiers had killed them.

What most of us did not see was the body of an Iraqi boy lying some distance away from that group. The boy's body lay close to a bicycle. He was probably between 12 and 15 years old.

But some soldiers from the battalion had seen the body. They said they had also seen which soldiers from the 101st had killed him and that he had posed no threat to U.S. forces. They reported the incident and, after a delay that alarmed some in the battalion, an investigation was launched. The military does not normally make it public when it starts investigations like these. But this one was reported, because several soldiers had come to know me well enough to trust me with the details.

Without the embedding system, the shooting of the boy may never have been reported to a wide, international audience.

It opened up the front lines on an unprecedented scale, and it brought to light incidents that could otherwise have been covered up. Embedding has continued since the end of major combat in Iraq, but on a smaller scale and with reporters spending shorter and much less intense periods with military units. The challenge for journalists now is to report on postwar Iraq and keep track of stories from the conflict—such as the investigation into the death of that boy in Kerbala—without the unique scrutiny granted by the wartime embedding program.

Chapter 4

BRENDA
GOES TO
BAGHDAD

By David Fox

A month before the invasion of Iraq, I had never heard of the expression "unilateral journalist." Two days into the conflict, I realized it was probably a good thing, as I would likely never have volunteered to become one if I had known what it would be like.

This thought bounced around my head at around midnight as I drove an armored car belonging to Reuters at the rear of a sorry convoy of frightened and bewildered unilateral journalists—myself included—being led through the southern Iraqi desert by British troops. Our temporary escort—about half a dozen military police—ordered total blackout conditions on the 33-vehicle convoy. No headlights, torches or illumination of any kind. No smoking even. Just a tortuously slow and meandering six-hour drive in the middle of the night, interrupted by the overhead roar of military jets, the crash of outgoing and incoming artillery fire and the occasional rattle of small-arms fire.

Every half hour or so the convoy would be stopped and one of the MPs would walk slowly down the line of cars, telling the occupants not to leave their vehicles, to maintain the blackout and complete silence, telling us "the enemy" was everywhere and that we were in real danger of being attacked at any moment. Occasionally, our motley convoy would pull over to make room for a military one, and through the dark you could see the impressive lumbering hulks of tanks, armored personnel carriers, trucks and support vehicles winding their way north to Basra and Baghdad. Sometimes they stopped alongside for a few minutes, and through our windows we could see the faces—some grim, some frightened, most expressionless—of young soldiers being sent into battle.

It was a situation calculated to frighten the wits out of even the most battle-hardened war correspondent, and calculated it was. The whole exercise, we believe, was staged by coalition forces to chase unilateral journalists out of southern Iraq. For the most part, it worked.

Before the war started, even the most experienced war correspondents around were unfamiliar with the concept of being either an "embedded" or a "unilateral" journalist. The way it was explained to us by the coalition forces media people was that embedded journalists would be virtually "adopted" by a military unit, which would be responsible for their security, sustenance and mobility. Many would get to see a lot—more than they bargained for in some cases—while others spent the war in rear positions, complaining of boredom and routine—much as any soldier will tell you that boredom is the greatest enemy. The unilateral journalists, we were led to believe, would be responsible for their own supplies, safety and shelter, but would be assisted whenever possible by coalition forces.

We had crossed into Iraq early the day after coalition forces launched their ground invasion following nearly a week of softening up Iraqi positions and morale with an air bombardment that was, in most cases, witheringly accurate.

Reuters had two teams of journalists positioned on the Iraqi border, just inside Kuwait, poised to cross over to Iraq at the first opportunity. While the news of the aerial attack was being broadcast live by colleagues in Baghdad, a report of the ground invasion beginning was going to be the next important event—the sort of thing that any news organization prides itself on being the first to get.

Establishing our position on the border had been a scoop in itself. Colleagues Bill Maclean and Michael Georgy persuaded a wealthy Kuwaiti to let us stay on his small farm, which ran alongside the border, and Michael moved out there permanently a few days before the air campaign started. Michael, an Egyptian-American, dressed like a working-class farm overseer, had scouted the lay of the land as ground forces started moving into position. Six more Reuters journalists—two photographers, two cameramen and two writers—would join him a few days before we anticipated the ground invasion would start. We were confident our collective instincts would know when that best time would be.

Our plans were disrupted as soon as the embedded journalists "reported for duty" with their respective units. It also gave us the first inkling of how different our understanding of the term unilateral journalist was to the authorities who had bestowed that accreditation upon us. While Kuwait has long had security checks and roadblocks on routes heading north to Iraq, U.S.-led forces took over manning the positions and turned away anyone but Kuwaitis. Every day, a long line of cars piled high with journalists could be seen begging to be let through. As we had, most also planned to camp out on the border and watch the ground invasion start before "invading" themselves in the footsteps of the troops.

While most of those journalists were in hired 4x4 civilian vehicles, Reuters had temporarily imported two armored Land Rover Defenders—the backbone of the British Army's vehicle fleet. Our cars were painted a sort of drab gray-brown, which proved to be both a blessing and a curse. Luckily for us, the color and distinctively British right-hand steering column made our vehicles—to a young U.S. soldier manning a checkpoint at dusk—appear to be a British military jeep. They just waved us through.

Once hidden on the farm itself, we had a front-seat view of the invasion and were witness to a spectacular artillery barrage that went over our heads as cover for the infantry. We were very close to Iraq's port city of Umm Qasr, the scene of some of the stiffest resistance of the war, and our pictures and video footage—delivered via satellite telephone from the farm—were snapped up by media organizations already looking for something different than Baghdad's blazing skyline.

The day after the invasion, we entered Iraq through a gap in the border's sand barriers created by combat engineers to let their forces through. There was no need for us to get right in the thick of the fighting—colleagues embedded with military units would be doing that. Our job was to find stories in the immediate wake of the invasion, to question what authorities were telling the world about how the war was going, to see things from an Iraqi civilian perspective—to get both sides of the story.

That was also, presumably, the aim of the other unilateral journalists who, through equal cunning and guile, made it into Iraq. We marked our cars distinctively with signs reading "TV" made out of black duct tape so that we could be spotted at a distance from the air as being journalists. Most of the other press cars did the same thing, but it quickly became clear that many of the journalists were just following each other around the countryside. As a news agency, Reuters is particularly vulnerable to that, as clients feel that because they take our service, they are entitled to tag along with our staff as well. Usually, we are happy to help out fellow journalists when we can—once we have done our own work—but being chased around the countryside by a convoy of reporters, some raw and poorly equipped, asking "What's going on?" is irritating at best and dangerous at worst. It is also why we found ourselves riding shotgun in the dead of night for a convoy of unilateral journalists in southern Iraq.

We camped the first two nights in a cloverleafed intersection north of the Kuwait border on the road to Basra. A group of friendly British MPs who were guarding a dozen Iraqi POWs were happy to have a few press vehicles camped nearby. We were a relative curiosity, and there was always a chance to call home on our satellite phones. But by the next night, there were nearly three dozen cars full of journalists encamped at the same spot. The place was fast turning into a garbage site. Without the discipline and duties of an army, an invasion of journalists generally leaves behind a lot of collateral damage—particularly to the environment. Some of them should never have been there. While some of the most distinguished and respected journalists of their generation reported in Iraq, there were also some others who were simply out of their depth.

Scaring the Pants Off Them

That was certainly not the case of the ITN crew that was caught in an exchange of fire that resulted in the death of Terry Lloyd.

Two others traveling with him were at the time of writing still missing. A few other close calls with unilateral journalists spooked the already jumpy military authorities into action. They decided to round them all up and send them back to Kuwait. Physically deporting nearly 100 journalists—whom you had previously accredited—would be a public relations nightmare, so we became convinced that they decided to make them go voluntarily by scaring the pants off them. In the main, they succeeded. Early in the evening, rumors circulated the campsite that our friendly MP guardians had turned hostile and said they wanted to give a security briefing to us all later that evening. One MP told me that they would be pulling out the next morning and we would be left to our own devices. Not the best news in the wake of the ITN incident.

But an hour later, the MPs rushed through the camp saying everyone had to leave immediately. They said they had heard reports of a group of Iraqi soldiers heading our way with the aim of attacking us. They said we had to leave everything behind, get in our cars and assemble in convoy about 200 yards up the road, where we would be given an escort to safer ground. We also had to do this in blackout conditions.

The result was chaos.

People panicked, lost their tempers, froze in fear and even openly wept in the mad scramble to get out of there. Our two vehicles were swiftly ready—we had no intention of losing anything and were already well-drilled in packing and unpacking them. Often, it appeared a constant activity. But around us there was mostly panic, and cars were driving off leaving behind tents, boxes of food, water and fuel. Although we could have driven off, we stayed because we didn't want to get caught up in the fender-bending melee that had resulted. From the center of the camp, we heard a plaintive "Help us. Can somebody please help us?" and discovered a team from a British newspaper unable to start their brand new 4x4 because they had been running their satellite phone batteries, computers and, amazingly, an immersion element kettle, off the car battery without the engine running.

We pull-started them out of the campsite, which brought us to the rear of the convoy in the middle of the desert in the middle of the night. The convoy finally settled down for the night in a spot about 30 miles west of where we left, and we were promised a security briefing in the morning. Before we turned in, the Reuters teams went aside and talked about the night's events—our bosses were clearly concerned for our security, as we were. We came to the unanimous agreement that the whole security alert had been staged in order to scare us. We suspected the next move would be to take us in convoy back across the border to Kuwait and then seal it properly and not let us back.

It is perhaps a scurrilous suggestion to make, but between the seven of us was a vast experience of dozens of conflicts around the globe, and nothing about our experiences that day seemed right. If there were reports of an attack on the camp, why not attack the attackers? There was certainly no sign of any Iraqi military presence, apart from POWs that we had seen, and we were already traveling vast distances each day. Despite our escort scaring us all night with talk of imminent or possible ambush, they were very lightly armed and the lead vehicle not even armored. There was no rear guard either—a standard for any convoy—so if they really were as concerned for our security as they insisted, why not do more to protect us? The next morning, a British officer briefed us all. As we had predicted, he issued a dire security outlook for our immediate vicinity and said a convoy would be formed heading back to Kuwait. We were free to stay, he said, but after a night like that, most were ready to go—particularly some of the less experienced. Only five cars stayed—including the two Reuters vehicles.

What followed was an experience we all hope will be a once in a lifetime one.

While we all agreed that the invasion forces had managed to get rid of most unilateral journalists out of genuine concern for their security, they became downright hostile to those that remained. There were some exceptions. I know of fellow journalists who virtually embedded themselves through resourcefulness and skill, while others were given food, water, and fuel by friendly troops. We also had a great deal of help from the troops, but at official level—or rather officer level—we had virtually no help at all. The message clearly was "don't give them any help and eventually they will have to leave."

Over the next few weeks, many other unilateral journalists managed to sneak back across the border, but the authorities made it clear that they expected unilaterals to be based in Kuwait and only attend coalition-organized media opportunities on day trips to Iraq. That plan turned out to be our salvation, as Reuters colleagues would come on an organized trip to see, say a mine-clearing operation in the port and bring supplies in for us that we could collect from prearranged drop points. We could not have survived without the support we got from our colleagues—even though not a day went by without our complaining, enviously, of the fact they were all staying in air-conditioned luxury 100 miles away. Over the course of the next few weeks, we slept by roadsides, in a port, opposite a POW camp, in a gas station forecourt, in a warehouse—anywhere but in comfort or luxury.

At first, the two Reuters teams tried to travel separately, but it became clear for security reasons that we were better off being together—at night at least. During the day we roamed apart. One vehicle was dubbed "Brenda," a sturdy diesel-powered Land Rover with half-inch Kevlar plate and bulletproof glass, while the other was a gasoline-driven version of the same. I traveled with Chris Helgren, a Canadian photographer, and Fedja Stanisic, a giant bear of a Serbian cameraman about the size of two normal people.

Brenda served us well but was very crowded as she had to carry all our equipment, fuel, food and water. Generally, when space gets tight, food and water are the first to go on the reckoning that you can always get something to eat along the way, or go hungry, but there is no point being there if you don't have the equipment to get your story out. In any multimedia team on the road, there is a cameraman with tripod, computers, editing machines, satellite phones and boxes of tapes. Photographers have bulky lenses and also need a computer and satellite phone to transmit their pictures. Reporters travel more lightly, but a laptop and satellite phone are essential. The cars were fitted with a global positioning satellite system that could pinpoint our location to within a few square feet, and adding to the clutter were three sets of body armor and biological suits and gas masks in the event of attack.

Our food at first was mostly canned, but we eventually became adept at trading short phone calls or chocolate with troops for their ration packs. Water was a bigger problem, and we were constantly on the lookout for an opportunity to "liberate" a box or two from the troops. For the first couple of weeks, there was nothing available locally. The Iraqi civilian population almost melted away in the face of the advance and reemerged blinking a few days after it went through. Their lives and their own supply lines had been devastated by the invasion, and their need for food and water was even more pressing than ours.

We Had a Good Run

The situation repeated itself at towns and villages heading north toward Baghdad. Invading forces would advance and snuff out any resistance or administration before passing through to the next town. Our embedded colleagues were reporting on the advance, so it was our job to see what happened in the vacuum left behind—while being prevented from doing so by the military. We had a good run. We were the first reporters in Basra, Baghdad's second-biggest city, but beat a hasty retreat when we came under fire from an Iraqi mortar attack aimed at some nearby British tanks. Our teams were also the first unilateral journalists to the Rumaillah oil fields and also the first into the South Basra refinery, which we confirmed had been undamaged in the invasion—news the oil market was waiting for.

The day we got into Basra was among our best and worst. We crossed the bridge over the Euphrates River, which is the entrance to the city, on foot and just walked into town behind two British tanks. Although they claimed the city, the reality was it had been virtually surrounded, but troops hadn't yet entered. They wouldn't let us pass in our car, but said they had no objection to our walking in. After a couple of miles, chatting to residents who told us of grave water and food shortages, I decided to go back to try to get our car through one more time. As I left, the mortars started. Chris and Fedja took cover under a blown up Iraqi tank, but I decided to carry on to get the car. The soldiers at the tanks tried to stop me from going, but they realized I had colleagues still stranded, and because the car was armored, they let me drive through. I managed to find Chris and Fedja, and we got out safely, although a group of Italian journalists who followed us and went even farther were captured by Iraqi authorities and whisked away to Baghdad. Almost comically, they were later given Iraqi accreditation—something scores of journalists had been clamoring for. If only we had known how easy it was! Chris's pictures of the attack (of a family running away) were on the front page of newspapers around the world, and Fedja's footage was also exclusive. My contribution was reporting that a mortar attack the military insisted had been aimed at civilians trying to flee the besieged city was more likely an attack on British positions guarding the entrance to Basra. The civilians fleeing the city—and there frequently seemed to be more trying to get back in—were being funneled by the invading forces right between their tanks.

On another day, our tire hit a piece of shrapnel from a U.S. laser-guided rocket as we were crossing the bridge, and we had to change it as another mortar attack raged. We changed that tire faster than a Formula One motor racing team in the pitlane.

At some point—tired, hungry, dirty and frustrated—our spirits started to waver. At first, the other car developed a problem and had to return to Kuwait, but they managed to sneak back across the border the next day—refreshed and recharged after a night of hotel luxury. When Brenda's air conditioner gave up, we needed no further excuse and did the same thing. Although it seemed embarrassing to have to admit we had gone back to get the AC fixed, the armor plate of the car meant the two-inch thick bulletproof windows couldn't be opened. In those desert temperatures, the car very quickly became impossible to stay in.

We also got back into Iraq easily—Brenda again fooling a U.S. soldier into thinking she was legitimate—but we decided to press north to Baghdad and report on events outside the city.

There are basically three routes into Baghdad from the south: the central main highway, the southern access and the northern route. U.S. Marines had stormed up the northern route and crossed the Tigris at the main bridge at al-Numan, around 60 miles from the city. The U.S. 3rd Infantry Division took the southern route—running into stiff opposition at Kerbala before bursting across the Euphrates. We tried to follow the Marines, and—through a combination of stealth, luck and a grueling 16-hour drive through the most inhospitable landscape I have ever seen in the middle of the worst sandstorm I've encountered—made it to al-Numan before we were caught and could go no farther. We tried everything we could to get across the bridge, but the American forces turned us away.

Trying the Southern Route

Trying the southern route—even though it was only about 60 miles west of us—would have meant backtracking almost as far as Kuwait—a journey of around three days. It was as low as we had been on the trip. We had got less than 60 miles from Baghdad and would have to drive 600 miles through the desert just to get 60 miles away in a different direction. In addition, we were hearing through our office via satellite phone that no journalists were getting access through that route anyway.

The central highway was uncharted territory. Although it is one of the best roads in Iraq, it was also reported to be the best defended, and as a result U.S. forces didn't use it, choosing instead a pincer movement on either side. No one had driven down that road. We had to decide what to do. Try the north again, do the epic journey and try the south, or take our chances and plunge through the middle.

On the way up, as we camped next to an oasis near a town called Hillal, we digested the shocking news of the day. Our colleague Taras had been killed and three others seriously injured in Baghdad. Our need to reach the city became more pressing.

We decided to take the direct route early the next morning, and we all agreed later we never want to have to drive through something like that again. About 90 miles south of the city, we passed a final U.S. checkpoint and were told that there were no further American forces until the airport in Baghdad. "We wouldn't do that journey in our tanks," was what one commander told us, but he agreed if he was a journalist, he would probably do the same.

In the field, we have always operated on the basis that if one of us feels uneasy about a situation and doesn't want to do it, the rest have to listen to the lowest common denominator and also bail out. After about 10 minutes of debate, we agreed to try. If we didn't make it, we'd head back to Kuwait and give up.

For the first half hour, we didn't see a single vehicle along the highway; then we drove past the wreck of a Russian T-54 tank that had been hit by something so big that its turret and gun barrel— which weigh three tons—had been blown 200 yards up the road.

From then on, it was a procession of ruin. Every mile or so we would pass another bombed tank or armored personnel carrier or artillery piece or missile carrier or army truck. There were also wrecked civilian cars—Toyotas, Ladas, Nissans—and buses and tractors and donkey carts.

It became very clear what had happened. Although U.S. forces had not gone down that road, they had flown over it about a day earlier and blitzed everything along it. It is testimony to the incredible accuracy of modern weaponry that the overwhelming majority of the approximately 200 vehicles we passed had been military ones, but it was clear there had been "collateral damage."

One bus we passed had been hit from above, and almost every seat contained a corpse, still sitting upright, caught completely unawares. From the piles of fly-blown, blackened flesh, it was clear there were men, women and children aboard.

As we carried on, we saw the first Iraqi bunkers. Then more. Then more. On both sides of the road. Piles of sand had been bulldozed onto the highway by the Iraqis to create a series of chicanes that forced the car to a crawl. It is almost impossible to describe the feeling of driving, slowly, the only car on the road, toward what from the front looks like a fortified bunker, every second expecting to see a flash of light as whoever was in it opened fire, only to drive past and from behind see it was empty. Every mile or so this shocking, debilitating build-up and release repeated itself. It was the most excruciating thing I have ever done. I kept having to force myself to release my grip on the steering wheel. The air conditioner was going at full blast, and the three of us were drenched in sweat. We were all chain-smoking, lighting one from another. We had a CD on full volume on the stereo in the hope that if we were going to be blasted into eternity, we wouldn't hear it coming. Ridiculous. Basic science tells you that you never will anyway.

Halfway to Baghdad we decided on another consultation on whether to proceed. I was concerned, but there was no way I wanted to go back. We had driven nearly 3,000 miles in the last three weeks, and Baghdad was so tantalizingly close. We drove on—to stop and talk about it was inviting disaster; we had to keep moving, in any direction—and I argued that the Americans had clearly hit every single piece of heavy hardware along the route, so we were not in danger from that. Chris then pointed out that we were in an armored car and were safe from light machine gun and rifle fire. The biggest hazard was an attack from a rocket-propelled grenade. Shooting us as we drove at a snail's pace through those bunkered chicanes would have been like shooting a barn door from two paces.

It carried on, four hours of agonizing build-up, release. Build-up, release. Build-up, release. I wanted to scream. Chris offered to drive for a while, but I selfishly refused. I wanted something to do, and if we were going to be ambushed, I wanted control and I wanted to blame no one for what followed but myself.

As we neared Baghdad, the chicanes started petering out. Still no sign of many cars on the road. No sign of anyone along the route.

The soldiers had all fled. Every one of them. All that remained were the hulks of dead tanks, APCs, artillery pieces, cars, trucks. Chicanes and bunkers. Smoke rising from the city in the distance. The inside of the car clouded by smoke. Music blasting out.

Then, in the distance we saw movement for the first time: two tanks blocking the road about a half mile ahead, but the turrets of both moving, their gun barrels swinging around and aiming straight at us. Through his binoculars, Chris could make out that they were both big American Abrams tanks. We slowed to a crawl. Middle of the road. Let them see us clearly. Let them look through their binoculars and see Brenda. British plates. Battleship grey. Friendly vehicle. Please, please, please, not friendly fire.

Then madness. Suddenly, we all made the same whimpering eee sound as a flash of light came from the barrel of one tank, followed almost instantly by an astonishing noise like nothing I have heard before. It was almost a non-noise, as if all noise had been obliterated. And then the car swayed from side to side like it was being blown by wind. Both Chris and Fedja screamed, "Stop!" at the moment I was slamming on brakes.

We sat there, scarcely daring to look ahead in case we saw a second flash. Seconds passed. Two hundred yards ahead, we could see the tank commander peering at us through binoculars. Chris and I slowly raised our hands and pressed them to the windscreen. Fedja in the back, chanted something in Serbian. Then Chris got out. Slowly. Arms above his head, he started walking, slowly, toward the tanks. As he got close, the tank commander pulled himself out of the turret and climbed down. Then we saw them shaking hands. Then Chris waved us to come forward.

"You guys are damned lucky I fired over your heads," said the tank commander, who couldn't have been more than 25. "Ain't no one come down that road since we took it out. Kind of caught us by surprise."

And then this happened, as we were driving to where we camped: We saw a jackal—a desert fox—trot across the road in front of us. "A good omen," I told Chris and Fedja.

We were in Baghdad.

Chapter 5

ARE WE NEARLY THERE?

By Matthew Green

"It's killing time boys!" yells a Marine named Donnie, his voice shrill with teenage adrenaline.

Safety catch off, bolt back, machine gun loaded.

Shots crack from somewhere in the mist, Marines run to sandbanks at the roadside, flinging themselves prone and pointing rifles into the haze.

It's the first time they've heard the Iraqi forces fire a shot.

It's a first for me too. I feel a lightness in my stomach, a giddiness as if I've just swerved my car to avoid an oncoming vehicle. Time seems to move in slow motion, reality wobbles.

I'm standing by an ammunition truck—stacked with thousands of bullets, assorted anti-tank missiles, and God knows what else. This is not the place to be hanging around in the middle of an ambush.

More shots ring out from down the road. I run for cover behind what looks like the safest bet—a pair of military ambulances—big red crosses emblazoned on their tan sides. At least I'll be first in the line if I get hit.

Three medics crouch behind the vehicles' tires, eyes wide, handguns drawn.

"Not much you can do with a freakin' nine mil," mutters one of the corpsmen, Taylor, sitting opposite me.

He's clutching a 9-mm caliber Beretta handgun—a weapon of last resort in a fight like this. The corpsmen—Navy paramedics who provide the Marines with medical backup—aren't supposed to carry anything bigger. Gripping the weapon obviously makes Taylor feel better. I have to make do with chewing my pencil.

Thuds reverberate from somewhere close by, a series of crashes like someone dropping filing cabinets from a sixth-story window. I lie flat, scribbling notes, trying to neutralize the creeping panic by recording every detail. Somehow, by writing, you gain an illusion of detachment, as if this was just part of the job of a reporter, rather than an attack that has caught the platoon truck convoy completely by surprise.

Steam rises from the warm soil where rain fell this morning, blanketing the road in mist. I can barely catch a glimpse of what's going on, but I can hear it. An explosion sends a wave of pressure through the air that makes my eardrums flex.

"Now I'm not having a good time anymore," says Taylor, trying to sound nonchalant, but looking worried.

By now I'm so wired I feel like I've drunk 10 espressos one after the other. My handwriting is all over the place. I don't smoke, but I wish I did. Taylor's right, this is less and less fun every minute.

The radio in the ambulances fizzes.

"Mike three, Mike three, this is Mike five, over. We've got the Marines moving up toward that flank," says the voice of a lieutenant, female, and reassuringly calm. Maybe this isn't the time or the place, but I suddenly think this is the kind of woman I could marry.

"Copy," said another voice through a sea of static.

My watch says 5:10 p.m.

"They got to have arty, no one would attack a convoy with an AK," said another voice from behind the ambulance, fearing the attackers wouldn't just have AK-47 rifles, but would start hitting the line of trucks with artillery shells.

"Bullshit, they're nuts, they just want to go to Allah, baby," says Taylor, the whites of his eyes roving left and right beneath the rim of his helmet.

Then another sound, a vibration like 20 pneumatic drills hammering the road. You can feel it getting closer.

"Wow, yeah baby, come on!" says Taylor, fear turning into elation.

An American tank thunders past, the name "War Pig" emblazoned on its barrel. Much as I want to remain neutral as a reporter amid all these Marines, it's impossible not to grin at Taylor. We share a moment of relief and he grins back.

"It's been a while since I been at war you know," he says, suddenly self-conscious about his earlier anxiety.

We're all scared, but in some ways it's a lot easier to be a reporter in a situation like this than one of the troops—all you have to do is hide—you don't get told to go and shoot at anybody. True, you don't share the wild camaraderie of running into gunfire, but I could live with that.

A jagged sound—high-pitched automatic weapons—and I crane my neck around the hood to see figures running in the mist. One screams some orders I can't make out, then bang—the loudest blast yet. I drop my notebook and cover my ears, fearing a closer shot will rip my eardrums.

"Okaaaaaay," says Taylor, eyes rolling upward, contemplating the sound like an ornithologist trying to identify a bird by its hoot. "That's a tank."

There's a screaming howl of engines powered by jet fuel, a crashing like ocean waves as the M-1A1 Main Battle Tank lurches off the tarmac, its 70 tons squashing the brush in search of hidden assailants.

"Mount up! Mount up!" comes the order, yelled from Marine to Marine. A hot bolt of relief—exhilaration blows away the chills. The platoon is moving out, and in my opinion, not a moment too soon.

As I sprint over the tarmac as best I can wearing a bulky flak jacket, Marines are rushing back from the bushes, hauling themselves up into their cabs. I jump up into our ammunition truck, and seconds later, I hear a shout.

"Start her up!" yells Grimes, the driver, from the road below.

I hesitate for a second. I'm a reporter, I'm not really supposed to be a part of all this. On the other hand, I don't want to stick around. There are no keys for military vehicles, so I reach onto the dashboard and turn the switch that starts the truck. I wonder briefly if that small act has transformed me from observer into participant.

Grimes hauls himself up, mud spattered on his flak jacket and helmet. He grabs the wheel as the engine shudders into life and the truck accelerates with aching slowness.

"I had eight rounds come over the top of me," he shouts. "We just watched them comin' in, they aimed straight at us!"

"I was five feet from getting my ankle blown off," replies Scott, the Marine in the passenger seat, panting like he's run a 100-yard race and pointing his M-16 rifle out of the window.

"Feels like huntin' in the reservation, drunk Indians shooting at you," says Grimes, who's 19 years old.

"A shot came next to me, I nearly shit my pants, except I had a shit yesterday," Scott mutters. He's only a few years older than Grimes.

They both seemed to be talking to themselves, caught up in the realization they had been in combat for the first time. For Marines, this was a coming of age—even if they had been forced to beat a hasty retreat. That surprise initiation began to glow inside, flickers of bravado eroding their fear. This was a feeling I would never share. I was writing, not fighting. They had crossed a line during the 30-minute firefight, become a different kind of Marine than the one they had been that morning. I was still just a reporter.

"You ever been shot at and they miss?" the normally reserved lieutenant asked me when we stopped, slapping me on the shoulder and grinning like a maniac, his brain high on a drug called narrow escape. The talk was of combat action ribbons—the decoration Marines get for being shot at, and shooting back—regardless of whether they ran away or not. I was more worried about sending a story, and preferably before any other reporters who might be around.

By now the truck is speeding, and I wish Grimes would shut up yapping and keep his eyes on the road.

"This is not what I expected in Iraq," he says. "I expected tanks and desert warfare, not jumping into ditches full of mud."

And he's right—this is not what many of the Marines had expected. Perhaps naïvely, a good number of them were anticipating a "Baghdad Run," four days from Kuwait to the capital, and nothing but white flags all the way up the six-lane. A road trip to glory.

The attack hit them on March 26, less than a week into the invasion. Looking back now at headlines saying "Victory after 21-day war," it looks like a lightning campaign. But there was a time in the early days when for at least some of the Marines, the war looked like it would take a lot longer, and be a lot tougher. And, some admitted afterward, if the Iraqi armed forces had tried harder, they could have made things a lot bloodier for the Americans.

The day of the attack, I had been asking the Marines about overstretched supply lines, how vulnerable they were. I felt acutely exposed in the cab of the truck, visible for miles. With typical bravado, they said they felt pretty secure, a "hard target" in Marine-speak.

"That's a 40-mm grenade launcher, that'll hurt you," said one of the gunnery sergeants with a gleam in his eye, pointing at the MK-19 mounted on the cab of one of the trucks.

"As we speak right now there's jet aircraft flying around about us, we can get on the radio if we see an Iraqi tank out there, within a couple of minutes it could come screaming out the sky and blow it up," he said, and a little circle of Marines nodded agreement.

"It would be a tough fight, but we could fight an Iraqi tank platoon," said one. "Our threat right now is not so much the Iraqi army, it's the terrorists and the fanatics that are runnin' around."

Seconds later, we heard the first shots, and they were diving for cover, some grabbing the Kevlar helmets they had carelessly removed and jamming them on their shaven heads. The platoon did not take any casualties, but it was a chastening experience—it showed the Iraqis were ready to fight.

There were plenty of reasons to feel afraid. Earlier the trucks had rolled over a drainage pipe under the road packed with explosives, a trap set by the Iraqi forces. Perhaps they had been waiting for the convoy to approach before detonating the charges, blasting a couple of the trucks into smithereens. As it happened, the observers manning the ambush had fled. A loud bang cracked the silence as Marines blew the explosives up at dusk, sending a cloud of smoke curling over the plain.

Thrill Tour

It had started out differently, like a thrill tour, a grand adventure for the Marine drivers on the roads of southern Iraq. We were travelers in a caravan of tanks and trucks and ugly, tracked monsters the Marines called "hogs"—streaming up the road in a steel river without a living Iraqi soldier in sight. The Marines took photos with disposable cameras to send home, some snapping themselves posing by the bodies of Iraqi soldiers lying in a ditch by the roadside. When questioned, they said it was for "memorabilia," but they wouldn't send that particular film back to their wives.

"This is the best fun I've had in my life, I'm loving every minute of it," Grimes said one day, as our truck rolled toward the horizon, one tiny cell in a giant metal artery pumping ammunition, food and fuel to the front.

He would drive listening to Alan Jackson country tunes on his headphones—a reminder of his days on the farm back home in Montana. I was worried he wouldn't notice if we started getting shot at, but he insisted with boyish self-assurance that he could hear just fine.

He had a favorite tune—a song about Sept. 11. It was his soundtrack to the early days of the invasion—played over and over on the portable CD as we rolled up the highway. The track was a slushy song about how the fall of the twin towers had made people reflect on what was really important in their lives, going to church, that kind of thing. It was mulchy, and gooey, but it seemed to help give the trip a purpose. To prevent another Sept. 11 was one of the stock answers that Marines would give when asked about why they were going to war. Saddam might help plan another one, right?

While Grimes was listening, Scott, who seemed more aware of the danger, was watching, constantly on guard. Sometimes his caution seemed to border on paranoia, but on the other hand, if they really are out to get you . . ..

"If we get overrun, you want to know how to use the .50 cal?" he said, looking at me from his place on the passenger side of the cab.

Perhaps to him it seemed like a real possibility that a reporter would end up firing the .50 caliber machine gun—one of the heaviest weapons carried by the convoy.

"You pull open the top, put in the rounds, pull it back, twice, then aim it in the direction you want to kill," he said.

I felt almost touched that he would imagine I would leap to the convoy's defense in a crisis, but I knew I would never lay a finger on the thing. That would be getting a bit too close to the story. I'd stick to my place behind the ambulance.

My short wave radio crackled with BBC reports of Tomahawk cruise missiles killing civilians in Baghdad, of heavy fighting in southern Iraq, of dead American soldiers. But on our little patch of the battle zone, the Marine truckers seemed to feel less like they were in a war, more like they were on an outing full of new sights and sounds—smoke on the horizon, the crump of artillery, the endless plain.

We crossed the Iraqi border by night. Joining an invading army would normally rate pretty high on the excitement scale, but I was so tired after days of waiting in the Kuwaiti desert, and staying awake watching the artillery bombardment of the first night, I was half asleep. I was annoyed at myself—I wanted it to be exciting, I wanted to feel the pulse of world events. Instead my eyelids drooped, the backs of my eyeballs were burning. I was nodding off in my front row seat to history.

Grimes was tired too—he had slept for a few hours during the first night of the war in a foxhole in his gas mask, fearing chemical attack. I gave it a try, but found it impossible to sleep with what felt like a black rubber octopus clamped to my face. Bombers rumbled overhead, it sounded like they were ripping the sky apart. I slept maskless, the night air chill on my skin. A rodent scurried around the edge of the hole.

That night, American armor choked the roads of southern Iraq. Prisoners huddled in the middle of rings of razor wire by the roadside. Bring a set of the Marines' night vision goggles to your eye, and an emerald sun would turn the dark into a world of fuzzy green shapes and soldiers. You would see yet more U.S. armored personnel carriers off to the side of the road, some flickering with an infrared light identifying them as friendly forces, a fluorescent beam only visible through the scope. All the time, I had a sense of unreality, as if I was watching all this as a spectator, not really there.

Days passed in a haze, up before dawn, sleeping on the desert by the truck, engines rumbling into life when the sun was just a pale disc on the horizon. I wrote news stories, and Oleg Popov, the veteran Reuters photographer traveling in the same convoy, took pictures.

"I need a hot shower, a cold beer, and a medium woman, not too hot, not too cold," someone said one bright morning, and he spoke for all of the Marines.

By night, oil fires blazed, hot coals in the darkness. Far or near, it was impossible to tell. The dark made Scott nervous. One time, we were walking around the truck. The pinprick beams of the Marines' crimson flashlights danced in the blackness. You could make out the silhouetted hulks of the trucks, but only just.

I stopped.

Scott's rifle was pointing straight at my chest.

"I was just about to shoot you," he whispered, relieved that it was me, and not an attacker sneaking up on the vehicle.

A sandstorm halted us for a day and we lay almost comatose in the cab, covered in dust, asleep but looking like victims of the volcano in Pompeii, preserved by a layer of ash.

Marines posted cardboard signs on their trucks that read "Spring Break 2003" or "Baghdad or Bust." They giggled at each other when they had to take a crap in a hole by the roadside.

Toilets were never a priority for Marines—who liked to think of themselves as warriors rather than sanitation experts. Many removed the base of an ammunition crate and used it as a kind of throne to avoid the discomfort of crouching in the dirt. "Lighthouse" toilet paper came in the ration packs, along with miniature bottles of Tabasco sauce.

Body Bags

Maybe the atmosphere would have been different if we had seen dead Americans. During 50 days with the Marines, traveling from Kuwait to Baghdad to Najaf and beyond, I never saw a single dead U.S. Marine or Army soldier. The closest I came to American death was in Kuwait, while we were still waiting for war.

I interviewed Lt. Col. John Cassady one Sunday morning. He was sitting in the MA tent. Mortuary Affairs—rather a delicate way of putting it, I thought. Sunlight filtered into the interior, golden specks of dust danced in the light, and Cassady offered me a cardboard box to sit on.

This was a story I really wanted—the story of the man in charge of sending dead Marines home. I wanted it because this was not an advertisement for the destructive power of U.S. weapons, or urban warfare training that Pentagon spin doctors perhaps hoped would intimidate the Iraqis, or life in the desert for U.S. troops. This was a story about what the war might be like.

Cassady is a large man, 52 years old, whom I imagine to look almost like an uncle, a friend of the family. He has an air of dignity about him. And he seems happy to talk about recovering the "fallen."

"The process is very personal, you do get to know the deceased, you get to go through personal effects," he said. "You'll find wallets, ID cards, favorite rings perhaps. We even read off the serial numbers on the money, there'll be drivers' licenses, it all builds up a picture of the person."

"You were saying that you feel almost like you get to know them," I said. "I wonder whether that means there was one in particular you remember?"

He paused for a few seconds.

The memory of a photograph is back.

"I've got a photo in my head right now from a Marine 12 years ago, it just happens to catch in your head, it was probably a girlfriend."

Cassady fell silent, transported for a moment to the 1991 Gulf War, when he was doing the same job. His eyes turned away from mine, and he seemed to be thinking, distracted by something.

"Can you remember the photo at all?" I asked.

"A young woman," he said. "A black woman, I suppose it must have been his wife or his girlfriend."

"Can you remember what she was wearing at all, any details like that?"

"Blue dress," he said, then paused again, he seemed to be holding his breath.

"A lot of the time you think she might be missing him," he said. He turned his head to look at something on one of the shelves. There was a silence between us.

"I tell my Marines not to look at these kinds of things too much," he said. "Photos go face down, it's best not to dwell."

It isn't just photos that stick in the minds of the men collecting the dead—other details bother them, Cassady said. "Particularly when very recent dead quiver. If you move them, air in their lungs might cause a sound, a groan or something like that, that's just a fact of what happens when you die."

"Quiver?"

"Well, sometimes you might get a finger, or an eyelid or something move after a Marine is deceased," he said.

Two Marines in the tent were discussing what would happen if a man was killed wearing a chemical warfare suit—how the gas from the putrefying body would swell up, forming a balloon of corrupted flesh and vapors.

As I walked out I asked Cassady what the metal stakes piled up in the corner were. They were the poles for stretchers to be used for carrying corpses. Outside the tent, crates held "remains pouches"—MA doesn't call them body bags. Cassady didn't want to say how many he'd brought with him.

By the time I was in Iraq, the memory of the conversation with Cassady was fading.

I watched the scenery turn from the desolation of northern Kuwait, where the only things to break the depressing desert vista were marching power pylons, to the irrigation ditches and greener countryside of Iraq.

I had never seen a more dismal sight than the Marines advancing through Kuwait: trucks of artillery shells, parked in a monochrome wasteland, their drivers wandering through the dust clouds in gas masks and chemical overalls, a vision of some future Apocalypse.

In Iraq, we sniffed the pine cone scent of coniferous trees in the plains around the southern city of Basra. I listened to something I had not heard for months: birds. There were fields and blue sky, it felt like a European summer.

"Funny, ain't it? This is almost like Star Wars, there's us coming up the road to take on this evil emperor type guy," said Scott one day as the truck trundled ever onward.

He paused to reflect.

"You know a thing I want to happen in my lifetime, I want people to actually be able to fight with light sabers."

We passed a herd of dromedaries, curved necks probing forward as they made stately progress through the desert.

"I remember in the film *Conan the Barbarian* when he knocks out a camel with a punch," said Scott. "That was cool."

Sometimes we talked about women. Scott taught me the Marine Corps songs. "I wish all the ladies were pies on a shelf, and I was a baker, I'd eat 'em all myself," he recited as we sat in the cab of the truck.

There were many variations of the tune.

"I wish all the ladies were bells in a tower, and I was a bell boy, I'd bang 'em every hour...."

We talked about the future, as if the war would soon be over and our lives suddenly transformed.

"I'll go back to the farm one day, or maybe work—work as a mechanic. Maybe I'll go to work on the oil in Wyoming, my cousin's got a company out there," Grimes said, puffing on one of his cheap cigars.

"What would you do?"

"Truck driver," Grimes said, twisting the wheel as the convoy veered off the road, weaving through the desert.

We told stupid jokes, saying anything to pass the time as we rolled forward into the white space on the map of Iraq, crossing the River Euphrates, heading for Baghdad. Scott reckoned that the distance to the capital was about the same journey from his home in upstate New York to Disneyland.

"I told my friend I'd bring him back a picture of Saddam and a skull," he said. "I figured I could fit it into my sea bag."

"I bet you couldn't get an Iraqi into the States," said Grimes.

"I wouldn't want to," said Scott.

Our conversations ranged wide.

"You ever put a frog in bleach or chlorine or something?" asked Scott one day. "It's pretty funny, they just dissolve."

"Military Sucks"

We passed tracked Amphibious Assault Vehicles with names like "Millennium Falcon" and "Baghdaddy" and a tank called "Saddamizer." Then we stopped.

There was talk of an "operational pause," the radio news was full of reports of fighting at Nassiriya, of the U.S. advance getting bogged down, of attacks by Fedayeen guerrillas. In Washington, questions were being asked over strategy. Had America sent enough troops? Had they attacked too early? Had Defense Secretary Donald Rumsfeld blundered?

Marines don't like stopping. Marines especially don't like stopping in fields, populated chiefly by irritating gnats, with rumors coming down the line that they might have to halt for a month. I didn't much like the idea either, and I wondered what I would write about in this patch of dirt. The Marines dug foxholes and waited. And as they waited, they thought less and less of Iraq.

Donnie was a lance corporal sent to ride in a supply truck in "Operation Iraqi Freedom." I'd met him for the first time when we were in Kuwait, two days before the invasion started. He was sitting in the desert next to his weapon, smoking a cigarette. He had a few blond hairs on his lip—a brave attempt at a moustache. Lots of the young Marines attempted moustaches, which invariably made them look even younger. He had scrubby hair, freckled skin and was 18.

"What the fuck is that in front of you?" yelled a sergeant.

"It's a MK-19, staff sergeant," Donnie replied.

"Then why the fuck aren't you cleaning it?" he said.

"Yes, staff sergeant."

Donnie began to remove the clips holding the grenade launcher's components in place. Taken apart, it looked more like a piece of machinery than a weapon—like bits of a lathe in a workshop, not something made to separate flesh from bone. Donnie pulled out the item that looks a bit like a toothbrush carried by all Marines and began scrubbing the surface of the metal, weighing the heavy block in his hand.

"That's what I want," he said.

"What do you want?" I replied.

"A Buzz Lightyear tattoo, right here," he pointed to his calf. "Soon as I get back, I'm gonna get Buzz Lightyear tattooed right here on my leg."

He pulled a catch and the heavy bolt slid out of the body of the weapon. I wondered what the intergalactic space ranger Buzz Lightyear had to do with Iraq.

"This sucks," he muttered.

"What sucks?"

"Military," he said. "Everything sucks in the military."

"You mean you don't like it out here?"

"I didn't think I was going to get deployed, then, they're like 'you're going.'"

He dropped the block, and began brushing over the MK-19's barrel, a heavy pipe with a flared end for firing the grenades—little golden cylinders packed with destruction.

"So how long you been in the Marines?"

"Seven months, and I got a wife and a kid back home."

To be 18 and married was common for a Marine. Having a wife gets you out of the barracks and into your own home, and more pay. The kids come naturally.

"So why did you join?"

He paused. Another couple of Marines next to him were performing similar tasks, flipping catches on 240-Golf machine guns, brushing the grit from working parts coated with grease.

"We're over here protecting people in America, if we won't do it, who would?" Donnie said, not sounding very convincing. "You like music?"

"Yeah. What kind of music?"

"You know, good music, like 'Disturbed.' 'Disturbed' really rock. You like 'Metallica?' I love 'Metallica,' they really rock too."

Some buried, decade-old memory of heavy metal music rose to the top of my mind.

"What about 'Slayer?' 'Reign in Blood?'" I said.

"Yeah, 'Slayer' rock too. Hey, you like cool music man."

"So whereabouts are you from in the States?"

"You know a place called Davenport? It's in Iowa, right on the Mississippi. Gets real hot down in Davenport, wife's there now, with our son, they both waiting for me that's for sure."

"So how come you ended up in the Marines. Was that it, defending America?"

"Well, yeah, and I didn't have much else to do. If I hadn't joined the Marines, I don't know what I would have done, I probably would have done something stupid and ended up in trouble, I probably wouldn't have been able to support my wife and son. The Marine Corps keeps me out of trouble."

"You think you're going to be in Iraq a long time?"

"I think we'll be in Iraq for two weeks, I'm hopin', at best. Everybody wants to go home. I miss home, I just mean wakin' up in the morning and havin' my wife yell at me for stealing the covers and stuff like that."

He rummaged in a pocket and produced a coil of orange plastic—a slinky.

A sergeant shouted from somewhere near a truck. The Marines rose.

"Will you watch my slinky for me?" he said, placing the toy on a tire lying on the ground. "Thanks."

Now, a week after crossing the border, we were stuck in a patch of wasteland. The day of the ambush had passed, the adrenaline fix for the platoon had subsided. There was no sign we were going anywhere fast, but there was a routine of sorts. Every half an hour or so, Huey helicopters thwack-thwacked overhead in pairs, sweeping low over the convoy to provide air cover. You could see the door gunners in helmets and goggles watching out of their hatches—a Hollywood image of Vietnam.

Sometimes Marines would spend an hour or so assembling a camouflage net to hide their trucks. Then they would be ordered to take it off. Then they would be told to put it back on. I liked the nets, the sunlight fell through them like dappled rays filtering through a woodland canopy.

One day during the pause, Donnie was sitting in a foxhole, eating a Meal, Ready-to-Eat (MRE), the ration packs they lived on in Iraq. He was smoking, looking out at the fields with a child's eyes. He was missing his wife, Kim, the name he'd given to his M-16 rifle.

"We went and watched the sunset together and all that crazy trash, we had fun. It's gonna be like three times when we get back," he said. "I'm going to take 'em to the San Diego zoo, I might take 'em to Sea World too."

He wanted to talk. It was often like that with the young Marines. I sometimes felt like they saw me—aged 27—like some kind of older brother, a person outside the military hierarchy, always happy to listen. I heard stories of court battles for custody of children, of assault charges pending back home, and endless tales of girlfriends. They didn't seem to mind that I wrote it all down, or they just didn't notice.

Donnie told me the story of how he had met Kim at Happy Joe's restaurant in Davenport, where they had both worked before he enlisted in the Marines. One day, they'd been in the kitchen, joking around.

"I didn't want to be a dork and bust out 'do you have a boyfriend?' so I said 'your boyfriend would be mad if he knew I was messin' around with you.'"

"I kissed her, we married and we have a son. Weird story, huh?"

He pulled a picture of her from his flak jacket. Almost every Marine had a picture of a girl in his flak jacket. I was single, with no girlfriend. Part of me felt deprived, part of me didn't care.

Kim was jumping up and down on a bed, the picture snapped in mid air. Like him, she was 18. He showed me a photo of his baby, Jayden, fat-faced and wrapped in a blanket, born last October. The camera flash had given him red eyes. There's a letter from Kim, in an envelope with a Stars-and-Stripes sticker and "We love you daddy!!" written on it.

"We had a water fight before I left, I was just messin' around in the shower. Next thing I knew it's a big water fight, it was so fun," Donnie said.

"Me and my wife are like kids though."

He took off his Kevlar helmet. He'd drawn an insignia of a skull and lightning bolts on the desert-patterned cover, with the motto "IOWA BOY" in felt-tip pen. One of his superiors had made him cross it out, but you could still make out the design.

"I hate this place," he said. "After we leave I hope this place goes straight to Hell for all I care."

I left him and walked down the line of foxholes. There were other Marines who felt the same. Others didn't care much about whether our convoy was stopped or moving, and threw clods of earth at each other for fun.

Time passed in the wasteland, and rumors flourished. I hitched a ride with Grimes down to an ammunition dump, set up by the roadside. There were lines of crates—boxes of 83-mm anti-tank rockets called SMAWs. There were snakes of grenades linked together by chains—fodder for the MK-19. Coffin-shaped boxes contained charges for clearing minefields. I sat on a crate of electric fuses and talked to Marines who just seemed to be hanging around among the boxes of artillery shells.

They said they'd heard an ice cream machine was coming, though they didn't really believe it. There was talk that Iraq's former Deputy Prime Minister Tareq Aziz was dead, and a story that Saddam had built moats of oil around Baghdad to set ablaze when we arrived, hoping to kill us.

A beefy sergeant with the word "Monty" scribbled in black marker on his helmet barged into our little gathering, a cigarette dangling from his lip. He broke the news brusquely. An armored personnel carrier had just accidentally run over a pair of Marines up the road.

"Killed one, ripped the legs off the other," Monty said, and the young Marines looked on with a mixture of awe and fear.

I wondered if it was true.

Living in a Hole

My radio proved to be not only a vital source of news to keep me informed and chase away the more outlandish tales, but a great bargaining chip. Many a gunnery sergeant would give me a dawn cup of coffee—"Joe" as the Marines called it—in return for the BBC headlines. It was an unspoken but sacred agreement. Only those with the foresight to bring little camping stoves could get hot drinks in Iraq. I was not one of them, and I craved caffeine as one of my few luxuries.

The Marines loved listening to the news because the troops out in the field had no idea what was going on beyond their little patch of desert. Even when nothing was happening, some of them felt pretty depressed about the situation.

"I feel like the longer I'm out here, the less chance I have of staying alive," said a Marine called Sanchez one day during the pause. "I got a girl back home and this really isn't helping out with the relationship, she's going to be there but it puts strains on us both."

"Anyone want a chocolate dairy shake?" came a shout from further down the line.

Sanchez ignored the offer, explaining how he prayed every day to get back home, with a Rosary given to him by his girl. His 21-year-old soul was filled with self-pity.

"I want to have my mind, some people come back from war all messed up," he said, strapping up his flak jacket after splashing himself with water from a container by his truck, his first wash in a week.

"I could be walking over there to my friend right there and there's a landmine. Right here the odds are against us, we don't know the terrain, we don't know the people, we don't know what they got coming for us."

His black eyes were sullen.

"I hate being out here, it sucks," he said.

It was a view I heard a lot over those few days—nobody wanted to be stuck in a desert.

"I hate this place!" shouted one Marine from a trench he had dug by the road. "Where's the exotic women, I thought they were supposed to do some belly dancing or something?" he said, to laughter from Marines reclining in the shallow trenches they called their "fighting holes."

Oleg was also feeling a little let down at this point—not much combat action to take shots of. That would come later. As a writer, I was okay—"U.S. troops wonder why they aren't in Baghdad yet" was a story, though perhaps not the kind of headline the propagandists in the Pentagon were hoping for.

When the Marines took away our Thuraya satellite phones the next day—attempting to sever my only means of sending stories and communicating with the outside world—we were suspicious. The phone is basically a mobile that uses a satellite signal, so it can work anywhere in the Middle East, even if there is no normal cell phone network. I used it as a modem, allowing me to log on to the Internet and send my stories from my laptop anywhere in Iraq, or to speak to the Reuters desk set up in Dubai to edit our stories.

The Marines said they were taking them because the Iraqis could use the phone signal to find our position and fire missiles at us. Something didn't smell right—partly because many other "embedded" reporters had been allowed to keep their Thurayas. We wondered whether someone higher up the chain of command was fed up with reporters writing stories about bored Marines stuck in the middle of nowhere, though we had no proof. Maybe they really were worried about security.

Fortunately, I had brought two Thurayas with me. I handed over one and kept the other hidden in my flak jacket, using it in secret for the rest of the war. Sometimes I would hide behind a palm tree, other times behind a house, always worried I would get discovered. I never did. In Baghdad, the commanders eventually said we could have the Thurayas back—but only if we were at least 250 yards away from the nearest Marine when we used them. Perhaps they thought there might be one last Scud missile waiting to lock on to the signal.

In their first few days in Baghdad, the Marines felt like heroes, as kids ran up to greet them in suburban streets, asking them to sign soccer balls or their arms. I watched one Marine entertaining them with a Michael Jackson-style "moonwalk," reveling in the attention of his pavement audience of laughing children.

In Baghdad it was easy to forget those six days in the desert, when it all seemed to be going slowly, so very slowly. The sound that sticks in my head is the periodic clunk of Scott's Kevlar helmet on the dashboard as he kept nodding off to sleep in the cab of the truck, catching up with shut eye lost on watch the previous night.

"Right now, I'm going to that crazy level, so if enemies come, they're done," Scott said one day, the fatigue wearing his nerves thin.

I spent a night out with the Marines on watch, I wanted to see what it was like. Usually I slept in the cab of the truck, where I could also spend time working on my stories. I had to put a jacket over my head to stifle the light from the laptop screen at night to avoid attracting the attention of anyone who might be out there, watching the invaders.

It was quiet on watch. Behind us lay the road and the trucks. Beyond a sand bank lay stars, blackness, the unknown.

There was a constant chirruping of insects, and in the distance you could hear the click and buzz of radios from the command post. Muttering drifted from the darkness, whispers traded by Marines sharing watch. The metal loop holding a rifle strap rubbed against a gun butt with a clinking sound. Tearing noises came from a foxhole as someone ripped open an MRE.

"This is worse than we were in 'Nam," said a voice, but it was a joke. This wasn't so bad, after all.

I slept on the ground in my sleeping bag, trying not to roll into the deep "fighting hole" Grimes had sunk in the ground. He always seemed to dig them like basements.

Then almost immediately it seemed, we were being woken— this time by the shout of "Ravioli, Ravioli"—a sergeant's idea of an amusing play on the word "reveille"—normally used by the Marines to wake up sleeping comrades. It was 4:10 a.m., there was not even a hint of sunrise in the eastern sky.

"I don't understand, how could anyone ruin such a beautiful dream so quickly," muttered Grimes, emerging from his hole. His face was covered in dirt.

The lieutenant walked past.

"You need to hygiene, Grimes," he said—using Marine parlance for washing, or at least cleaning yourself with the baby wipes they used to scrub themselves.

"I live in a hole, sir," replied Grimes, which seemed like a good answer.

Some Marines even found religion in the Iraqi wilderness, or at least, rediscovered it. It was a sight I'll always remember. A priest in a combat helmet holding hands with a young Marine as a helicopter flies overhead by a roadside in southern Iraq.

As the roar of the rotor blades died, I made out a phrase.

"May all your sins be dissolved."

The Marine told me later that he didn't want to lose his spot in Heaven in case he was doing the wrong thing by following orders. Maybe it wasn't such a just war, after all.

Then, suddenly, we were moving.

Oleg and I left the platoon, moving to an infantry outfit that had paused at the same patch of wasteland for those six days of sun and sand.

That night we joined the "trigger-pullers," the "grunts," the combat troops. For me it was a chance to see the front line, the Marines on the offensive. We didn't know it then, but Baghdad was exactly two weeks away.

I said goodbye to Grimes, who gave me a terse "okay, bye." I left a business card for Scott, he wasn't around. I hoped he'd e-mail me, I'd got to like him. Taylor wasn't around either. And I said goodbye to Donnie.

"Here, take this," he said.

He handed me a brass casing from a bullet for an M-16.

"That's the first round I ever fired," he said.

I felt almost guilty about accepting it, thinking that this should probably have been an heirloom for his grandchildren. But it seemed rude to turn it down. I popped it in the zip-up pocket of my flak jacket and walked away.

Chapter 6

EYE OF THE STORM

By Nadim Ladki

President Bush's ultimatum to Saddam Hussein to step down or face an invasion was just 90 minutes old when day broke over Baghdad. From my balcony in the Palestine Hotel, I watched the Tigris River flowing unhurriedly through the battered city.

Over on the western bank, lights were still on at the huge presidential complex, Saddam's main headquarters and the oldest of dozens of lavish palaces across Iraq he called home.

Throughout the night of March 19–20 we had reports of raids by U.S. and British warplanes in the no-fly zone that extended from the Kuwaiti border to the southern edge of Baghdad. While intense, the strikes seemed only part of the softening-up attacks that had been going on for weeks in preparation for D-day.

Like most people, I thought hostilities would start with a night-time barrage, and that meant nothing would happen for at least another 14 hours. I left the balcony and went into my room, dreading the waiting game that now seemed inevitable.

I had just sunk into a chair when an angry screeching drove me to my feet. Rushing to the balcony, I saw that explosions were shaking the city. Black smoke billowed over the suburb of Dora to the south.

"A raid on Baghdad?" I remember thinking. "This is the opening shot of the war."

All the tiredness after a sleepless night vanished in a second. With my heart pounding, I took a deep breath and picked up the telephone to file the critical news. Saddam's third war, and almost certainly his last, had begun. A new chapter in Middle East history had opened.

What that was to mean for me was long nights and days of bombardment, shortages of food and water, close scrutiny and interference by authorities and ultimately the death and wounding of some of my colleagues.

Hundreds of reporters, camera crews and photographers had flocked to Baghdad in anticipation of the war. Only a few believed that U.S. and British threats were just saber-rattling.

As weeks of waiting had turned to months, journalists became restless, pushing the official reporting restrictions to the limit, even touching on taboo subjects such as Saddam's state of mind as reflected in his almost daily television appearances.

As hostilities approached, Baghdadis seemed confused. For the vast majority who only listened to the official media, war seemed unlikely.

"They have threatened us many times before," said a restaurant owner. "They are just trying to scare us. I don't think the U.S. and Britain have the stomach to invade Iraq."

"Bush is a coward," was a typical remark from a pro-government Iraqi journalist. "He will not dare to send his troops to Iraq because he knows what the cost will be."

But Iraqi government departments had been preparing for war, and the Information Ministry was no different. Since October, Baghdad had opened its doors to the international media, giving out hundreds of visas after years of mostly keeping foreign journalists out.

Iraqi officials knew that as war became more likely, they had to show that they were cooperating with United Nations weapons inspectors. Under intense pressure, Saddam allowed inspectors back into the country for the first time in four years to look for weapons of mass destruction, even though he denied he had them. Wanting the world to see that inspectors could work unimpeded, Iraqi authorities allowed journalists to cover their activities. But journalists had to be accompanied by Iraqi "minders" who monitored what they filmed and whom they interviewed, intimidating ordinary people into following the government line.

Iraq's Information Ministry naturally worked on the assumption that Saddam's government would survive. It forced the Western media to operate from a press center at the ministry and even built more offices to house the large numbers of journalists.

When the drive to prove Iraq did not have doomsday weapons failed to stop Washington and London from going ahead with invasion plans, the Information Ministry prepared to manage how the war would be reported. It believed that a prolonged war with many civilian casualties would provoke world opinion into forcing a negotiated end to the conflict that would leave Saddam and his Baath Party in power.

Propaganda Machine

On the morning after the opening raid, the propaganda machine was ready to roll with the official Iraqi version of the conflict. The director-general of the Information Ministry, Uday al-Taei, was at the press center in khaki shirt and pants, overseeing even tighter controls over the 250 foreign journalists in Baghdad. Camera crews, photographers and reporters would now only be allowed to leave the press center to go on tours organized by the ministry. Government buses would take journalists wherever the ministry saw fit—mainly to civilian areas where there were civilian casualties.

Journalists viewed these trips as propaganda exercises but decided they could not afford to pass them up in case—as happened on two or three occasions—there was some real news to be had.

In other restrictions, officials insisted that satellite communications equipment should not be removed from the ministry. Handheld satellite telephones with global positioning systems were banned because they could determine the exact locations of potential targets.

Taei brushed aside suggestions that the ministry could be a U.S. target and refused to allow journalists to move their offices to the Palestine Hotel, where they felt less exposed. Officials said privately they hoped the ministry would not become a target while foreign journalists were on the premises. Another aim was to keep the flow of information out of Baghdad under close scrutiny.

Journalists who went through Baghdad during that period believed that Taei considered himself to be God's gift to journalism. He had worked as a journalist in the official Iraqi press, served as a press attaché in the Iraqi Embassy in Paris, and headed the Iraqi News Agency. Journalists dreaded him and made a point not to run into him. Almost daily he would summon some correspondent whose reports he did not like and deliver a lecture on journalism. "A pen is a pen, so call it that and only that," was a favorite phrase of his. "You should report what you actually see and hear here and don't try to find twisted explanations or report hearsay," he would add. Everything that did not follow the official Iraqi line was "hearsay," according to Taei.

Most journalists had to put up with Taei and his restrictions. They resented him, but they knew a major confrontation could get them thrown out and possibly result in their organizations being banned. So they put up with him and his rules.

How this played out often depended on what kind of minder a journalist had. While some were true to the cause, others were more relaxed.

One, in charge of overseeing Reuters television feeds, told us privately, "I will not stop you, but please think before you feed whether the material would hurt me."

Some of the minders even switched sides during the war. "Have you heard, Ali is working for the Americans in Najaf," one said. "He is translating for the invading forces and showing them around."

During the war, the main sources of information by day were the state television, the official news agency INA, and briefings by the Information Minister, Mohammed Saeed al-Sahaf. By night, when the journalists retreated to their hotel, it was a different story. Reporters used the vantage point of the towering Palestine Hotel to film and report the bombing of Baghdad. Using smuggled satellite telephones, they crouched on balconies to call in details of the air raids. Television teams broadcast via portable satellite transmitters, freed from the shackles of minders overlooking every feed from the ministry.

Iraqi officials, who could still watch broadcasts from abroad, soon found out what was happening. They sent in intelligence officers to raid rooms and confiscate "illegal" communications equipment. One journalist said he was more worried that his hidden phone would be seized than that the building might be hit. "I fear the intelligence men more than the bombs," he said.

One night three officers stormed the Reuters office at the hotel. I slipped two satellite phones into my pockets but could not hide a third. In the end they confiscated two telephones. During a single night that week 14 illegal phones were seized. As the bombardment of Baghdad unfolded, news from southern Iraq in the early days of the war seemed to encourage officials in the captial.

U.S. and British forces made stunning advances in the first 48 hours. But when they failed to take Umm Qasr and Basra swiftly, the Iraqi propaganda machine jumped on the apparent setback and claimed Saddam's forces were confronting the enemy and inflicting casualties.

Footage of dead and captured U.S. soldiers on state television—which surprisingly was not knocked off the air for the first two weeks of the war—added to the reluctance of oppressed Shi'ites to rebel against Saddam. It also raised the hopes of pro-Saddam Arabs and prompted questions about the military plan in the West.

No one did more to put the Iraqi spin on the reports from the front than Information Minister Sahaf. He became a local and international hit—seen in Arab eyes as a symbol of defiance, while mocked in the West for denying the obvious.

A black beret on his head and a pistol strapped around his waist, Sahaf held daily briefings broadcast live to the world. Constantly describing invading soldiers in such colorful terms as "leeches," Sahaf said the U.S. and British forces were like a snake slithering through a desert and would be chopped into pieces. He later proclaimed: "The infidels are committing suicide by the hundreds at the gates of Baghdad."

Derided in the West as "Baghdad Bob" or "Comical Ali," Sahaf, a 63-year-old former foreign minister, became for three weeks the face of Saddam's ebbing power: lonely, detached from reality and ultimately humiliated.

"He's good entertainment," one foreign reporter said. "But the sad thing is that we have to report this crap."

Though many Baghdadis believed him at first, his local audience shrank as the war progressed. Sahaf could not convince even Iraqis that the setbacks were victories in disguise.

"They are prisoners in their tanks," Sahaf said of U.S. soldiers in Baghdad in his last televised appearance. "Their ammunition has run out, and our forces will deal with them shortly."

The next day, Baghdad fell.

It was hard to determine for sure whether Sahaf was simply misinformed or was twisting facts to serve his fading government's policy of appearing in charge to the last minute. He told lie after lie without blinking. It was difficult to accept that a man of his status in government did not know the facts, although he may have been out of the loop. He only found himself in the information job after falling out with Uday Hussein in 2001.

Casualties Mount

As air raids intensified, civilian casualties mounted, and Information Ministry officials were quick to turn this to their advantage. Whenever a civilian neighborhood was hit, they would take journalists to where the bombs had hit and to the hospitals. Whenever a government or a military target was bombed, they said they didn't have any information.

When a missile hit a market in a poor northern suburb, killing scores of civilians—mostly women and children—Iraqi authorities blamed the Americans and gave the media full access. Washington blamed an errant Iraqi missile. Days later a similar incident drew similar exchanges.

A day after the second bombing, which caused many civilian casualties, I was having a haircut at one of the few barber shops still open. Even though they were being bombed, local men went there to bring some normalcy back into their lives. A group of men was chatting with an Iraqi air force officer. But when they mentioned the "American crime," the officer said a stray Iraqi air-defense missile was to blame. And when they told him that the war was going well for Iraq in the south, he stunned them again. "News from the south is good, but remember it is early days yet and our enemy is mighty. We have to wait and see how things unfold over the next few days before we can call this war," he said.

Not every military officer was buying into Sahaf's line.

Many Baghdadis started to pack up and head for the provinces, fearing a lengthy siege or a bloody battle for the city. Streams of cars loaded with families and their belongings left the capital. Some people with nowhere to go just camped outside the city. Virtually all shops were closed, and at night, dogs roamed the dusty, cratered streets.

Journalists had to work at the Information Ministry—with an anti-aircraft gun mounted on its roof, it seemed only a matter of time before it attracted the attention of the Americans—and director-general Taei threatened to expel news organizations that refused to remain. CNN had been ordered out after removing most of its equipment from the ministry.

Journalists reluctantly showed up at the ministry for a few hours every day, but evacuated the building whenever air raid sirens sounded or planes appeared overhead.

Only when the ministry was bombed in the early hours of March 30 did Taei relent by moving the press center to the Palestine Hotel to the relief of the press corps.

"It's the Information Ministry!" a journalist shouted from his balcony at the Palestine as he saw smoke rise from the building.

"At last," came the reply from another room. "Now we don't have to go there, thank God."

The ministry was hit again a few days later.

Canned Food and Bottled Water

Basic services in Baghdad remained almost intact until the second week of the war when bombs and missiles began to knock out the telephone network. But life was still bearable for journalists who had stocked up on canned food and bottled water. And the capital still had electricity. That is, until the night U.S. forces reached the airport on the outskirts of the city.

Shortly before 8 p.m. on April 3, power was cut. There was no bombing and no fighting inside the city, but as one district after another lost power, the capital went dark. Suddenly, the battle for Baghdad, the prize of the U.S.-led invasion, seemed imminent.

U.S. forces moved into the airport that night. While the thud of explosions came from that direction, a remarkable silence hung over Baghdad itself. Americans were on the outskirts of the city, but not a single artillery gun or rocket launcher opened up against them. No tanks or troops were seen taking up positions to defend the capital. Earlier that afternoon, busloads of Saddam's Fedayeen, a militia commanded by the president's son, Uday, headed to the airport, but U.S. planes bombed the convoy. Hospital officials told us 83 fighters were killed. We saw the bloodied corpses of dozens of young men sent to their death in buses against the world's mightiest military machine. As these brave but misguided youths headed out to fight, regular Iraqi forces, including Saddam's special Republican Guards, were laying down their weapons and going home.

That incident, and the lack of any Iraqi military movement in Baghdad, convinced me that a U.S.-British victory was only days away.

The next day an Iraqi military spokesman announced that the U.S. forces suffered heavy casualties at the airport. Sahaf declared that the facility had been retaken and promised journalists that "within hours" they would be escorted there to verify the claim. We waited. And waited.

The Interests of Iraq

That same day, Uday al-Taei summoned me to his makeshift office at the Palestine Hotel and asked me for copies of my articles from the previous day. Then, on April 4, Taei advised me that my reports "did not serve the interests of Iraq" and told me I should leave. He refused to give any further explanation and did not single out anything I had written. This was the fourth time he had told me to leave over the past three months. I asked a senior contact to pull strings to get Taei off my back, but I heard repeatedly that he did not like my attitude, which was described to him as that of someone eager for war and to see Saddam out of power. It seemed my private, professional opinion—which was widely shared by colleagues—that war was inevitable and that its outcome a foregone conclusion, was not to his liking.

This time, with American forces knocking on the doors of Baghdad, he spent the whole day insisting that I leave. Every reporter was charged $125 a day to stay in Baghdad, and he gave me a piece of paper that verified that I had settled my fees even though I had not paid a penny of the more than $7,000 I owed the ministry.

On April 5, as a U.S. convoy drove through the southern suburbs of Baghdad almost unchallenged, Iraqi officials were nervous. Taei insisted that I should leave or Reuters operations would be shut down. I also feared for my own security. We did not know how officials would react once the Americans were in the city. I decided to leave the next morning.

One of the unanswered questions of the war is whether Saddam and his inner circle really did believe they could survive the invasion. But for lower level government officials, the idea that 35 years of Baath Party rule were about to end did not seem to have crossed their minds.

As I checked out of the hotel on April 6, Mohsen Tourfah, head of the press center, walked up to me, shook my hand and said, "Nadim, don't worry, we'll issue you a visa in a week's time and you'll be allowed back."

Tourfah was well known for taking payments under the table to fix journalists' problems. Another official who was among the greediest—and the most realistic—had confided in one of my colleagues as war approached, telling him, "There is so little time and so much money to make."

I set off with my Jordanian driver, Saud, in his SUV and headed toward northern Baghdad. Reports that the main road from Baghdad to Amman had been heavily bombed made us take a detour through heavily populated areas north of Baghdad before heading for the highway and, hopefully, safety.

In the northern outskirts, workers with cranes were tearing down road signs. "Maybe they don't want the Americans to find their way easily if they storm Baghdad," said Saud as we drove past the "Mother of All Battles" mosque with its minarets depicting Scud missiles on launchers.

A few hundred yards past the mosque, two large anti-aircraft guns stood on a makeshift soccer pitch. Iraqi soldiers were hanging around a military truck, taking their lunch. As we turned around to head north, I noticed artillery positions on the other side of the highway. Before I could tell Saud about them, we heard the screech of a warplane overhead and a split second later, the car shook. Two missiles hit the soccer pitch to our left, two more hit the artillery pieces 30 yards to our right. The soldiers hit the floor. We did not stop to see if they had been hit or were diving for cover. I had witnessed air raids before, but I had never been in the middle of one.

When the first missiles exploded, Saud appeared stunned and brought the car to a halt as shrapnel whizzed around us and dust blocked our view.

"What are you doing?" I screamed. "Don't stop. Go, go, go."

He sped off, but a few hundred yards on we saw more white smoke and cars coming in the opposite direction signaled to us to get back. Seconds later we found out why. There were seven Iraqi tanks, parked among houses, smoldering. Each had taken a direct hit. Their turrets lay on the side of the road, but the tanks seemed to have been abandoned by their crews. Shrapnel hit a civilian car, but the driver was unhurt.

"You should have had a camera. You would have got an exclusive," Saud commented. I thanked God for precision bombs and told him, "I wouldn't have had the heart to film."

As we made our way toward the western town of Falluja, fields were dotted with tanks, guns and soldiers. Camouflaged but still clearly visible, the vehicles must have looked like sitting ducks to the American pilots overhead. As we passed Falluja and took to the highway, green fields gave way to desert, but there seemed no end to the Iraqi tanks, now camouflaged with mud and dirt. Only when we passed Ramadi, 60 miles west of Baghdad, did the Iraqi military disappear.

As we approached the town of Rutba, 30 miles from the Jordanian border, two Arabs dressed in smart military fatigues with pistols at their waists and wielding assault weapons stopped us at a roadblock. I asked them where they were from, and they said they were Iraqis attached to allied Special Forces. After we showed them our IDs, they waved us on to another checkpoint. This time a British Special Forces soldier told Saud in Arabic to open the back of the car. Other soldiers appeared to be Americans and Australians. They asked how things were in Baghdad. I asked them how long they had been in Iraq, and one answered: "Too long." They had clearly been in Iraq well before the war started.

We made it to the border to find that Iraqi officials were on duty there. They checked our car and fined me $70 for overstaying my visa. Before we were sent on our way, an Iraqi border inspector who had clearly been listening to the Iraqi information minister, asked me, "Did you see how we destroyed them at the airport?"

Too tired to tell him there was a Western checkpoint only a few miles down the road, I smiled and drove to safety under the gaze of a large painting of a beaming Saddam.

Chapter 7

THROUGH ARAB EYES

By Caroline Drees

Twenty-one floors of glass and concrete tend to muffle the bustle of downtown Cairo. But the day the war in Iraq began, waves of voices, shouting and chanting, crashed through the windows of our tower block office. Down in the street, a torrent of anger flooded through the air long before the crowds appeared in view. From every direction, through narrow alleys and usually busy boulevards, protesters' voices carried for blocks and blocks, their fury spilling into the Egyptian capital and dozens of other cities across this region.

"With our spirit and our blood, we sacrifice ourselves for you, oh Saddam!" shouted a group of men, some in traditional robes and others sporting sweatshirts and baseball caps. A group of office workers stormed down one street, shouting, "Where are the Arab armies?"

The furor increased as the war pressed on and casualties mounted. Around the Arab world, at mosques, near U.S. embassies and in major thoroughfares blocked to traffic, men and women, young and old, clashed with riot police who fought back with water cannons, batons, tear gas or dogs.

In Arab countries from the Atlantic to the Gulf, the conflict was not just on TV. It was on your street and in your home, shrouding your life, day after day. At times, the smell of burning tires from towering smoke plumes filled your nostrils. In the medieval Yemeni capital Sanaa, a young boy was shot dead near the American embassy. He had gone out to fetch groceries.

The war fought, felt and seen in the Middle East was worlds away from the campaign shown on Western television. Sitting on a barstool in a Cairo café, chewing *qat* leaves in a Yemeni *majlis* parlor or smoking a water-pipe in a Palestinian refugee camp, most Arabs saw a war that bore no resemblance to the high-tech Blitzkrieg seen in suburban America.

As bombs at night turned Baghdad's sky orange, Arabs saw the dawn of a new era of colonialism. In advancing tanks, soldiers and U.S. flags, they saw occupation. While "Operation Iraqi Freedom" unfolded in front of U.S. eyes, Arabs saw their world come crashing down and took to the streets from Marrakesh to Damascus in the most widespread outpouring of frustration seen in years.

I usually bristle at suggestions that there is one Arab world and that it is possible to generalize what Arabs think and feel. But the Iraq war galvanized feelings of Arab unity more strongly than any other event in recent memory. Many Arabs were united in their opposition to the war and felt collectively attacked when the first bombs fell.

This part of the world gave birth to ancient civilizations, powerful empires and three of the world's main religions. For most citizens, the war was not about the military defeat of a government Arabs had hated for decades. It was about pride, frustration and lost hope.

Saddam Hussein's efforts to hold back the world's most formidable army turned a reviled despot into an Arab hero. Iraq's resistance to the invaders captured the imaginations of millions of disenfranchised, restive people angry after years of political, economic and social decline at home. And for most Arabs, the failure of their David to vanquish the Western Goliath came to symbolize Arab failure far beyond the battlefield.

When a U.S. armored vehicle was used to toppled a statue of Saddam in central Baghdad, most Western media focused on cheering opposition figures and made sweeping comparisons to the jubilant crowds at the fall of the Berlin Wall. But away from the spotlight of Paradise Square, much of the Arab world wept.

"They shouldn't have shown that on TV here," said Egyptian lawyer Mariam, throwing her usual love of press freedom to the wind. "It was a disgrace for all of us Arabs. Pure humiliation. Why rub our faces in it?"

Adnan Hamed, a salesman in an upmarket area of Amman, clenched his fists in anger and flung a box at a television showing jubilant Iraqis around the statue.

Ali Jaddah, an engineer, called the day the statue fell a "day of shame." "Arabs have become slaves. The only man who dared to say 'no' to the Americans' face has vanished today. What is left is a bunch of bowing and scraping Arab leaders."

When American soldiers briefly draped the Stars and Stripes over the statue's face, it left a bad taste in the Arab world that overpowered any joy at the removal of a tyrant. One Arab TV commentator said, "Everything that happens from now on will have an American smell."

Anger Erupts

The extent, vehemence and duration of the Iraq war protests in the Arab world took many inside and outside the region by surprise. The secular regime of Saddam Hussein had been unpopular among most Arabs, and the Iraq issue did not traditionally have the same emotional resonance as the Israeli-Palestinian conflict, for example.

Many people were torn between their distaste for Saddam and their concerns about a U.S.-led invasion and imposition of a Pax Americana. In the run-up to the war, Arab protests had been muted and overshadowed by a need to make ends meet in economically dire times.

When I asked shopkeepers, taxi drivers or civil servants about whether they would be protesting in the weeks before the war, the answer was invariably, "I've got to work and feed my family," or "What's the point?"

But the symbolism of the war, coupled with these financial woes, a rare opportunity to vent anger in public and the ability for the first time to watch a war unfold live, 24 hours a day on several Arab satellite channels, ignited popular protests as soon as the bombs started falling.

When the U.S. ultimatum to Saddam expired on March 20 and bombs began slamming into Baghdad, I sped to the office through the streets of Cairo before dawn while the teeming city still slumbered and armed police officers yawned at their posts.

As the ground shook in the Iraqi capital in Washington's first full onslaught to destroy Saddam's rule, Egyptian state-run television was featuring a program on acid reflux problems. But the calm was short-lived. As the Middle East woke up, a new reality took hold.

When most Arabs thought of Iraq, they didn't think of Saddam or a cache of weapons of mass destruction. Instead, they saw a country crippled by more than a decade of sanctions, its people toiling in miserable conditions while more and more children died. And now this wretched land was under attack.

Months of Arab diplomacy, vehement opposition and warnings by Arab League chief Amr Moussa that "the gates of hell" would open in the region if America attacked, had failed to spare ordinary Iraqis the misery of war. U.S. promises of a better tomorrow without Saddam fell on ears deafened by the wails of Iraqi suffering, and the region awoke with seething anger against Washington, its allies and their own autocratic governments.

Within a few hours and for much of the war, the groundswell of anger brought thousands upon thousands of Arabs to the streets, defying widespread bans on political demonstrations. Scoffing at the danger of arrest, men and women confronted teams of riot policemen in standoffs so tense they shocked even veterans of this troubled region.

On the first Friday of the war, tens of thousands of Arab Muslims marked the Islamic holy day by protesting against the war and against Arab leaders across the Middle East. At the ancient al-Azhar mosque in the heart of old Cairo, the venerated seat of Sunni Islamic learning, worshippers hurled chairs, wooden crates and bricks from the roof of the majestic building at police officers standing below.

From inside the mosque, hundreds of men pelted policemen with the shoes they had taken off before prayers. Police—the symbol of a government they resented for failing to avert the war—responded with jets of water. They knocked down protesters, drenched worshippers and pummeled the mosque's fragile façade.

The face-off between police and demonstrators highlighted the frustration many protesters felt with their own governments. "*Wahid, itneen, al geesh al arabi feen?*" ("One, two, where are the Arab armies?"), shouted the protesters. As policemen in Cairo unleashed dogs on them or beat them with batons, some shouted, "Look! Look! Egyptians are hitting Egyptians!"

Demonstrators set a truck on fire outside the ruling National Democratic Party headquarters in central Cairo in a powerful political expression I had never seen in years of covering Egypt. Protesters also tore down party posters and smashed windows in a nearby hotel. In a country where criticizing the president is taboo, protesters jumped on car hoods and berated President Hosni Mubarak. "Oh, Mubarak, you coward! You are an agent of the Americans," shouted a crowd parading down the central Kasr el-Nil street. They accused the president of humiliating Arabs and "smearing our heads with dirt."

Unlike most demonstrations in the politically disenfranchised Arab world, which are staged by governments, political parties or other interest groups, the first days of antiwar protests were a spontaneous and genuine outpouring of anger. Our reporter in Yemen was amazed by the sustained protests, which continued late into the day when Yemenis usually drop all other activities and gather in a *majlis* lounge for their national pastime: chewing the mild narcotic *qat* for hours and hours. "We thought they'd just forget their anger and start chewing *qat* leaves as usual in the afternoon. But no. The protests kept going on and on," our reporter said.

In Cairo, the Arab world's biggest city with some 17 million people, the protests lasted into the middle of the night that first day of the war, until policemen charged on the demonstrators and dispersed them into the city's underground system and myriad of alleyways.

As demonstrators widened their protests to include attacks against the government, the authorities seemed to lose patience quickly. Reporters who witnessed the crackdowns said they feared for their safety as police, who had clearly had enough after standoffs, verbal abuse and being spat at by usually docile citizens, attacked the crowds.

As the civilian death toll rose in Iraq, so did anger across the Arab world. News that U.S. and British aircraft had bombed a bus in Iraq, killing five Syrian laborers being ferried home, fueled fury in Damascus. Thousands of protesters poured into the streets, enraged by Washington's explanation that the bombing was an accident. Waving Syrian and Iraqi flags, some protesters carried banners saying, "Stop murdering Iraqis now" and "Iraq is the symbol of the Arab nation." Others burned U.S. and British flags and spat on pictures of President Bush covered with red paint symbolizing blood.

When an air assault devastated a busy Baghdad market and with some 60 people killed, Arabs called it a massacre by colonial tyrants and a crime against humanity. "Everyone now wants to be like Osama bin Laden," said Muhanad Abdullah, a Jordanian computer programmer. "They have made thousands of bin Ladens. They will see what the future will bring upon them."

Speaking Out

The antiwar movement was also unique because it enveloped all segments of society. These protesters were not party apparatchiks or Muslim activists with an agenda. A glance across any crowd of protesters revealed a broad mix of citizens from all social strata and age groups. They were simply Arabs who were fed up.

Amr, a 20-year-old Egyptian student, was one of many young Arabs who wanted to take their protest further and lined up at Iraqi embassies to volunteer to fight in the war. Speaking about "American aggression against Palestinians and Iraqis," he got so animated his thick glasses slipped off his face. The pen in his shirt pocket made him look more like an accountant than a warrior.

Even Arabs who studied in the United States, worked for U.S. companies or had a penchant for all things Western—like the so-called golden youth—were filled with distaste for the unfolding war. For them, the war further tarnished the image of a country they had long admired, but which they felt had turned against Muslims and Arabs after the Sept. 11 attacks. "It's not only the war in Iraq. People are beginning to view the States as a hostile entity because of the increased prejudice after September 11," said Maha Abdel Rahman, assistant sociology professor at the elite American University in Cairo.

Mai Ezz el-Din, a 29-year-old woman working for an American insurance firm, said Washington's policies were whittling away her trust. "Before the war, I was undecided about America's commitment to its promises . . . . Now I have seen them breaking their word and changing their stance. I don't believe what they say anymore."

Women, who often keep to the political sidelines of male-dominated Arab societies, protested in numbers rarely seen in the Middle East. In Sanaa, in Yemen, a traditional city wrapped in the aura of 1001 Nights, women staged their own antiwar rallies, day after day. From girls to grandmothers, from housewives to academics, thousands gathered from all over the vast, poor country on the southern flank of the Arabian peninsula. Most were completely veiled in black, but their determined daily protests showed they were anything but the oppressed, downtrodden victims many Westerners associate with traditional Islam. Holding Korans in their outstretched hands and wearing green headbands reading "There is no God but God" over their black *hijab* scarves, the women shouted antiwar slogans as loudly as they could while female police in military fatigues kept watch. In Cairo's downtown business district, women rallied growing crowds of demonstrators against the United States and Egypt's government, the second largest recipient of U.S. aid in the world after Israel. "Hey, Mubarak, are you an American? Are you Jewish? Are you with us or with them?" one woman shouted, as the crowd repeated her chant.

The protests also broadened to some sidelined members of society who sensed a rare opportunity to speak out. In Lebanon, dozens of gay rights protesters—an uncommon sight in this conservative region—joined the demonstrations, raising the rainbow flag above the crowds. "Since we are calling for freedom and calling for war to stop, let the secret war on us stop too," one gay rights campaigner chanted. "We have rights too," his partner said. "Now that everything is changing, let people know we exist."

Numbers of protesters were hard to estimate because there were so many bystanders in the crowded streets of Arab cities, fascinated by this unusual display of public discontent. For some reporters stuck in the middle of the masses, a few dozen people could feel and sound like a revolution. Estimates fluctuated wildly in multiples of thousands between our reporters on the scene and other journalists covering the same events.

Some media also unwittingly inflated the number and impact of protesters because they were not used to the usual chaos of cities like Cairo and were unable to distinguish a bustling street scene from a massive demonstration. One Western satellite channel broadcast footage of a typical clogged bridge spanning the Nile in the Egyptian capital, with cars bumper to bumper in usual Cairo gridlock, with a voice-over saying, "It looks as though the protests have really brought Cairo to a standstill!" It was comments like these that made Arab viewers more wary than ever of the accuracy of Western reporting.

But from where I sat, the bottom line was not the size of the protests or the number of demonstrators. What made this antiwar outcry important was that it was widespread, passionate and spontaneous. It reflected an underlying political, social and economic discontent that pointed to longer-term problems ahead.

Addicted to the War

From the first bombing of Baghdad until the invasion of the capital and end of major combat operations, life in the Arab world centered on the war. You could drive by any Arab café throughout the day and night, and see smoke-filled rooms of men, huddled around backgammon tables and water-pipes, glued to television coverage of Iraq. At schools, universities, homes and restaurants, men, women and children talked about nothing but the latest news of the war, their pride in Iraqi resistance and what the battles meant for the troubled Middle East. The addiction to the war was unlike anything I had witnessed in almost two decades of studying, covering, traveling or living in the Arab world.

More than Afghanistan, and even more than the Arab-Israeli conflict, this war touched on all the major emotive issues that have formed a collective Arab self-understanding. Even though many, if not most, Arabs detested Saddam, the standoff with Washington turned him into a symbol of Arab nationalism, confrontation with the West and the impotence of other Arab rulers. Even if he couldn't win the war, many Arabs admired Saddam for putting up a fight. For many in the region, the United States seemed more of a threat to the Middle East than Saddam ever was.

In some Arab cities, street vendors began selling plastic hand puppets of the Iraqi president as a boxer, complete with big black gloves, and dolls of Bush as his antagonist. "I bought dolls of Saddam and Bush. My sons fight over who plays the role of Saddam. They hate to be Bush," a customer in the Gaza Strip said. Palestinian teacher Ahmed Shahin explained why so many Arabs reveled in Saddam's face-off with Washington. "They support him because he represents the kind of leader they wished to have themselves."

In the West Bank and Gaza Strip, Saddam had long been far more popular than in other Arab states. Palestinians sided with Iraq in the 1991 Gulf War, and Saddam provided millions of dollars in aid to families of Palestinian militants and civilians killed in an uprising against Israeli occupation that erupted in September 2000. More recently, Palestinians—and many other Arabs—saw Iraq's conflict with the United States as a new version of the Palestinian fight against Israeli occupation. Throughout the Iraq war, the sale of Iraqi flags, pictures of Saddam and T-shirts bearing his face skyrocketed in the Gaza Strip. Some Palestinians even started a telephone campaign, calling people at random in Iraq to express their sympathy and to praise their resistance. Tareq Abu Dayya, who owns a flag shop in Gaza City, said the sale of Iraqi paraphernalia had been particularly good after Iraqi television showed footage of dead and captured U.S. soldiers, a move that many other Arabs said was distasteful and un-Islamic. Abdel-Hadi al-Waheidi, a 51-year-old engineer who bought a small Iraqi flag for his 13-year-old son's bicycle, called Saddam "a symbol of defiance."

Identifying with Saddam took on a new meaning for Palestinian Turki Abu Rbeya', a 49-year-old electrician. As a refugee living in Bureij camp in the central Gaza Strip, he revered Saddam as one of the few Arab leaders whom he felt had stood up to the West—and to Israel, which faced a barrage of Iraqi missiles in the 1991 Gulf War. After living and working in Iraq for several years, he named two of his seven children Uday and Qusay after Saddam's sons. To friends, family and customers in Gaza, Abu Rbeya' became known simply as Abu Uday, "the father of Uday," a nickname he shared with Saddam. He said he identified with the struggling Iraqi leader and wished him success in fending off the U.S.-led forces. "How's it going, Abu Uday? Are you sure you will survive?" his friends joked at the start of the war. "Hide, Abu Uday, hide! The Americans are coming to get you." Abu Rbeya' said each American advance in Iraq was like a personal setback. "When Baghdad collapsed, people looked at me sadly. I almost believed I was Saddam. Some people even paid me condolences," he said. "I still support Saddam and hope he returns to liberate Iraq."

Like Abu Rbeya', many Arabs felt the war targeted them and highlighted the collapse of much they held dear. The failure of repeated, halfhearted Arab diplomatic attempts to avert the war struck a blow to latent hopes of pan-Arab nationalism, an idea that is close to Arab hearts even though it has rarely borne fruit. The war also hit Arab pride, especially after Iraqi resistance early on in the war failed to turn the tide against the U.S.-led advance. For a time, Arabs had felt a sense of unity again, which gave them something to rally around at a time of deep malaise at home. But the brief shining moment faded before the might of the U.S. military.

The war also undermined Arab hopes of struggling against imperialism. Many in the region believe they have never discarded the imperialist yoke and that Washington now controls the area economically and politically. Some Arabs also view Israel as an imperial state in their midst, which is occupying Arab land with U.S. help. Many fear the war and occupation of Iraq heralded a neocolonial era in the region. A popular joke spread by text messages on mobile telephones in the Arab world said the new slogan of the U.S. tourism board was "Visit America—before America visits YOU!" The joke played on the deep-seated fear among many Arabs that Iraq was only the first step in a larger U.S. campaign to subjugate their region.

The coming of age of Arab satellite television heightened the personal identification with Iraq. For the first time, Arabs were able to watch news unfold on competing, Arabic-language satellite channels as well as on local TV channels, which showed the war from an Arab perspective. While the first Gulf War in 1991 had made CNN's name and Qatar's Al Jazeera made its mark in the Afghanistan war, no less than three, 24-hour Arab satellite channels were competing with CNN during the Iraq war.

The ability to watch the war on "our own" channels, in Arabic, gave Arab audiences a sense of pride that they were no longer piggybacking on the West. It also gave them much more graphic coverage of Iraqi casualties and scenes of destruction than most Western media, which many people in the Middle East thought were biased toward the U.S.-led forces. Arab stations tilted heavily towards Iraqi resistance, Western setbacks and Arab suffering. Comparing what they saw on Al Jazeera, or Al Arabiya, or Abu Dhabi TV to the coverage on CNN, many Arabs wondered if these networks were actually covering the same war. The often one-sided coverage by Arab media, including stomach-turning images of charred bodies, bloodstained clothes, and suffering children in devastated hospitals increased Arabs' sympathy with Iraq and heightened the hatred of the U.S.-led invaders.

The Iraq war became a conflict of "us against them," spin versus counter-spin. America and its "coalition of the willing"—an expression that never failed to elicit sarcasm if not scorn in the Arab world—had promised people dancing in the streets at the sight of U.S. troops. Instead they saw incessant footage on Arab channels of wailing women, bombed residential areas, mangled bodies and overcrowded hospitals.

Many Arabs were also convinced that "liberating Iraq" really meant grabbing its oil. While Washington tried to sell the war as a step toward Arab political emancipation, many in the region said its main goal was emasculation. American promises of spreading democracy rang hollow in a region that feared the U.S. government wanted to turn Iraq into a satellite state, cripple the region's economies and dominate one country after another.

The war was also further proof in the eyes of many Arabs that their own governments were, at best, politically impotent to influence U.S. policymaking, and at worst, colluding to further Washington's goals. Arabs also refused to accept the stated U.S. justification for attacking Iraq and considered allegations of weapons of mass destruction a pack of lies rather than a casus belli.

Depending on where you sat, Saddam was a dictator or a hero. Iraqis attacking U.S. forces were either "pockets of Baathist sympathizers" or "resistance fighters" and "martyrs." For many Arabs, the war also fed into persistent stereotypes that Americans were trying to subjugate and weaken Arab states for the benefit of Israel. Why did Arab states have to stick to U.N. resolutions if Israel did not, they asked? Many Arabs saw Israel as the only clear victor in the war, arguing that without lifting a finger, Israel eliminated an arch enemy and rattled the Arab world.

The perceived links between the United States' Iraq policy and Israel became even clearer in the aftermath of the war. Arab newspapers and television use strikingly similar vocabulary and images to describe U.S.-led troops in Iraq and Israeli troops in the West Bank and Gaza. The daily footage of U.S. soldiers patrolling among Arab citizens in Baghdad, with deadly skirmishes and heavy use of words such as occupation, conjure up images of the Israeli-Palestinian conflict and leave the Arab world with a disturbing sense of déjà vu.

On a more practical level, the war hammered regional economies already mired in stagnation. Sitting in his tiny shop in a small alley of Cairo's Khan el-Khalili bazaar, bead salesman Amr el-Saeed watched coverage of the war on a black-and-white television wedged into a hole in the wall. Surrounded by thousands of strings of pearls, stones, coral beads and glass, Saeed said business had come to a standstill since the war erupted. "You're the only person who's come into my shop today," he told me, as he twiddled his thumbs and gazed out into the empty bazaar. "Since the war started, we lost at least 90 percent of our tourists and revenues. And it's not like it was good before. Since September 11 and Afghanistan, business has been miserable." Tourism all but ground to a halt in the region, choking off a valuable source of foreign exchange. Hotels offered bargain deals, but the television footage of protesting Arabs in tourist destinations like Egypt and Morocco kept wary foreigners away. Stock markets sagged, foreign investors steered clear, local businesses shriveled and frustration grew.

Aftermath

Now, the war may be over, but the region must deal with its legacy. "It has opened a Pandora's box. . . . You can never tell what will be in it or come out of it," Arab League chief Moussa told me over coffee, puffing at his cigar and staring off into the distance. While he is fond of hyperbole, I think most people in the region would tend to agree with Moussa's assessment and are waiting nervously for what may lie ahead.

Some things seem to be returning to normal. The King Tutankhamun exhibit at the Egyptian Museum is again packed with tourists craning their necks to catch a glimpse of his golden mask and throne. State-run Arab television channels have stopped blow-by-blow coverage of the war and have returned to their daily dull diet of new agriculture projects or sewage treatment plants. Conversations no longer center on Iraq, and now the only events attracting crowds in the thousands are soccer matches.

But people say the war has changed the region. Some analysts speculate it has widened the gap between rulers and ruled, although empirical evidence is hard to find. The violent protests witnessed in the first days of the war fizzled as governments cracked down on demonstrators in a bid to keep the calm. In some cases, states co-opted the protests by organizing their own mass antiwar marches to show the authorities shared the public's anger. Many Arabs say suppressing the genuine protests only left people seething and waiting for the next opportunity to vent their frustration, especially at the governments that tried to shut them up.

The jury is still out on whether regional governments are genuinely threatened. The battle for the "middle ground" of public opinion is still raging. Washington's ability to return stability to Iraq and Arab states' ability to improve local economic and political conditions will help determine who wins. Whether or not ordinary Arabs rise up against their governments could also be linked to progress on the Arab-Israeli conflict. Many had hoped a renewed peace process could rise from the ashes of the Iraq war, akin to the progress seen in the aftermath of the 1991 Gulf War.

More obvious than a gap between Arab governments and their people is the war's destruction of residual goodwill toward the United States after Sept. 11. Ask a group of 16-year-olds where they'd like to study, and few of them will tell you they're heading to the United States—once the favorite place for wealthy young Arabs to pursue higher education. "This is my major concern," one Saudi businessman said over a recent dinner. "Going to college in the States ensured that generations of Arabs returned home with a sense of understanding about America. They wanted to pursue business deals with Americans, read American books and go there on vacation. Not anymore. This can only lead to alienation, more misunderstanding and potential for conflict."

The war was also a watershed because for the first time in recent memory, the line between the United States or Britain and their citizens blurred. For the first time, you felt you had become the face of a government people despised. Until the war, if an Egyptian asked you "Where are you from?" it was often a prelude to "Come and see my papyrus shop" or a story about some brother, cousin or uncle who lived in America or England. But once the bombs started falling, "Where are you from?" meant "Are you American or British?" And if the answer was yes, you were in for a tongue lashing for what "you" were doing to the Middle East. Until the war, I had never felt uncomfortable as a foreigner in the Middle East, and for the most part I still don't, but the attack on Iraq hardened the line between "us" and "them" for many ordinary Arabs and gave rise to discomfort that was new to me. As an American living in Egypt, I felt pushed to defend my country whether or not I opposed the war, and I felt equally pushed to explain Arab views to friends back home, whether or not I agreed with them. Both sides seemed so alienated from each other, fixated on black and white representations of the conflict. Nuance had become a luxury for most, and insightful discourse was rare.

But black-and-white never paints the full picture. I got into a cab around 2 a.m. to head home from work one night in the first week of the war. Before I even settled into my seat, I could see the driver was seething. He was shaking his head, hitting the wobbly steering wheel with the heel of his hand and muttering angrily in Arabic. "Damn the Americans. Damn the British. May God destroy their houses," he cursed. "May they all be damned." Feeling nervous at this unusual outburst, but worried I wouldn't find another taxi at this hour, I slouched into my seat and let him rail. "Damn every single American and British person. I wish a giant earthquake would swallow them all up. We should kick them all out. Every American. Every one," he insisted, just missing several cars as he sped through the inner city. I became angry and scared. I told him to stop the car because he was frightening me and I wanted to get out. After all, I said, I was one of the foreigners he so obviously despised. "Ohhh, I didn't mean YOU!" he said. He almost wept as he described how powerless and frustrated he felt at seeing the bloodshed in Iraq and fearing Egypt or another Arab state could be next. "Please don't be scared. It's just that things are so horrible."

The war left behind a region more disillusioned than ever with the West and with Arab leaders. Thirty-four-year-old Salma Mokdad broke down in tears in Beirut when she saw footage of American troops approaching the sacred mosque of Imam Ali in Najaf. "Now the Americans have made our holy sites impure," she wailed. Salma said she fasted for three days and prayed at night that God might save Iraq. But when U.S. forces took Baghdad, she said all her hopes and prayers had been for naught. After more than a year of boycotting U.S. goods, she went out and bought American cigarettes again. As she lit up her first Marlboro, she said, "To hell with everyone. Americans, British, Arabs . . . . I will not believe in anything at all from now on."

(With contributions from Reuters' bureaux throughout the Arab world.
Special thanks to Mariam Karouny in Beirut,
Nidal al-Mughrabi in Gaza, Mohammed Sudam in Sanaa,
Inal Ersan in Damascus, and Amil Khan and Tom Perry in Cairo.)

Chapter 8

DOHA:
A PLATFORM
FOR TRUTH

By John Chalmers

"Where y'all from?" The GI with the sniffer dog smirked, friendly yet also curious, and then an afterthought: "Hope it ain't France."

That was our welcome to U.S. Central Command's Coalition Media Center in Qatar, unquestionably the safest front-line position for a journalist covering the invasion of Iraq but perhaps one of the most frustrating.

Correspondents from around the world converged on a converted warehouse on the desert-dusted outskirts of Doha to watch the war unfold from a briefing stage designed by a Hollywood art director. Trumpeted by war commander Gen. Tommy Franks as "a platform for truth," the media center provided us with more polished spin than genuine news.

There were valuable insights into what was being touted as a new theory of warfare, one whose key ingredients are speed, agility and state-of-the-art technology. But, from what we could glean, Operation Iraqi Freedom appeared in the end to be a highly professional, well-planned but mostly conventional war against an impoverished country with weak and demoralized armed forces.

Arriving in the tiny emirate of 800,000 people—a peninsula jutting into the Gulf along the Saudi Arabian coast and, at 400 miles southeast of Iraq, just about within reach of a well-aimed Scud missile—you could have been forgiven for failing to notice that a massive military operation was in preparation here.

Although anxious to keep good relations with Washington, the emirate was painfully sensitive to Arab world dismay over the conflict: It was not until five days after President Saddam Hussein was toppled that the emir finally broke his public silence, describing the situation in Iraq as a humanitarian crisis but carefully avoiding any direct criticism of the United States.

Yet, the military activity in Qatar in the weeks before the war was frenetic. Traffic at Doha International Airport had doubled as U.S. Air Force transport planes ferried supplies in and out of the country, and two "Commando Solo" propaganda broadcast aircraft sat on the tarmac next to Qatar's own Mirage-2000 fighters.

"With their air force, our air force, civilian airliners and small craft all moving at different speeds, it's like *Mission Impossible*," one airport official told Reuters correspondent Douglas Hamilton on the eve of the first strike.

Late that night the sprawling al-Udeid air base south of the capital sprang to life, sending up wave after wave of F-15 strike planes and F-117A stealth bombers. Hamilton watched patiently from the perimeter of al-Udeid, the tip of his cigar glowing occasionally in the hot gloom. At last he saw one F-117A take off for what may well have been the opening bid to kill Saddam and his aides in Baghdad.

From al-Udeid, a brief jostle along the desert highway with some of the oil-rich state's ubiquitous SUVs brought you to Camp As Sayliya.

U.S. Central Command set up the nerve center of the war here, a Qatari military base encircled by barbed wire and high cement barricades and guarded by troops. The mobile forward headquarters inside, bristling with cutting-edge control and communications technology, had been tested in a computer-simulated war game called "Internal Look" more than three months before the conflict began.

The media center would have been just a three-minute walk from the installation's entrance, but elaborate security checks and an obligatory shuttle bus ride meant that journalists sometimes waited in the sapping heat for more than an hour. If you arrived at the gate when the sniffer dog was having his lunch, you could wait even longer. Many of the 700 or so journalists accredited in Doha bellyached about the hassle of getting past the ring of security which, in retrospect, seems churlish given that most of us were staying in swanky Doha hotels while our embedded colleagues were dicing with death on real front lines in Iraq.

Teddy Bears, Muffins, No News

But we grumbled even more over what we found inside the $1.5 million media center. On Day One of the conflict you could buy as many fatigues-clad souvenir teddy bears and blueberry muffins as you wanted (U.S. dollars preferred). You could lean against the coffee bar sipping caffe latte and watching the war unfold on a bank of televisions blaring the big networks. But there was precious little news to be had for the army of journalists eager for a slice of the action.

"We're not giving operational details, sir," came the reply to every question put to officers manning the media desk, no matter how ingeniously they were worded.

Late that day a news release was issued naming the six ships that had fired the opening volley of Tomahawk missiles. There weren't many copies around, and a Japanese correspondent had to be stopped from tearing one off a bathroom door. "Man, you have to take a pee to find out what the news is!" said one American journalist as he headed in to relieve himself.

Meanwhile, we watched live footage on CNN of U.S. armored columns tearing across the sands of Iraq's western desert. Such images must have delighted the Pentagon because of the powerful message they sent to both the Iraqis and skeptics in the wider world who had warned of a difficult war. In fact no one had ever predicted much resistance to the U.S.-led forces in the desert, where Saddam's troops were sitting ducks in the 1991 Gulf War, but there was no one at the Camp As Sayliya briefing podium for us to challenge.

The amiable, not-quite-polished main spokesman for the British forces, Group Captain Al Lockwood, helped fill the void left in the first 60 hours by the near silence of the Americans, making himself available for on-camera interviews in front of a Humvee parked outside the media center. By the end of the war, Lockwood had stood in the sun so long he had a nut-brown tan.

In those early days, the big news networks as well as the news agencies vied for the opening interview slot with Lockwood: He would trot out the same well-rehearsed lines for all of us.

It was a tough start for the Royal Air Force officer, who drew sniggers from the British press for doggedly pronouncing Iraq as only some Americans do: *Eye-raq*.

Although British troops had established a beachhead on Iraq's Faw Peninsula, close to the border with Kuwait, he was quizzed repeatedly on the bad news: a helicopter crash in which eight British and four U.S. soldiers had been killed. On the same day, he made a big blunder, answering glibly a question on when U.S.-led troops would roll into Baghdad: "If I were a betting man—which I'm not— hopefully in the next three or four days," he told reporters. Lockwood was upbraided in front of the British journalists by Downing Street's onsite spin-doctor, Simon Wren, even while his unfortunate comment was being flashed around the world.

The next day Lockwood had a corrected message ready. "That was a foolish remark that was said off-camera," he told me with a sheepish grin. "We must be prepared for a prolonged campaign, there will be resistance. Not everything will go the allies' way as we go forward."

Dressed in sneakers and civvies, Wren kept a watchful eye on the British press from the shadows in the media center.

His counterpart on the U.S. side, Central Command Communications Director Jim Wilkinson, was even less visible, but he too made his presence felt. A former spokesman for the U.S. National Republican Congressional Committee and a recent transplant from the White House, Wilkinson's boyish looks and silky self-confidence disguised a salty tongue. He had warned reporters before the war that if any of them wrote an unfair story "I will seek you out." And, true to his word, Wilkinson called me into his office for an expletive-peppered tirade over a Reuters story that incorrectly described him as "a political appointee brought in by the Bush administration."

Podium Ploys

In the early hours of Thursday, March 20, Franks threw away the much-touted "shock and awe" war script and launched a narrow-focus missile attack on what U.S. intelligence believed could be Saddam's location. But it was late Saturday before he made an appearance on the media center briefing stage.

Painted battleship gray and decked with five large plasma display screens, the slick *Star Trek*-like set was the work of Hollywood scenic designer George Allison, whose portfolio includes White House backdrops and the World Trade Center Memorial Wall. The cost of the stage was somewhere around $200,000, and *USA Today* reported that it had cost $47,000 to ship it from Chicago by FedEx.

A self-effacing Texan, Franks was admired by fellow officers for his dawn-to-dusk devotion to planning detail and a fastidious routine that would impress even the fiercest military disciplinarian. His low-key style could hardly have been more different from that of Norman Schwarzkopf, the swashbuckling general who commanded U.S. forces in the Gulf War. According to accounts from that conflict, "Stormin' Norman" spent a lot of time barking down the phone and screaming at aides who feared his volcanic temper.

Franks gave few operational details of the Iraqi Freedom campaign in that first appearance, using phrases that were to become rhetorical fixtures of the daily briefing: "We believe that we are on our timeline" and "The outcome is not in doubt."

He was flanked on the stage by commanders from Britain, Australia, Denmark and the Netherlands, apparently a gesture aimed at demonstrating the breadth of the "coalition" backing Washington for a war much of the world did not want. The four never appeared together again, and the Dane and the Dutchman simply vanished. No wonder a *New York Times* editorial before the war had described the coalition as "a scattering of mainly powerless supporters cheering the effort from the sidelines."

Franks briefed only three times during the three-week main combat phase of the operation, leaving it to the telegenic Brig. Gen. Vincent Brooks to become the face of the war effort in briefings timed for U.S. breakfast shows.

Just 44, this one-star general had had a meteoric career in the U.S. Army. He was the first black leader of cadets in his senior year at the West Point military college, he studied at Harvard as a national security fellow, and his assignments had taken him across the globe from Korea to Kosovo. Articulate, polite, cool and occasionally witty, Brooks was a safe pair of hands for Central Command.

He was asked at one briefing to describe his personal thoughts at that iconic moment of the war, beamed live around the world, when a giant statue of Saddam was felled in Baghdad. "You know that generals don't have personal feelings," he quipped. "I was personally excited about it but quickly got over it and got back to my normal mode."

The Brooks briefings were in fact quite sober, repetitive sessions, usually starting out with videos depicting precision bombings—impressive in the 1991 Gulf War but largely ignored as old hat 12 years later—but never, despite requests, images of bombs missing a target. He also routinely showed slides and videos of humanitarian operations ("This scene is being repeated all over Iraq…and it is the truth."). Toward the end of the war, the monotony of filming the same guy on the same platform saying the same thing every day prompted one television crew to paste a sign on its workroom door: "Camp Groundhog."

There was only one moment of high drama at the camp, a blast at an industrial compound about a mile away from the base. There were several minutes of alarm as journalists, some clutching gas masks, poured outside to look at a pall of smoke hanging in the haze. But it was nothing sinister, just a gas cylinder exploding at a car-crushing plant.

Shortly before the first briefing of the war, U.S. Marine Capt. Stewart Upton, a member of Wilkinson's team, had popped his head into the Reuters office long enough to say just three words: "Nassiriya has fallen." Some news!

But it hadn't fallen. At least, not yet. Before the weekend was out, Franks's deputy, Army Lt. Gen. John Abizaid, was at the media center podium describing the fighting around the southern city as the "sharpest engagement of the war thus far." Iraq put five U.S. captives on television and showed up to eight bloodied corpses of what it said were U.S. soldiers killed near Nassiriya.

It was not the last time that Britain and the United States would have to row back from triumphal claims after jumping the gun in the propaganda war.

British Prime Minister Tony Blair at one point said two dead British soldiers shown on the Arab TV network Al Jazeera had been "executed" by Iraq. His government later backed away from the accusation after a relative of one of the soldiers told a British newspaper that she had been informed that he died in action.

Then there was the mass uprising that, according to various military sources, was taking place in Basra. Iraq dismissed the reports as "hallucinations," while Arab television channels showed images of quiet streets in the besieged southern city. Blair later conceded that it had been only a "limited uprising."

There was the repeated fall of the port city of Umm Qasr, the false-positive discoveries of weapons of mass destruction and the claim by U.S. officials that an Iraqi commander had surrendered, which was quietly forgotten when he turned up on Al Jazeera.

Part of the problem was that both countries, under huge political pressure to make the war a success, struggled to keep up with the furious pace of media covering minute-by-minute developments on rolling television news broadcasts.

London, Washington and Doha coordinated around the clock on the "lines to take" and the message of the day, and there was a daily conference call which usually included Pentagon spokeswoman Victoria "Torie" Clarke, the State Department, the White House, Downing Street and the British Foreign Office.

But it could take the best part of 24 hours to package this as a neat script, which meant that information was not only sanitized but also hopelessly out of date when it was presented at the daily briefings.

The media center operatives were sometimes caught off guard by bad news from the battlefield. Determined not to let their message of the day be hijacked, they would put a different spin on events (the looting in Baghdad and Basra was "merely natural exuberance," "people taking back what they think they are owed after 25 years of Saddam's rule"), or they simply played for time.

On March 26, when at least 15 people were killed in a Baghdad marketplace by an apparently errant missile, Brooks said he could "honestly" provide no information on the incident. There was nothing to move the story on there. But the next day he had his line ready: "We think it's entirely possible that this may have been, in fact, an Iraqi missile." Hamilton, watching the briefing live from the

Reuters bureau in a Doha hotel, flashed me a message at the media center: "I was just waiting for that."

Brooks was also tripped up by the furor when a U.S. tank had fired at the 15th floor of Baghdad's Palestine Hotel, which was packed with foreign journalists. Reuters cameraman Taras Protsyuk and Spanish channel Telecinco's Jose Couso were killed, and three other Reuters staff were wounded in the shelling. Brooks said initial reports indicated that U.S. forces "operating near the hotel took fire from the lobby of the hotel and returned fire." Asked just a minute later to explain why the tank round was directed at an upper floor, he conceded: "I may have misspoken." Journalists at the scene said they had heard no fire coming from the hotel.

The strategy of embedding reporters with U.S. and British forces on the battlefield produced a torrent of action-hero style television images that were lapped up by audiences back home. Independent television crews in the theater of operations who were not restrained by attachment to a military unit were, in Wilkinson's words, "a pain in our rear."

When there were no television crews on hand to film "good news" stories, the U.S. military handed out footage shot by its own forces.

Twelve days into the war, when initial optimism had been dampened by fiercer-than-expected Iraqi resistance, blinding sandstorms and concerns about overstretched supply lines, just such an opportunity presented itself: the rescue of an injured U.S. Army supply clerk from an Iraqi hospital. Captured on black and green night-vision film, the Special Forces operation was billed as a daring and heroic act, and it turned 20-year-old Pfc. Jessica Lynch of Palestine, West Virginia, into an instant symbol of patriotic pride.

Journalists were awakened in their Doha hotel beds that night and urged to get down to As Sayliya for some big news. Many of us were convinced that Saddam must have been captured.

The reality TV worked. Four days later a *Los Angeles Times* opinion poll, which had been conducted while news of the rescue filled the air waves, showed an upsurge of support among Americans for the war and a steep rise in President Bush's approval rating.

In Doha, Central Command milked the snatch operation for all it was worth for days. Before an on-camera interview with Reuters, Media Director Capt. Frank Thorp suggested that we might pitch him a question on Lynch's condition. We complied, and duly got the answer he wanted to give: "She's free."

A scathing BBC documentary on the U.S.-British spin machine later concluded, after interviewing Iraqis, that the Lynch rescue was "a script made for Hollywood, made by the Pentagon." It portrayed a rescue in which there was little danger to the soldiers and quoted a local doctor as saying troops cried, "Go, go, go!" and fired blank rounds to "make a show." The report also said the U.S. military knew before going in that there were no Iraqi forces guarding the hospital.

The Pentagon branded the claims "ludicrous and insulting."

One video clip that Central Command may have regretted showing was the aerial bombing of three Iraqi aircraft sitting in the middle of runways, which British military analyst Paul Beaver immediately dismissed as useless old decoys. "I'm surprised that they would put this up on television when, to the trained eye, these were at least two or three generations old," the former publisher of *Jane's Defence Weekly* told a news network. One of the aircraft looked like an old British Hawker Hunter, planes Beaver said were in service "when there was a kingdom of Iraq in the 1950s."

Why Should We Stay?

Despite the flow of images from "embeds," the world was getting only a worm's-eye view from the front lines. Critical information gaps were rarely filled back at Doha because of the selective approach to providing detail. As the BBC documentary put it, the set-up for journalists covering the war was "close up at the front for action shots or tied up in the rear for the not-so-big picture."

The disconnect between the situation on the ground and Doha's "we're-still-consistent-with-our-plan" mantra was starkly illustrated by a comment made by Lt. Gen. William S. Wallace, commander of the U.S. Army's V Corps. "The enemy we're fighting is a bit different from the one we'd war-gamed against," he said, adding that a longer war was now more likely.

Brooks reassured the press, "What we would say is that we haven't had anything that's hindered our operations to date."

Lockwood was more frank, conceding that what the U.S.-led forces were encountering was "slightly different from what was initially anticipated."

Indeed, British media officers at Doha were privately critical of their U.S. counterparts' modus operandi and accused them of alienating journalists by treating them with condescension. Wren told Britain's *The Guardian* newspaper that the "hugely overblown" Lynch incident was symptomatic of a bigger problem. "The Americans never got out there and explained what was going on in the war," he said. "All they needed was to be open and honest. They were too vague, too scared of engaging with the media." Wren said he had tried on several occasions to persuade Wilkinson and Brooks to change tack.

But the British were not really any better themselves at giving the big picture. British journalists there felt so starved of information that they put up a sign on their reporting room quoting the British forces commander, Air Marshal Brian Burridge: "We don't do detail."

A week into the war, Michael Wolf of the *New York Magazine* asked Brooks the question that many journalists had been asking themselves: "Why should we stay? What's the value to us for what we learn at this million-dollar press center?"

Characteristically unruffled by the round of applause that followed, Brooks replied, "I would say it's your choice."

"I think some of you may have been...looking for very, very precise information about the operations," he said. "But we should never forget, the more we tell you, if we're precise about the frontline trace and where units are operating, exactly what our strength is, you're not the only one being informed."

But one U.S. television network had already voted with its feet and reduced its staff in Doha. Others were increasingly cutting away from the live-broadcast briefings in favor of more compelling news than the sight of U.S. officers repeating that the campaign is "on plan."

Wolf, who was told after his "why-should-we-stay?" outburst that he would not be allowed to ask any more questions at the briefings, had nothing good to say about his experience at Camp As Sayliya. "Every day, every hour, whatever you knew had begun to degrade, and so you knew less and less, and somewhere at the end of your stay in Doha you would know absolutely nothing," he said.

Central Command had an armory of devices to remain master of the news agenda or recapture it when events appeared to be turning against U.S.-led forces.

By Goran Tomasevic (March 21)

I knew that Baghdad would soon come under heavy bombardment. So at around 7 o'clock in the evening I made my way to the 12th floor of the Palestine Hotel, where the media were camped out.

I had to force open several locked doors to find the best position from which to shoot my pictures. A French cameraman on the balcony I chose tried to make me leave, but I set up my tripod anyway.

Soon afterward, the bombing began. I could not believe what was happening: yellow flashes, the balcony shaking, huge blasts in the sky. Baghdad was under attack and it felt like the end of the world. Amazing images exploded in front of me and I furiously took pictures.

My problem now was getting past the Information Ministry officials who were searching the hotel for journalists to stop them filming the bombing. As I left the room where I had been taking pictures, they were already on the same floor. I managed to slip past them with my equipment and my digital picture memory cards tucked out of sight. "Hello habibi Goran," one of them said. It was one of the most memorable nights of my life.

Journalist Luke Baker inspects the site of a battle between U.S. troops and Iraqi forces just north of Najaf. Iraqis had set up an ambush at the mouth of an escarpment, using anti-aircraft guns on the backs of small trucks, but they were no match for U.S. Abrams tanks, which left a sea of tangled, incinerated metal in their wake. REUTERS

Journalist Rosalind Russell talks to a British soldier outside Basra. REUTERS

Journalist Saul Hudson scours a map with U.S. soldiers just outside Tikrit. Hudson flagged down the armored vehicle convoy to ask for directions to a suspected Iraqi banned weapons site nearby. He had interrupted reporting on Iraqis celebrating Saddam's birthday to look for the site, where the U.S. military said later Iraq had not stored any proscribed weapons. REUTERS

Photographer Nikola Solic and journalist Mike Collett-White run for cover from sniper fire on hills overlooking the northern Iraqi city of Kirkuk. REUTERS

By Goran Tomasevic (April 9)

This was one of the worst days of my life.

The day before, an American tank had killed my friend, Taras, a Reuters cameraman who was filming from the balcony of the Palestine Hotel. Taras was an outstanding person and a great professional and we had worked together in hot spots around the world.

I woke up feeling terrible because of the tragedy and I knew it would be a long day. I started work early in the morning in one of the poorest and most dangerous places in Iraq at that time—Saddam City. I then went back to the Palestine and realized that American troops were nearby.

Tired, indignant and angry with the Americans over the death of my friend, I ran out of the hotel to watch about 100 Iraqis and some Marines trying to topple a huge statue of Saddam Hussein. After a while they managed it with a U.S. military vehicle and a tow rope. These became the iconic pictures from the Iraq war, but I am still trying to forget that day.

Journalist Samia Nakhoul, wounded in the face and head when an American tank round hit the Reuters office at the Palestine Hotel in Baghdad, is evacuated to the hospital. Reuters television cameraman Taras Protsyuk was killed in the incident along with Spanish Tele 5 cameraman Jose Couso. Two other Reuters staff were wounded in the explosion. REUTERS

Damage caused by the U.S. tank round that struck the Palestine Hotel in Baghdad. The round killed a Reuters cameraman, a Spanish cameraman and wounded three Reuters employees. REUTERS

Photographer Faleh Kheiber, wounded by shrapnel from an American tank shell that hit the Reuters office at the Palestine Hotel, is evacuated by U.S. forces in an ambulance for treatment outside Baghdad. Next to him, Samia Nakhoul and Paul Pasquale (lying down), were both wounded. A Reuters cameraman and a Spanish cameraman were killed in the incident. REUTERS

Journalist Matthew Green writes a story on his laptop computer on top of a Marine armored vehicle at an Iraqi military base about six miles from the center of Baghdad. REUTERS

By Damir Sagolj (March 29)

This was the aftermath of furious and confused crossfire that ripped apart an Iraqi family.

The Marines I was with had pitched camp just before a hostile village on the way to Baghdad. The soldiers were twitchy about suicide bombers or fighters using human shields. Checkpoints and positions were set up. A sandstorm had died down and it was a sunny day under blue skies.

In the afternoon, just as we thought that we had an easy day with no shooting, machine-gun fire erupted. Suddenly all hell was let loose with a massive firestorm from U.S. positions. When the gunfire subsided we saw the family and their devastated vehicle. Behind that was a mangled Iraqi truck, and two dead Iraqi soldiers. Three soldiers were taken prisoner and some escaped.

We never really found out just what happened, but Marines said they returned fire when the gunmen started to shoot after forcing the family toward the Marines check-point.

A 4-year-old girl, blood streaming from an eye wound, screamed for her dead mother while her father, in shock with wounds to the leg, waved his white shirt from no-man's land. Although the site was dangerous and Iraqi troops could still be around, Marines rushed to tend wounds.

In the chaos as Marines treated the family and rounded up Iraqi troops, a medic, clearly touched and somehow strangely separated from the scenes around him, simply sat down and cradled the second daughter, who was miraculously unscathed. I could only imagine the conflicting emotions going through his mind. Was he thinking of his own daughter?

I would normally go right up close to them and use my wide-angle lens, but the scene was so powerful I didn't want to interfere. With my long lens I took this image that I will always carry with me in my mind. It was so sad, so tragic.

Journalist Sean Maguire works on a story in a ruined Baghdad building that served as a base for the Marines unit he was embedded with. REUTERS

Reuters photographer Damir Sagolj sits inside an armored vehicle during the ride from south to central Iraq. REUTERS

Photographer Desmond Boylan transmits pictures, watched by a U.S. Marine at a makeshift camp near Nassiriya. REUTERS

Photographer Desmond Boylan stands in front of a devastated U.S. armored personnel carrier knocked out on "Ambush Alley" in Nassiriya. REUTERS

By Desmond Boylan (March 21)

I was fortunate enough to be there when a Marine raised the Stars and Stripes over the port of Umm Qasr—marking the first significant U.S. military success of the Iraq war.

After accompanying Marines who fought their way into Umm Qasr, I was standing in a truck as they searched the port to make sure it was safe. Marines were ripping down a big canvas portrait of Saddam Hussein when another image caught my eye.

A Marine was climbing up the walled entrance to the port carrying a flag. I shot three or four frames as he took down the Iraqi flag and replaced it with the Marine Corps pennant attached to the Stars and Stripes. Fifteen minutes later, orders came to take it down again, presumably to avoid inflaming Arab feelings.

Technically it wasn't a difficult shot. The difficulty was to be there, and to be the only one to capture an image of victory that was used around the world.

ع العبور البحري

OR MARINE TER

Reporter Adrian Croft stands on a bridge spanning the Euphrates in Nassiriya during a Marines' patrol. REUTERS

Journalist Matthew Green covers fighting for a bridge outside Baghdad. U.S. Marines battled Iraqi defenders for control of two bridges over the River Diyala, a tributary of the River Tigris lying along the southeastern outskirts of the city. REUTERS

Journalist Luke Baker calls in news via satellite phone from inside a shelter set up to protect against fierce sandstorms. REUTERS

Journalist Saul Hudson with Laleh Tarighi on top of a Brazilian-made, wheeled tank at the headquarters of the Iranian rebel group, the People's Mujahideen, in Ashraf, about 55 miles north of Baghdad. Before joining the Iranian rebels, Tarighi lived in Cambridge, England, and extraordinarily enjoyed cappuccinos at a cafe that was also a regular hangout for Hudson. REUTERS

By Desmond Boylan (March 23)

A boat carrying U.S. Navy Seals arrived in the port of Umm Qasr a couple of days after it had been taken. Also aboard was a mysterious group of masked men, dressed in black and bristling with weapons.

They started unloading prisoners and said they were Polish forces working with the Seals. At that point, there was no inkling these forces were involved in the fighting, so I shot pictures as they handed over the Iraqi prisoners.

It was only later I discovered the photos had caused a scandal in Poland because the Polish government had said the 200 troops it had sent to the Gulf would have a non-combat role. Pictures of Polish special forces in action were splashed across Poland's front pages the next day, forcing the Defense Ministry to confirm its elite GROM (Thunder) commando unit had taken part in U.S.-led operations.

The Polish and U.S. commandos came ashore and stood in a group in front of a huge picture of Saddam Hussein, taking "happy snaps" of each other. Despite their secretive role, they were quite keen on their souvenirs and quite happy to let me snap away too.

Journalist Nadim Ladki eats a dish of spaghetti as he works on a story in his Palestine Hotel room in Baghdad. REUTERS

Journalist Samia Nakhoul files a story from the Reuters bureau in Baghdad as advancing U.S. troops push toward the capital to topple Saddam. REUTERS

Photographer Peter Andrews works on pictures from the hood of a jeep near the city of Najaf. REUTERS

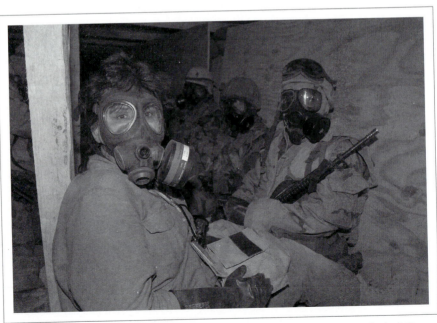

Photographer Stephanie McGehee in a Scud bunker after sirens sounded at Camp Doha Patriot missile site. REUTERS

By Oleg Popov (April 2)

I arrived just after the Marines seized a key crossing point at Numaniya, 75 miles southeast of Baghdad.

There were several abandoned Iraqi T-55 tanks and burnt-out military trucks, one still radiating heat from the explosion that destroyed it. Marines were on their guard, fearing Iraqi forces might still be in the palm groves and fields surrounding our position.

Marines had to fight hard to secure two more bridges over the Diyala River, a tributary of the Tigris on the eastern outskirts of Baghdad. Iraqi defenders laid anti-tank mines and fired at the advancing Americans before blasting large holes in the bridges with explosives.

Our close call came when Iraqi defenders fired a volley of rocket-propelled grenades that screeched low over our vehicle, detonating harmlessly on the other side. The Marines were not so lucky. A 155-mm artillery shell apparently fired by their own side slammed into one of their armored vehicles by the river, killing two men inside and wounding three others.

Photographer Faleh Kheiber inspects the Reuters office in the Iraqi Information Ministry after a U.S. air strike. REUTERS

Photographer Kai Pfaffenbach washes clothes in the desert just south of Kerbala. After days of sitting in vehicles without a change of clothes, soldiers had time to do some laundry, but had to be ready to get back into their Nuclear, Biological and Chemical warfare suits at a moment's notice. REUTERS

REUTERS

By Oleg Popov (April 8)

Urban warfare is one of the most dangerous aspects of conflict. Known as Mout, or Military Operations in Urban Terrain, the term is ugly and the fighting more so.

Street-by-street house searches are a nightmare for soldiers, giving defenders multiple opportunities for sniping and ambushes and increasing the chances of civilian casualties and incidents of "friendly fire."

It was intense work snatching photographs as Marines broke down doors and smashed windows with the butts of their M-16 rifles. As they searched a housing complex for Iraqi soldiers, there was no knowing what was around the next corner.

But as U.S. forces advanced into Baghdad, their worst fear—a house-to-house battle for the capital—failed to materialize.

The first resistance was at the city's Martyrs' Monument, when a sniper opened up at Marines standing on a tank. Luckily for the Marines, and for reporters on the scene, his shots missed their mark.

Journalist John Chalmers and Berlin-based cameraman Martin Schlicht interview British spokesman Group Captain Al Lockwood. REUTERS

Journalist Luke Baker listens to Col. Mark Hildenbrand, commander of the 937th Engineer Group, as he describes a firefight between U.S. and Iraqi forces south of Najaf. REUTERS

By Faleh Kheiber (March 24)

When the Iraqi Information Ministry announced that two U.S. helicopters had been shot down in Kerbala, I raced to the area, hoping for an exclusive.

Arriving ahead of other photographers, I was terrified that the Americans would order an air strike to destroy the helicopters to prevent them from falling into enemy hands.

Local people were oblivious to this possibility, celebrating victory and dancing up and down wildly. I discovered that the Iraqi man waving an AK-47 rifle was called Mingash. He had been identified by the ministry as the man who had shot down one of the aircraft.

I was acutely aware that a storm of American bombs could spoil the impromptu party the impoverished farmers were throwing after helicopters from the world's most powerful army came down in their backyard. But undeterred, some villagers clambered on top of one of the aircraft.

Iraqi authorities had offered a $50,000 reward to anyone who shot down a U.S. aircraft. But Mingash later admitted that he had nothing to do with shooting the plane down and it had just landed in his backyard. He did not collect the money.

Photographer Kai Pfaffenbach stands in front of a burnt-out Iraqi pickup truck in the desert north of Najaf. Iraqis had loaded anti-aircraft guns onto the back of pickup trucks in the hope of surprising U.S. forces with their fire power, but the makeshift weaponry was no match for U.S. Abrams tanks. REUTERS

Journalist Christine Hauser speaks to an Iraqi man working at an American military checkpoint where soldiers search Iraqi passengers outside the Shi'ite city of Najaf. Hundreds of thousands of pilgrims flocked to shrines in the city and also in Kerbala after the war ended Saddam's rule. REUTERS

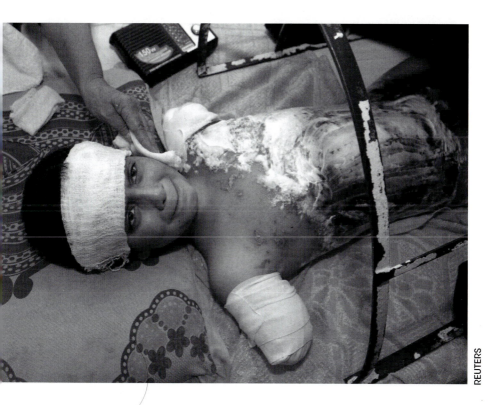

By Faleh Kheiber (April 6)

I find it hard to describe just how shocked I was walking into the burns unit of al Kindee hospital in Baghdad. Lying on a bed was little Ali.

He just looked at me and cried and that made me cry.

"Is there any way that I can get my arms back?" he asked me. "I like to play volleyball."

I thought of my own children. With tears welling in my eyes, I told Ali to be patient and that God will help him. I told Ali that he would be a symbol for Iraq.

"Faleh tell the doctor to try and give me back my arms," he said, wincing from the pain.

I needed to show the world the inner pain and hurt he was suffering. So I took out my camera and took a picture. But I had to leave in a hurry. I simply could not bear to see Ali in so much distress.

Main events in the Iraq war

Map labels:

TURKEY

SYRIA

IRAN

IRAQ

KUWAIT

SAUDI ARABIA

The Gulf

Dohuk

Arbil

Sulaimaniya

Khanaqin

Tigris River

Qaim

Haditha

Euphrates River

Falluja

Baghdad

Hilla

Kut

Amara

Samawa

Kuwait

Map legend:

→ Main advances by U.S.-led forces

▨ Kurdish-held area at start of war

⛏ Main oilfields

100 miles

5 miles

BAGHDAD

Tigris River

Dates on map:

Apr 11, Apr 10, Apr 14, Apr 4, Apr 2, Apr 2, Mar 25, Apr 7, Mar 21, Apr 9, Apr 7, Apr 9, Apr 5, Apr 4

March 20 President Bush announces start of campaign to oust Saddam Hussein. Selected targets hit by air raids in attempt "to decapitate" Iraqi leadership (**1**).

March 21 Invasion forces enter southern Iraq. U.S. Marines attack port of Umm Qasr (**2**). British troops capture Faw peninsula (**3**) and take control of oil installations.

U.S.-led forces unleash devastating blitz on Baghdad (**1**). Missiles hit Saddam's palaces and key government buildings.

March 25 Umm Qasr (**2**), where U.S. and British forces have been trying to put down Iraqi resistance so that aid can be shipped in, is declared "safe and open".

A big convoy of Marines crosses Euphrates River at Nassiriya (**4**), resuming advance on Baghdad.

March 26 About 1,000 U.S. troops parachute into Kurdish-held northern Iraq and take control of Harir airfield (**5**).

April 2 Marines seize bridge over Tigris River (**6**) and take control of main highway from Kut to Baghdad.

U.S. troops attack forces loyal to Saddam in Najaf (**7**), drawing fire from fighters hiding in one of world's holiest Muslim shrines. U.S. commanders say they did not fire back on the Ali Mosque. U.S. forces encircle Kerbala (**8**).

April 4 U.S. forces take Saddam International airport and rename it Baghdad International (**9**).

April 5 U.S. forces enter Baghdad for first time. Also take "Medina" Republican Guard division headquarters in Suwayra (**10**).

April 7 U.S. forces storm center of Baghdad, seizing two of Saddam's palace complexes (**11**).

British paratroopers walk unopposed into center of Iraq's second city, Basra (**12**), where residents warmly welcome them.

April 9 Saddam's rule collapses as U.S. forces sweep into heart of Baghdad (**13**).

April 10 Kurdish fighters take northern oil city of Kirkuk (**14**).

April 11 U.S. and Kurdish forces take Mosul (**15**) without a fight, sealing their victory in the north.

April 14 Marines enter and take control of Tikrit (**16**), Saddam's hometown and power base.

May 1 Bush says "major combat operations in Iraq have ended".

Although one spokesman had assured us that he and his colleagues would "come running out to tell you when there's good news and running out to tell you when there's bad news," it was always the former. Thorp mentioned, almost casually, to Reuters on April 3 that U.S. troops were outside Baghdad's main airport, and the next day he told us that about 2,500 Iraqi Republican Guards had surrendered. Both were "good news" scoops.

When there was growing talk that U.S. forces were getting bogged down south of Baghdad, a senior Central Command official called a background briefing to quietly brace the British and American publics for the worst. "We're prepared to pay a very high price," he said. "There will come a time maybe when things are going to be much more shocking. In World War II there would be nights when we'd lose 1,000 people."

A few hours after an Apache Longbow helicopter had been shot down south of Baghdad and Saddam—with apparently more lives than a cat—had delivered a defiant speech hailing his troops' tough stand, the briefing plans of the day were suddenly changed and Franks was rolled out in front of the cameras.

Less subtle was Central Command's use of language that depicted Iraqi forces in the darkest possible hues. They were fighting in civilian clothes, sneaking up, doing hit-and-run raids, shooting their own surrendering troops, showing prisoners on television to depress the morale of the enemy at home. These acts were "treacherous." These Iraqis were "terrorists," a label that had powerful connotations for the American people post-Sept. 11. "Although we knew, coming into this, that some of the tactics that would be used by this regime are quite frankly horrible, they were perhaps beyond the comprehension of what we thought, as humans, people would actually do," Thorp told us in one interview.

There was also a tendency at the Central Command podium to use language that served to justify the war ("There is a certain knowledge in the Iraqi forces that chemical weapons will be used" and "Basra has been one of the cities that has been most oppressed by the Iraqi regime"), blurring the line between the military and their political masters. This was in stark contrast to the NATO bombing of Yugoslavia in 1999, during which the allies went to considerable efforts to separate military from political statements, with a civilian and a uniformed officer each giving a daily briefing on developments.

The Propaganda War

In the early days of Operation Iraqi Freedom some of the propaganda battles were in fact squarely won by Baghdad despite its rudimentary approach.

With his trademark beret and sly smile, Iraqi Information Minister Mohammed Saeed al-Sahaf astonished and later delighted Western television viewers by appearing behind a forest of microphones often to deny events that were patently true. Even Bush admitted he was a fan of the man who regularly berated the invaders as "infidels" and vowed that "God will roast their stomachs in hell."

But his gathering comic absurdity was almost certainly lost on the Iraqi people, who could still see state television—despite bombing raids aimed at knocking the network out—and had little access to other media. Millions of Iraqis were glued to the television after the war broke out, watching Saddam urge them to defend the motherland and seeing footage of bombed buildings, bloodied Iraqis and slain or captured enemy troops. Television anchormen, who switched jackets and ties for military fatigues, relentlessly drove home the message that Americans were trying to subjugate the people of Iraq and steal their oil wealth against the will of the United Nations.

A U.S. military plane, a specially modified EC-130 called Commando Solo, flew over Iraq during the war, broadcasting what one British newspaper dubbed the "Tony and George show." But the lack of power meant that most people in the country were unable to watch the replays of messages from Bush and Blair and slides of propaganda leaflets.

Iraqi state television's gruesome images were beamed by fledgling satellite channels such as Al Jazeera into millions of Arab world homes.

Even the British government's master of spin, Alastair Campbell, conceded that Washington and London were facing a "huge uphill battle" to win hearts and minds in the region. "Democracies cannot tell lies in the way that dictatorships tell lies all the time, both about themselves and about us, and I think that gives them . . . an advantage in the way this thing is prosecuted," he told the Australian Broadcasting Corporation.

But it was more than the "dictatorship lies" that made the propaganda war so tricky for the United States and Britain.

Unlike the 1991 war, when the world's eyes were focused on CNN, Arab viewers were now turning to three broadcasters for news which critics said was carefully packaged to chime with regional fury over the invasion.

It is hardly surprising that the Arab street wanted something other than American news networks, which the head of the BBC blasted after the war for their "unquestioning" coverage and blatant patriotism. On one occasion a CNN early morning anchor grew impatient with the live broadcast of an Iraqi news conference just as Sahaf was harping on the "stupidity" of the American invaders. She told viewers, "All right, we are going to interrupt this press briefing right now because, of course, the U.S. government would disagree with most of what he is saying."

The Arabic-language alternatives—newly launched Dubai-based Al Arabiya, Qatar's widely watched Al Jazeera and the up and coming Abu Dhabi TV—had huge operations in Iraq. They often broke news that was quickly picked up by news agencies and household names like CNN and the BBC.

Al Jazeera, whose lively Western-style reporting had irked the secretive governments of the region for years, made its name as "the Arab CNN" during the U.S.-led war in Afghanistan by airing exclusive comments from Osama bin Laden. At the outset of the war it had an audience of 35 million in the Arab world, and it was winning millions of new subscribers among Muslim communities in Europe and elsewhere.

The network's broadcast of Iraqi television footage of U.S. prisoners of war and dead British soldiers with gaping holes in their heads infuriated the Bush and Blair governments. Washington said the "disgusting" images violated U.N. conventions and, shortly afterwards, Al Jazeera's reporters were expelled from the trading floor of the New York Stock Exchange.

Al Jazeera's spokesman told Reuters correspondent Jim Wolf in Qatar that the station would not censor the horrors of war. "I think the audience has the right to see all aspects of the battle," said Jihad Ballout. "We're not catering for any specific side or any specific ideology. If there's a perceived imbalance, it's purely a function of access."

Central Command made sure Al Jazeera got plenty of "access" at the media center, offering it interviews and assigning it a front-row seat for the briefings along with the world's big-name news agencies and broadcasters. And Abizaid, an Arabic speaker of Lebanese descent who has since succeeded Franks as head of Central Command, at one briefing specifically sought questions from Arab media.

It looked bad, though, for the Americans when Al Jazeera journalist Tarek Ayoub was killed in his Baghdad office by a U.S. air raid. At a glum memorial meeting in downtown Doha that night, Ayoub's sobbing widow spoke by phone from her home in Amman, lambasting the American Dream as not "life, liberty and the pursuit of happiness" but "blood, destruction and shattered hearts." Al Jazeera Chairman Hamad Bin Thamir al-Thani told journalists there that the network would never know if its reporter had been attacked deliberately, but added, "I would like to remind you that our bureau in Kabul was targeted in the Afghanistan war two years ago."

Central Command expressed regret for the Baghdad incident but said its forces had come under significant enemy fire from the building.

Was the War Brilliant?

In his first briefing, Franks had promised "a campaign unlike any other in history, a campaign characterized by shock, by surprise, by flexibility, by the employment of precise munitions on a scale never before seen, and by the application of overwhelming force."

Five weeks later, Defense Secretary Donald Rumsfeld stood triumphant beside his war commander in Qatar. "There were a lot of hand-wringers around, weren't there?" he said with a grin and to rousing cheers from headquarters troops. Noting Winston Churchill's remark about the Battle of Britain against Nazi Germany that "never in the field of human conflict was so much owed by so many to so few," he fired a barb at critics of the military strategy: "Never have so many been so wrong about so much."

On the eve of war, a number of retired generals, including Wesley Clark, who commanded NATO's campaign against the former Yugoslavia, noted uneasily that several heavy divisions were still not in place. Such pundits were routinely dismissed during the conflict as "armchair generals embedded in television network studios."

Unlike the 1991 Gulf War, which relied on the "overwhelming force" strategy favored by Colin Powell, then chairman of the U.S. Joint Chiefs of Staff, the invasion to oust Saddam was a gamble on a much lighter but speedier thrust toward Baghdad. The gamble paid off. Although the Pentagon still had to go in with large numbers, it deployed less than half of the ground forces used in the 1991 Gulf War for a far more difficult objective, in less time and with fewer casualties.

Military historians will examine this conflict, Rumsfeld crowed in Doha, because of its unprecedented combination of power, precision, speed, flexibility and compassion. The British commander, Burridge, paid tribute to the "audacity and brilliance" of the U.S. advance on the Iraqi capital and said it would become a required case study for military strategists (though he did tell a parliamentary committee later that British generals had acted as the "conscience" of the United States, influencing what was targeted for attack).

Iraq was indeed the dog that didn't bark. There were no chemical weapons attacks, no strikes on Israel, there was no "war within a war" between Turkey and the Kurds, no refugee crisis, no mass destruction of oil wells, bridges or dams, and there was no "Stalingrad" urban bloodbath.

In one of the few background briefings at Doha that shed any light on the military strategy, officials stressed that they had relied on speed, creativity and a potent combination of arms to avert such worst-case scenarios.

The command structure of Saddam's giant military machine was modeled along Soviet lines, one where divisional commanders waited for orders and were not expected, perhaps not trusted, to take initiatives. And so by quickly ripping Iraq's command and control capability to shreds—mostly with devastating air power—the U.S.-led forces reduced the chances that any orders to use weapons of mass destruction (assuming there were any) or blow up infrastructure would ever reach its front lines.

Franks also applied several lessons learned in the Afghanistan conflict of 2001. One was the extensive use of special operations forces, teams of 10 or 12 people which one source said waged "a guerrilla war of their own." These secretive elite units moved early on in the conflict, often under the cover of darkness, to destroy command and control centers, seize oil infrastructure and dams, take airfields, establish a presence inside Baghdad and provide targeting information.

Another was the readiness to look for opportunities and pursue advantages rather than stick to rigid battle plans and timelines. The opening attempt to decapitate the enemy, launched on the basis of fresh intelligence information, is one example. Franks also used this tactic when the formidable line of Republican Guards with which Saddam had hoped to defend the southern outskirts of Baghdad collapsed and pulled back in disarray to the city: Seeing that the enemy was on the defensive, the general sent his troops dashing into the capital before the Iraqis could prepare an urban battlefield.

The rapid disintegration of Iraq's command and control meant that the U.S.-led forces were always 48 to 72 hours ahead of their enemy, which never had a real-time picture of the battlefield. And so Saddam was probably astonished to find U.S. troops at the gates of Baghdad so quickly.

For champions of a military transformation in the United States like Rumsfeld, the campaign was nothing short of vindication. One of his co-champions, Vice President Dick Cheney, told the Heritage Foundation think tank on the day Bush declared major combat operations in Iraq over that Saddam had been expecting a replay of Desert Storm. But the Iraqi leader was outwitted by the stealth and agility of his enemy and by its extensive application of new war technology. Cheney reeled off the list of new combat capabilities that included widespread use of lasers for targeting bombs and other weapons, a broad range of unmanned planes, and real-time computer displays telling ground commanders of the location of all forces.

Cheney could have added Abrams M-1 tanks equipped with guns that fired 50 percent farther than what had been available in 1991 and the successful deployment of B-1B bombers, which combined supersonic speed, long range and a large bomb load.

Fairly early on in the conflict, the U.S. strategy of dashing north to Baghdad without securing population centers along the way appeared to have gone wrong. Iraqi forces and Fedayeen militia were using unsecured cities and desert space to inflict stinging attacks on the exposed flanks of the advance. There were also supply shortages at the tip of the spear: The use of gas-guzzling armored vehicles had to be restricted, and soldiers in one infantry unit had their food rations cut from three meal packets a day to one. Even Bush and Blair were tempering the optimism with which they had launched the campaign, warning of tough battles ahead.

Embedded correspondents were told that commanders had ordered a pause of between four to six days in the northward push to Baghdad. The "pause" was repeatedly denied in Doha, but with some units doubling back from forward positions to root out resistance in urban areas they had swept past, it was clear that mopping up was playing a bigger role than foreseen in the war script.

As it turned out, the pause made the job no easier for Saddam, and just 17 days into the war U.S. forces were making a daylight foray into Baghdad in what was widely seen as a ploy to buckle the resolve of their enemy and convince the Iraqi people that Saddam was finished.

But to get there they had unleashed a formidable force of essentially traditional combat capabilities. It was a point made in a report by one of the war's most cited military analysts, Michael O'Hanlon of The Brookings Institution:

"Yes, Special Forces and modern air power were important, but so were Abrams tanks, five-ton supply trucks, rifle-wielding soldiers and Marines and old-fashioned infantry combat skills. When U.S. forces met the Republican Guard's Medina al-Munawara Armored and Baghdad Infantry divisions south of the Iraqi capital in the decisive battle of the war, they did so with numerical superiority, dominant air support and tremendous firepower," he said.

The point is that much of the weaponry was Cold War stuff, but these same combat platforms have been souped up by the application of information and communications technologies.

Before Pentagon planners draw lessons from Iraq about the shape of future wars, though, they would do well to consider the enemy they had taken on.

Iraq started out at a huge disadvantage despite its overwhelming advantage in numbers. It had old weapons and tanks, its troops were poorly motivated and disciplined, and its air defenses had been softened up by 12 years of no-fly-zone bombing.

Saddam's army had learned new tactics since its thumping in the open desert in 1991. Although it could boast a history of fighting ferociously in static defensive positions, this was no use against an enemy that was brilliant in fluid battlefield conditions. So, they chose to fight dirty and fight in urban areas to grind down a casualty-averse nation still haunted by the horror of the Black Hawk Down battle in Mogadishu.

On the eve of the 1991 war, Saddam told the U.S. chargé d'affaires in Baghdad, Joseph Wilson, "Yours is a society that can't take 1,000 deaths." As he faced off with the United States in 2003, he was probably calculating again that he could hold his opponents to at least a draw by inflicting heavy casualties.

His plan failed, largely because Iraq's military was so badly degraded and so bad at organizing itself into a coherent fighting force. As Abizaid put it at a Doha briefing, "We have not seen on the battlefield one coherent military move."

Chapter 9

THIS WASN'T IN THE SCRIPT

By Adrian Croft

A shell burst in the sky, sending a cascade of bright fragments into the smoke-blackened air. U.S. Marines had just crossed the Iraqi border, and this was not in the script. Commanders had not expected Iraqi forces to counter their advance with an artillery barrage.

For reporters traveling with Marines, this was the first indication that the mission to capture the southern Iraqi port of Umm Qasr might not be as easy as we had been led to believe.

It was vital to the U.S.-led forces' strategy to capture the port quickly and with its modern facilities intact. U.S. commanders wanted to get the port operating within a week for ships to bring in humanitarian aid that could be distributed to needy Iraqis as allied forces pushed towards Baghdad. The aid was to be a key plank in a "hearts and minds" campaign aimed at showing ordinary Iraqis that the Americans and British were interested in their welfare. The plan called for a convoy of open five-ton trucks crammed with Marines to occupy Iraq's only deep-water port, but the unexpected resistance led to a hasty rethink.

Heavily armed Marines dived out of the trucks and fanned out across the sandy scrubland, pinned back almost on the border as they responded to Iraqi machine-gun, mortar and artillery fire. Clouds of swirling black smoke obscured the sun.

Reuters photographer Desmond Boylan and I scrambled out of our truck and took cover behind a sandy bank, cursing the heavy bulletproof vests and helmets we wore, which made it difficult to run.

One Marine originally assumed the artillery fire was "friendly" and radioed British units supporting them to tell them their fire was dropping short only to be told that British guns were not firing in the area.

The Marines had to wait for two M1 Abrams tanks to be called up to punch through the Iraqi resistance before they could be on their way to Umm Qasr again.

This was war reporting first hand, a taste of action after 10 uncomfortable days of waiting in the searing heat of the Kuwaiti desert. It was what we had signed up for when we "embedded" for a unique inside view of the conflict with the 15th U.S. Marine Expeditionary Unit (MEU).

With its own planes, helicopters, tanks and armored personnel carriers, the Camp Pendleton, California-based unit was a 2,100-strong force. It was among the first to cross the border into Iraq on the morning of Friday, March 21, a day after President Bush's ultimatum to Iraqi President Saddam Hussein expired.

The 15th MEU's piece of the grand scheme to invade Iraq had been meticulously planned and rehearsed during the long wait in the Kuwaiti desert. U.S. Marine commanders became intimately familiar with the ground they would have to cover through satellite photographs of the port. Those pictures showed that, perhaps surprisingly, Saddam had done little to defend Umm Qasr.

A military planner told us nine days before the attack that there was "not much of an organized military threat down there." The Marines' main concern was that a police station and a Coast Guard facility in the town might be turned into Iraqi strongholds.

It was only in the final days before the attack that the United States received intelligence indicating Saddam had strengthened his defenses in the south. These reports indicated an Iraqi infantry unit had moved in to former United Nations quarters in Umm Qasr and that an Iraqi battalion was reinforcing the border.

But grizzled Marine commanders, saying it was common for intelligence to focus on such scare-mongering reports as the prospect of military action loomed, played down the information and stuck to their plan.

"Am I Scared?"

From the moment we were embedded 10 days before the attack, there had been no doubt in my mind that the war was going to happen. It seemed to me unlikely that Bush and British Prime Minister Tony Blair would order tens of thousands of service men and women out into Kuwait if they did not intend to go through with an invasion—and less likely still that they would invite hundreds of journalists to join them.

A day after we joined, the unit moved from a large, established camp in Kuwait with showers, toilets and a mess to Camp Viking, a forward camp closer to the Iraqi border that had no such facilities.

When I arrived at Camp Viking after an exhausting four-hour drive along desert roads, it was already dark. The camp was buzzing with activity, as it was still being built. I was given sleeping quarters with other journalists in a military tent and was just settling down to sleep when a gale-force wind whipped up from nowhere, tearing into the tent as if it were a huge sail. The tent was beginning to collapse and seemed about to be blown away—with us in it.

We struggled to find the way out. Outside, in the stinging sandstorm and darkness, Marines were driving metal stakes through guy ropes to keep the tent down. Another photographer who was with us confided to me, "This is the worst experience of my life."

We went back into the tent and found two massive metal posts inside had collapsed. One of them lay across a sleeping bag where a reporter had until recently been lying. We decided it was safer to be outside and curled up in our sleeping bags in a hollow in the ground until the sandstorm blew itself out.

The days in the Kuwaiti desert passed slowly. Desmond and I were attached to Fox company of the 2nd Battalion, 1st U.S. Marine Regiment, made up mainly of men in their 20s or late teens. The Marines spent their days training, exercising, playing cards and eating MREs, the brown-packaged military rations that were to be our staple diet.

The mood changed dramatically on Tuesday, March 18. When I woke up, I heard on the radio that Bush had just given Saddam an ultimatum to flee his country by 4 a.m. local time Thursday.

A sense of urgency gripped the camp. Now it was for real. Marines checked equipment, cleaned and recleaned their guns and staged dress rehearsals of what they would do when they crossed the border.

On the surface, all was confidence and bravado.

"As a Marine, this is what we train for. This is what we look forward to," 19-year-old Joseph McCarthy from St. Johns, Arizona, told me. "I myself—and I'm pretty sure all the other Marines around me—are ready to go, ready to get this thing kicked off and taken care of and finally get Saddam out of where he's at."

But the young Marines, most of whom had never seen action before, could not disguise a touch of nerves about what lay ahead.

One Marine who borrowed a journalist's satellite phone to call home was shocked because his father broke down in sobs as he wished him good luck.

This was the first time I had seen war from such an insider's position and, while modern warfare relies on cutting-edge technology, I was struck by how little, at a human level, the build-up to war has changed since Shakespeare's day.

There was still growing tension throughout the camp in the final hours before the attack as young Marines secretly wondered if they would come out alive. Extra religious services were laid on at which a chaplain reassured Christians that "being a warrior of the Lord does not put you in conflict with being a warrior for your country."

A "Henry V" moment fell to Fox company commander Capt. Rick Crevier when he gathered his men around him in a howling sandstorm on Wednesday, March 19, to give them final instructions. Rather than a pep talk, his sober speech was intended to dampen any overconfidence among his Marines.

"I bring you together so that you understand you are not going into a benign environment. There is a company of the 45th or 47th [Iraqi] infantry brigade in Umm Qasr....Once we cross the breach, we will be in [Iraqi] Sagger missile range and will remain so," he said.

"Some people accept fate, that when the time comes, your life's got to be expired. You all have to accept this in your own way.... I'd be a liar if I told you I wasn't a little apprehensive about crossing the border. Am I scared? No."

The small tents that had served as home for a week were pulled down, and everything was loaded into trucks to move to forward positions. The move was all of 500 yards farther north. I did not know whether this exercise had a valid aim in making sure the Marines were ready to move more quickly or was just designed to keep them busy.

Camouflage nets were taken down, revealing the awesome force of tanks and armored vehicles that the Americans and British had assembled. Convoys formed and moved off.

Wednesday, March 19, the Marines were growing tense. A decision would be made at 6 p.m. whether they would go into Iraq that night, I heard. As evening drew on, it was clear nothing was to happen and the invasion had been postponed.

I learned a possible reason why when we heard on a short-wave radio the next morning that Bush had ordered air strikes targeting Saddam and some of his top lieutenants.

So it was more waiting. I had already packed my sleeping bag in the trailer, meaning that night I could barely sleep for cold. The ground was hard, and my helmet was a poor substitute for a pillow.

I rose early Thursday morning to find the war had begun, heralding an anxious wait until night fell again and the Marines could move forward. Crucially, the delay appeared to give the initiative to Saddam and put the Marines on the defensive.

At least 14 times throughout the day, the cry of "gas, gas, gas" went up whenever there were suspicions that an Iraqi missile had been fired over our heads. The alerts were a precaution in case a warhead containing a toxic chemical landed near us. Each time the cry went up, we strapped on our gas masks, dived into foxholes and waited up to 30 minutes for the "all clear."

Word spread through the camp that the attack was on for that night. "We're about to go into the mouth of the cat," Crevier, a lean and energetic officer, told his Marines.

The Marines, who had been wearing desert camouflage fatigues, changed into chemical warfare suits. Taking no chances with Saddam's alleged arsenal, they went into Iraq wearing the suits and kept them on until the fighting was nearly over.

Journalists too were issued U.S. military chemical kits. Gas masks hung from our belts, and we carried rubber overboots and gloves ready to put on if we came under chemical or biological attack.

In the late afternoon, Marines were allowed to fire practice rounds with M-16s and machine guns, taking turns to blaze away into the desert. One Marine offered me a rifle to fire. I politely declined.

Preparation for war made an interesting psychological study. How do you turn young men from some of the most pampered societies on earth into killers? After spending weeks in the Kuwaiti desert in harsh conditions, deprived of virtually all contact with the outside world, Marines were brimming with pent-up aggression by the time they crossed the border into Iraq.

Nightfall ushered in more cold and restless dozing, interrupted repeatedly by gas alerts that forced us to dive into foxholes. At one point, there was panic as Marines detected an unidentified vehicle heading towards us that they feared could be a pre-emptive Iraqi incursion into Kuwait. Marines scrambled in the dark to assemble mortars and prepared to fire. But the vehicle, or whatever it was, moved away, and the scare passed.

During the night, a fearsome artillery barrage was heard as U.S. and British artillery pounded southern Iraq in preparation for the attack.

Before dawn on Friday, March 21, we were up again, packing and clambering into trucks. Marines painstakingly daubed their faces with black, green and brown camouflage paint, making themselves look fierce.

The convoy moved off along rutted desert roads, past a British artillery unit firing salvos into Iraq and past Kuwaiti army units whose role was limited to defending Kuwaiti territory.

Combat engineers had dug several holes through a sand bank protecting the border to keep Iraqis guessing where the attacking forces would come through, but there didn't seem to be much element of surprise.

It was after dawn now, but it never really got light that day because of the smoke from so much ordnance. "The sky is black with smoke and dust. There is a very strange light here," I reported as I called in details of the attack to the Reuters editing desk, using my satellite phone.

The truck crossed the pontoon bridge that British engineers had laid over a dry riverbed on the border, and I was in Iraqi territory.

Almost instantly, the rattle of machine gunfire and the crack of exploding shells erupted.

The convoy scrambled, and Marines poured out of the trucks, exchanging fire with Iraqis holding a ridge several hundred yards ahead. Artillery fire was thought to have come from a battery of Iraqi guns dug in on the Faw Peninsula that had not been spotted by U.S. intelligence. I crouched in a field for about two hours while two M-1 Abrams tanks were called in to destroy opposition on the ridge. Cobra helicopters flew overhead. A Marine officer said later that he believed around 60 Iraqis may have died in the clash, but no one went close enough to see any bodies.

Once the shooting had died down, the convoy reformed. One of the Marines' eight trucks chose this moment to break down, and we had to load another four or five Marines into our already overcrowded truck. The trucks pressed on past ruined buildings, eventually joining an asphalt road.

On the outskirts of Umm Qasr, which lies just a few miles over the border, I saw about 30 uniformed Iraqi soldiers, including some senior officers, who had surrendered to U.S. Marines. They were marched down the road towards Umm Qasr with hands on heads.

A man in civilian clothes lay face down in the middle of the highway, a U.S. Marine with a rifle standing over him. Other civilians waved makeshift white flags.

Approaching the town, we saw a blazing truck with the horribly burned body of a man lying beside it. Nearby, a portly man in civilian dress lay on his back with arms spread wide, dead but with no obvious wound.

Nearby, a well-dressed Iraqi family appealed to U.S. Marines to help a young man who was lying badly wounded by the road, his white shirt covered in blood. A U.S. medic got down from the truck to help.

The casualties were people who had tried, too late, to flee the town and were fired on by U.S. forces who said their vehicles failed to stop.

Raising the Flag

The convoy drove round a corner, and we found ourselves at the entrance to the new port of Umm Qasr, the Marines' main objective. Cranes and other facilities of the modern container port were intact. Six port workers emerged with their hands up. Most of the U.S. fighting force had gone on ahead, and it was eerily quiet now.

In front was an archway bearing the words "Aluboor Marine Terminal" with an Iraqi flag flying. To the left, under an eagle's head, was a large portrait painted on canvas of Saddam Hussein. The wall around it was riddled with bullets.

Some Marines passed the time by cutting out the Saddam portrait and rolling it up as a memento, while another Marine climbed on top of the archway, hauled down the Iraqi flag and replaced it with the Stars and Stripes and a red Marine flag.

I was on the satellite phone to Reuters editing desk in Dubai at the time, and the news that the U.S. flag had been raised at the new port of Umm Qasr was flashed instantly around the world. It provided eyewitness proof of how the fighting was going at a time when the invasion force and Iraqi government were making competing claims about who was in control of the port. Desmond, standing in the truck next to me, captured a dramatic exclusive picture of the moment that was shown on television stations and printed in newspapers worldwide.

Raising the U.S. flag has been a time-honored tradition of victorious U.S. forces, but it was not the most diplomatic move at a time when America was stressing that it was engaged in a war of liberation, not conquest, in Iraq. Within an hour or so, the U.S. flag had been brought down again. We heard later that their superiors had rapped unit commanders over the knuckles. But rank-and-file Marines were unrepentant, and one, the owner of the flag that was raised at Umm Qasr, thought he saw the way to riches with a scheme to auction it on Internet site eBay for $1 million!

Marines entered the warehouse area of the new port. They used five-ton trucks to bulldoze cars parked in the lot out of the way to create a landing strip so that helicopters carrying Marine reinforcements could land. They then laboriously went through the port complex, building by building and room by room, checking for any enemy or booby traps.

As Marines were busy extending their control, Iraq's Interior Minister, Mahmoud Diyab al-Ahmed, vowed the port would not fall. "This is silly talk. Umm Qasr is an Iraqi port and is going to remain an Iraqi port," he told a news conference in Baghdad, waving a rifle.

But Defense Secretary Donald Rumsfeld's assertion on March 21 that U.S. and British forces had captured Umm Qasr was also premature.

U.S. forces only occupied the new port of Umm Qasr on that first day, and it was to take them several more days to pacify the old port and the residential area of the town. Occasional bursts of gunfire rang out on Saturday, March 22, as Marines gradually tightened their grip over Umm Qasr.

Marine officers said there were pockets of resistance from a mixture of Fedayeen militia, regular soldiers and fighters from Saddam's ruling Baath Party. It did not seem to be essential to wear a military uniform to be considered a combatant. Marine commanders said defenders were switching into civilian clothes.

One warehouse at the new port had been turned into a temporary holding center for Iraqi prisoners of war, and it was gradually filling up. British forces sailed 10 rubber dinghies into the port carrying 50 prisoners of war they had taken in fighting on the nearby Faw Peninsula.

The prisoners—some in uniform but most in civilian dress—had their hands bound with plastic handcuffs. Many were barefoot, and some looked in a poor state. Two men were carried ashore on stretchers, and another limped with a foot injury.

The next day, two boats came into port carrying more prisoners. The crew consisted of U.S. Navy SEAL Special Forces and a number of sinister-looking men dressed from head to toe in black and armed to the teeth. These turned out to be Polish commandos—part of the allied forces in the Gulf—whose mission was to board suspicious ships in the Khawr az Zubayr waterway.

In a surreal moment, the commandos came ashore, scrawled graffiti on a huge portrait of Saddam Hussein that faced the harbor, posed for photographs in front of it and then got back on their ships and sailed off.

For a second time, Desmond's photographs sparked controversy, and again the Stars and Stripes was partly the cause. Poland's Defense Ministry was forced to confirm that its top-secret GROM (Thunder) commando unit had taken part in allied operations after the pictures were splashed across newspapers. Poland had sent 200 troops to the Gulf in what it originally said was a supporting, noncombat role.

A picture of the elite Polish commandos posing with U.S. Navy SEALs holding the American flag touched on national sensitivities. "These photos shouldn't have happened," Polish Defense Minister Jerzy Szmajdzinski said. "The next time it will definitely be with the Polish flag."

Walking Tour

By Sunday, Crevier, the company commander, felt confident enough to allow Desmond and me on a walking tour of part of the port. But we had gone just 100 yards across an open space when shooting broke out. Some kind of missile whizzed by us. We took cover in a hurry.

On top of a nearby gantry, we had a good view over the residential area of Umm Qasr, and Crevier directed operations from there by radio.

Crevier said a captured Iraqi officer told the Marines that 120 Republican Guards had taken refuge in the town, a cluster of low, sandy-colored buildings. Iraqi fighters were said to be holed up in several spots, including an official building with an Iraqi flag flying in front. U.S. Marines were exchanging fire with them from a road bridge.

Crevier called in tanks, and a few minutes later, two M-1 Abrams rumbled down a road toward the residential area. The tanks opened up with their heavy machine guns, and then there was a flash, white smoke and an explosion as one tank fired a shell.

"Great effects, tanks, great effects," Crevier said, looking through binoculars to survey the damage they had done.

The earth shook as tank shells demolished the tower of the building where the Iraqis were thought to be taking cover. Crevier said there were more dug-in Iraqi troops at another location and called in U.S. Marine Harrier jets.

"Rather than send men in there, we're just going to destroy it," he said.

We took cover behind a building well out of range of the bombs. Soon afterward, I saw the glint of aircraft overhead as two Harriers swept by, each dropping a 500-pound bomb and sending columns of black smoke curling into the air. Some Iraqis came out waving white flags, and the fighting died down.

But at dusk, Marines were again using machine-gun, artillery and mortar fire to flush another group of Iraqi fighters from a hideout in the town. American snipers, using powerful rifles that can kill at a range of more than a mile, fired an occasional round from their vantage point on the road bridge.

No Marines from Fox company were killed in the battle for Umm Qasr, and only a few suffered light injuries. Its sister company, Echo, was not so lucky.

Echo's armored personnel carriers had the task of blocking the road north of Umm Qasr to stop any Iraqi reinforcements arriving from Basra. Marines from Echo company were returning from assaulting an Iraqi trench when one of them was mistaken for an Iraqi soldier and accidentally shot by another American, a Marine officer said.

The dead Marine was Guatemalan-born Jose Gutierrez, a lance corporal from Lomita, California. The U.S. government gave the 22-year-old—one of a number of Marines fighting in Iraq who were not American citizens—posthumous citizenship.

Iraqi casualties were harder to assess. I saw few, but U.S. forces often did not go into the areas they had bombarded, so there was no way of knowing how many dead and injured there were.

I later got some idea of the scale of suffering inflicted on the Iraqi civilian population in the war, when the unit moved to the southern Iraqi city of Nassiriya. There, at an open-air clinic set up by U.S. medics, 39-year-old Hafid Katham was being treated for severe burns to his face and hands. Nearby, his nephew Talal Ali Katham lay face down on a stretcher, suffering from severe burns over much of his body.

Katham said both were burned in a U.S. air strike on his home in Nassiriya in late March. The air strike killed 11 people, including his mother and father. He said the group was relaxing at home at the time and had no weapons.

Hand Over and Move Out

On Monday, March 24, I learned the unit was pulling out of Umm Qasr. With only scattered resistance left in the town, Marines considered their job done and were handing over control of the town to British Royal Marines, who could already be seen in their desert-camouflaged Land Rovers.

The idea was that British forces, with their experience of urban guerrilla warfare in Northern Ireland, would be better qualified to root out any remaining fighters in Umm Qasr and to keep the peace.

A lot of work still had to be done in Umm Qasr, clearing explosives, maintaining equipment and rehiring workers, before the port could reopen. A first ship bringing humanitarian supplies, the British naval supply vessel *Sir Galahad*, docked on March 28, but the full reopening of the port was delayed because mines needed to be cleared from its approaches.

The Marines of Fox company climbed back into their five-ton trucks on March 24 and headed north, first to the former Iraqi naval base at Az Zubayr and finally to Nassiriya, where they relieved other U.S. Marines and helped gradually to tighten U.S. control over the city.

As Saddam's authority crumbled before the U.S.-led onslaught in April, the focus of operations in Nassiriya turned to humanitarian and reconstruction tasks, allowing young Marines of Fox company time to reflect on their first experience of war.

"Everybody expects it to be fast-paced battle after battle when, in actuality, it's not. It's sitting, waiting for this, waiting for that, going here and there, and not knowing why you're doing it," said Cpl. Jeffrey Wright, 21, from San Jose, California. "It's boredom and confusion, really," was his considered verdict.

The war was winding down, and for Desmond and me, after five weeks with Fox company, it was time to return to our more sedate life in the Reuters office in Madrid.

Our dozen or so different camping spots included a mosquito- and fly-ridden Iraqi army base populated by squads of howling wild dogs, a rat-infested warehouse and an uncomfortable muddy bank. Treated pretty much in the same way as the "grunts," I was constantly hauling around bulky equipment in temperatures above 100 degrees and trying to find a space for my gear in Fox company's heavily loaded vehicles.

Physically, it had been the most demanding assignment I had ever been on. I never had a shower in the entire time I was embedded. Toilet facilities were, at best, a trench in the ground, and toward the end I went down with a severe dose of gastro-enteritis that laid low two-thirds of Fox company.

Before hitching a ride back to Kuwait on a U.S. transport plane from Tallil air base, I was able to visit the spectacular remains of the ancient Mesopotamian city of Ur, near Nassiriya.

The sight of the city, whose oldest buildings date back 6,000 years, reminded me that the U.S. and British invasion was just another turbulent episode in Iraq's history.

Chapter 10

OPERATION RUN THE GAUNTLET

By Sean Maguire

A column of black smoke rose ahead of us and helicopter gunships suddenly clattered by, low and ominous. The convoy halted unexpectedly. It was day four of the war on Iraq, and I had barely heard a shot fired. That was about to change.

The Marine infantry battalion I was traveling with reached the outskirts of Nassiriya on the morning of March 23, just as U.S. forces were pitched into an intense battle in the city center. Marines from Task Force Tarawa sped across the southern bridge that led into the dusty low-rise town and were ambushed by Iraqi militiamen firing rocket-propelled grenades from the dirt-brick houses that lined the roads. Marines fought along a strip of exposed roadway, with their vehicles raked by machine-gun fire, until they seized the bridge on the northern exit from town. It was mission accomplished, but at a cost.

That Sunday's assault on Nassiriya left 18 Marines dead. Some were killed when an American A-10 tank-busting jet struck a

U.S. vehicle by mistake. Others died as they attempted to rescue the U.S. Army's 507th Maintenance Company, which had taken a wrong turn in early morning darkness and found itself trapped under fire among the city's canals and waterways. Eleven U.S. soldiers from the lost Army convoy died. Iraqi forces captured six soldiers, including soon-to-be-famous Pfc. Jessica Lynch. With 29 fatalities, it was America's deadliest day of the war. About a quarter of the combat losses from the war were suffered in less than 18 hours in a town where little resistance had been expected.

It was also the first real taste of urban combat in Iraq for U.S. forces. They had trained for it in mock towns built of plywood in the deserts of Kuwait, but found themselves fighting amid palm trees and irrigation ditches. The U.S military's superiority in numbers and equipment was undermined by an enemy prepared to come close, hide among the local population and refuse to confront it openly. U.S. troops complained they were shot at by children, by men in civilian clothes and by groups who pretended to surrender. Trained for orthodox combat, they were surprised to meet guerrilla fighters whose only hope was to engage in unconventional warfare. The Iraqis knew to aim for weak points, for the soft-skinned trucks and Humvees at the tail of convoys. They knew artillery could not attack them if they fought at tight range. U.S. forces had hoped to be greeted as liberators but found determined, low-tech, low-intensity resistance from the gunmen of Saddam Hussein's Baath Party, regime loyalists known as Fedayeen and remnant units of the Republican Guard. This was not in the U.S. battle plan.

The generals had hoped to skirt Iraq's towns and cities, sending their troop columns in wide sweeps through the desert to avoid population centers. They feared being trapped in an urban quagmire amid a mounting civilian death toll that would spark a political backlash against the war. But the strategy for toppling Saddam—a pincer movement on Baghdad—relied on opening the eastern flank of Iraq to U.S. forces. The Army had open terrain in western Iraq. But to mount the eastern assault on Baghdad, the Marines needed to secure routes across both the Euphrates and the Tigris, the two great rivers that watered the ancient civilization of Mesopotamia from which modern Iraq developed. Nassiriya, on the Euphrates, sits astride the roads the Marines needed to let them strike north. Once they encountered resistance that could cut supply lines, the Marines had to shift tactics and attempt to capture the 350,000-strong city.

I sat on top of a Marine armored vehicle and wondered why we had stopped. Something was wrong. The medical crews from the artillery battalion we were supposed to escort through Nassiriya rushed forward to treat the wounded. The great armored cavalcade that had trundled unopposed through the southern Iraqi desert was halted, vehicles backed up for miles along the highway. The sound of shells hitting concrete blew back to us on the wind. More smoke spirals corkscrewed into the air over the city. Reports filtered through of deaths, resistance and unconventional tactics. Black Hawk helicopters flew over us repeatedly to field treatment tents. The men of the 3rd Battalion, 1st Marine Regiment (3/1), my hosts for the duration of the war in Iraq, knew they had to enter Nassiriya as well. It was a well-trained, well-led unit, but it had not seen combat before. Nerves were on edge.

The Attack

I held tight to the lip of the hatch as the vehicle rushed over the bridge at first light. The unit swerved past the smoldering wreckage of an Iraqi anti-aircraft gun, the tracks of our speeding vehicle biting the concrete and spitting rubble behind. "Ride these hogs like a rental car you don't care about," Kilo company commander Capt. Mike Martin told his crews before they gunned their vehicles toward the combat zone. The unit dipped right and rode past the wreckage of a Marine armored personnel carrier. A grenade had pierced its metal frame, and its armor had peeled back like dried skin. Nobody inside had survived. The burned remains of a Marine lay on the road. It would be nearly two weeks before it was safe to retrieve his body. It was a chilling reminder of the vulnerability of the vehicle I rode in to rocket-propelled grenade attack.

The unit pressed on, taking position along an open stretch of "Ambush Alley," the road linking the northern and southern bridges in Nassiriya. The bridges were in U.S. hands, but the road was a free-fire zone. The Marine tactic was to line the road with combat forces, lay down covering fire and then drive through the logistical support for a whole regiment, several hundred vehicles in all. The 1st Marine

Regiment had to get north of Nassiriya—the war timetable was already slipping. "It's 'Operation Run the Gauntlet,'" joked Martin, grimly.

The noise of battle rose to a crescendo. Capt. Dan Schneider whooped as he pumped .50 caliber rounds from the armored personnel carrier's main gun into a house with red gates. "We saw a head pop up. I think we got him third time," said Schneider. An M1 tank lumbered forward, Marines lying in ditches ran back for cover, and the tank's main gun put a shell into a building less than 100 yards away. Humvees and trucks rumbled past, their machine guns blasting holes in silent roadside homes. Sgt. Maj. Jose Martinez screamed, "What the hell are you doing?" at a trigger-happy enlisted man who fired his M16 carbine overhead, risking the lives of his colleagues. Martinez was sheltering in the lee of an APC, where a Marine was lying on the ground having a foot injury treated. Cobra helicopters wheeled above with their front machine guns waggling from side to side as the pilots searched out targets. A pair of choppers flew in low. A hundred feet above my head they fired their rockets with a whoosh that sounded like fabric ripping. Ducking back inside the cramped, windowless APC, I saw the crewmen staring at each other, bug-eyed with fear. Cpl. Mike Britt heaved a garbage can of empty shell casings over the side, and the heavy brass cartridges scattered across the road in a noisy staccato.

Marines ducked into houses and searched for attackers. I followed. A middle-aged man lay dead in his scruffy living room, a victim of the hail of American bullets. His brother had been killed in a nearby bedroom. Their elderly mother was in the hallway, holding a beseeching arm up at passing troops. Her husband lay under a blanket, still alive. A Marine medic had treated his bullet wound, and the couple would later be evacuated to safety.

Outside, Marines sheltered against walls, chewing tobacco or lighting cigarettes. "I just killed my first man," a lance corporal said nonchalantly. Capt. Joe Bevan pointed up the street to where a body lay, clad in the black favored by Fedayeen fighters. "There are 10 to 15 guys in black clothes in a stronghold three to four hundred meters north. One guy tried to run to the building, but he got hit. He tried to low-crawl in but didn't make it." Bevan directed heavy machine-gun fire onto the building, and clumps of concrete fell off its walls. The last of the convoy the Marines were shielding sped by, the drivers scrunched down inside their soft-skinned vehicles, keenly aware they had only helmets and flak jackets to protect them.

It would take 10 days for the Marines to subdue Nassiriya completely. All convoys had to brave attacks as they were escorted north under armed guard. The Iraqi resistance slowed the U.S. advance, muddled the order of battle and strained supply lines to breaking point. Nassiriya was one of very few places where the Iraqis managed to mount a coherent defense. It defied the U.S. military with more persistence than anywhere else before it finally succumbed under the weight of the assault. Hundreds of Iraqi civilians were reported to have died as artillery shells, mortar rounds and air strikes hit the city. U.S. forces say the targets were carefully selected to minimize the risk to noncombatants.

The Long and Dusty Road

I traveled with Damir Sagolj, a Reuters photographer from Sarajevo, and by the time we reached Nassiriya, we were hardened road warriors. We had been living in the desert for two weeks and were caked in dust and sweat. Our bodies were heavy with the fatigue of interrupted sleep and hours of grinding, bumpy travel. In our last night in a Kuwaiti camp we were awakened at 1:30 a.m. and listened on short-wave radio to President Bush declaring war had begun. He warned of a long struggle. In the desert, before we crossed the border into Iraq, Father Wayne Haddad, a military chaplain, celebrated Roman Catholic Mass, serving communion from an ammo can. He blessed the vehicles "to keep you all safe" and told his small congregation of young men to pray for their enemies.

Just hours later, as the clock ticked toward departure, a cry of "Gas, gas, gas" rang out, and we struggled to pull masks out of the cumbersome satchels strapped to our legs. The company pigeon was fetched from the back of a truck and watched for signs of asphyxiation. We breathed heavily inside our rubber casing as the sweat trickled over our faces. At the "All clear" the desert wind coated us with sand.

Damir and I were attached to a front-line Marine infantry battalion as embedded journalists. The Pentagon told us we would be given no special treatment, and it was true to its word. We ate, slept and worked with the troops, dug our own sleeping holes in the dirt, fetched our own food and shared the dangers of war. It's a truism that military life consists of days of tedium punctuated by moments of terror. We lived out the adage inside a Marine APC.

Fifteen Marines and two reporters crammed into a tin can on tracks officially known as an armored amphibious vehicle (AAV). Over the weeks that the group traveled together, it evolved into a mutually supportive micro-community that sublimated differences in rank, nationality and ideology. The opening move of the campaign fused us together. We drove through two nights and a day, barely stopping. The AAVs, designed for beach landings, not for arduous desert treks, were torture to travel in. I sat on numbing steel benches, with clouds of sand billowing down on us through hatches kept open to prevent suffocation. Those who stood up on rear sentry duty choked on hot exhaust fumes that a design flaw appeared to funnel directly into the vehicle. The sun turned the troop compartment into an oven. Men sweated profusely in their chemical weapons protection suits and sucked desperately on water bottles to keep dehydration at bay. If reporters and troops, two very different breeds, could tolerate each other through that opening ordeal, I realized we could survive all the way to Baghdad.

Highway of the Dead

The fight through Nassiriya had bloodied the Marines. Behind them lay their dead colleagues, not yet recovered. The 1st Marine Regiment's mission was to forge north from Nassiriya along Highway 7 toward the city of Kut. They were to act as a large-scale diversion to hold in place the Baghdad Division of the Republican Guard defending Kut and prevent it reinforcing the Iraqi capital. Feinting attacks were supposed to draw the Guard into the open where it could be pummeled by coalition air power. Along the road to Kut lay a string of potentially hostile towns and miles of unknown territory. The men were on edge, quick to fire to protect themselves. Their tactics were aggressive.

Fast-moving scouting vehicles in the vanguard left mayhem behind them. The first bus we saw was burned out and looked empty at the side of the road. As we got closer, I could see the bullet holes, the crater in the road and the charred corpses. It was hard to keep count of the dead as we rode past. A headless man here, a body without legs over by the reeds. Then there was another bus with dead poking through the windows. A forlorn group of two dozen men, some in Fedayeen black, were in U.S. custody. They appeared to be the lucky survivors among Iraqi reinforcements blasted by U.S. fire as they tried to reach Nassiriya. Some lay on stretchers, badly hurt.

We drove north, past burning trucks and an abandoned family car with its lights still on and the dead driver, a civilian, on his face in the mud. That night we slept in the rain, with big drops of water sluicing into my sleeping bag. By dawn, we were on the move and swerving past more cars and buses wrecked by U.S. fire. The ground around them was littered with dead. Two men knelt by the side of the road with their hands in the air, hoping not to be targeted. A bus heading north, away from the approaching forces, had been hit in the rear by heavy cannon fire. A dead man lay across the twisted metal in a grotesque tableau.

On our second morning north of Nassiriya, we refueled beside another bus full of dead passengers. I counted four dead men on the ground and 16 lying lifeless in pools of blood and shattered glass inside the bus. Their belongings lay scattered around—clothes, wallets full of family photographs, a watch. A few of the dead men were in uniform, and some had Republican Guard insignia. I saw no weapons, though a Marine told me two handguns were found. The bus, like the others on previous days, appeared to pose no real threat to U.S. forces. In 3/1, disquiet was growing at what the Marines had witnessed. A supply officer wondered aloud why the Iraqis had not been given the chance to surrender. The battalion commander, Lt. Col. Lew Craparotta, pointedly told his men to fire only if they had a clear target and if they were shot at. A senior commander visiting his troops, Brig. Gen. John Kelly, conceded some vehicles should not have been hit. But Marines had been attacked with suicide bombs, by civilians and by men pretending to give themselves up, he told me. "That's the problem we face here. We have very little time to decide if a truck or bus is going to be hostile."

Hold-ups on the Way

It was March 27, 3/1 had been in Iraq a week and apart from prisoners of war, the Marines had not yet talked to a local person. In each town we came to, the regiment adopted the same tactic as in Nassiriya. The lead unit set up a cordon and blasted roadside buildings to allow the main convoy through safely. Our progress was slow as units fell behind, vehicles broke down and battalions crisscrossed each other. In the confusion, we slogged forward.

The battalion was ordered to cordon the small town of Qal'at Sukkar, 60 miles north of Nassiriya. Kilo Company had the midsection of town, facing a jumble of houses, shops and mosques. The APC drove fast into the shelter of a culvert, and I stepped out into ankle-deep mud. It was already late, and I knew the night would be miserable. I heard no Iraqi shots, but the Marines started firing heavily. The captain directed heavy machine-gun bullets into the minaret of a mosque, which he said was being used as an observation platform. Nobody could have stayed alive in the minaret, but the fire continued, chewing at the brickwork. That night I slept sitting in a corner of the APC, heat leaching out of me into the metal. The Marines had to lie outside in the mud all night and struggled to stay alert. "It was cold. Marines were falling asleep, and that's dangerous," said Lt. Brian Von Kraus. "We need to keep our guard up."

The 3/1 forged forward through the green fields of young wheat. The Marines felt alone and isolated. They were the northernmost unit in that part of Iraq, so far forward that an A-10 tank-buster plane had dropped a 250-pound bomb behind them. By the evening of Friday March 28, they had outrun their supply lines. "We've run out of chow," Martin announced. And as for getting mail, he told his disheartened men, "Don't even think about it."

The battalion had no fuel, and tankers were 24 hours away. Radio batteries were in short supply and had to be recycled. Rations were cut to one MRE a day, a third of the recommended daily intake for a fighting man. For two days, we went hungry. When deliveries reached us, by helicopter, we went to two MREs daily, and the squabbling over who got which flavor of ration intensified. The Marines felt bogged down and directionless, unsure of their next move. The coalition's top land commander called a four-to-six day pause in offensive operations to let his forces regroup. The order was not supposed to leak to the press, but it quickly did. Central Command, fearful the U.S. public would get a whiff of defeat, denied there was a break in the action or any problem with supplies. The distortion was galling for troops who had empty stomachs. The end of the war seemed increasingly distant for men who had been away from home for months.

Checkpoint Casualties

Having ground to a halt, frontline U.S. forces were forced to have a relationship with the civilian inhabitants of the country they had invaded, a challenge they met reluctantly and were ill-prepared for. The battle plan relied on constant movement and assumed attack troops would confront armed opposition. Dealing with civilians was largely to be left to forces following later. But assault units found themselves manning checkpoints, corralling frightened women and children and trying to determine if sullen crowds were hostile or intimidated. Troops were trained to fight but not to defuse the tension of an angry mob. They were already nervous, and a suicide bombing in the central city of Najaf that killed four U.S. servicemen set them further on edge.

Along Highway 7 the Marines tried to keep the curious away with prerecorded Arabic warning messages. But local people were unable to get to market, to return to their homes or even to flee Baath Party repression because U.S. forces blocked movement along roads. Civilians were unable to understand U.S. instructions or to explain themselves to the troops because there were too few translators. A genial Kuwaiti worked with 3/1 but needed to be in several places at once to be effective.

American troops assumed Iraqis would know it was dangerous to approach the U.S. military. They expected the Iraqis to be cautious. It was a delusion that led to several needless deaths, including the shooting of seven women and children in Najaf when their vehicle failed to stop at a desert checkpoint. U.S. forces were accused of being trigger-happy and struggled to explain that they were responding to a genuine perception of threat. Arab fury rose over U.S. "aggression" toward Iraqi civilians.

Ignorance and inexperience played an uncomfortably large part in some civilian shootings. I saw one such death before breakfast on April 1. The Marine checkpoint was a single strand of barbed wire, barely visible in the bright sunlight. No stop sign had been posted. A white pick-up truck failed to see the wire or the U.S. vehicles nestled down beside the verge, and it kept coming. The car was hit with blasts of machine gun fire and rolled to a halt. "I thought it was a suicide bomb," said the gunner. Inside were two elderly Iraqi men who had set out with an empty vehicle on an early morning errand. The driver was dead. A Marine screamed in English at the passenger to get out, but his spine was severed by bullets and he could not move.

Some deaths defied explanation and resisted easy allocation of blame. One of the most haunting images of the war was a close-up of the bloody face of a young Iraqi girl with multiple gunshot wounds. Tears and blood welled out of the socket of an eye that had been torn apart. Damir took the picture after the girl and her father and young brother were retrieved from no-man's land where they were caught in withering crossfire. The Rahi family had approached a U.S. checkpoint but stopped their car some distance back. An Iraqi truck drew up behind them and a soldier got out of the truck and approached, poking his Kalashnikov through the car window. Marines said the Iraqi soldier shot at the family, and Americans then opened fire. The barrage raked the car and the truck. It is not clear if it was U.S. or Iraqi bullets that hit the 6-year-old and killed her mother. The father, Haytham Rahi, was shot in the leg. We never discovered why the family was on the road or why the soldier shot at them. The incident was symptomatic of the limitations of embedded journalism. I wanted to follow the story, hoping it would illustrate the complexities of Iraqi society in turmoil. But that was impossible—the family was whisked away for treatment, our unit was quickly on the move elsewhere and I had no choice but to go with them. It was only six weeks later that I learned, via a colleague, the little girl's name was Tghreed. She survived, but has no right eye.

Hearts and Minds

The problematic handling of civilians impeded one of the central war aims, which was to win the Iraqis over to the U.S. side. It was the oft-repeated belief that Iraqis would welcome the U.S. forces as liberators. Local people would throw off their Baath Party oppressors, I was told, if only they could be persuaded of U.S. benign intentions. Killing civilians and riding through their towns, shooting up their buildings, appeared a poor way to convince them. The citizenry never did rebel, but despite the checkpoint disasters, many of them eventually applauded the Americans for toppling Saddam.

U.S. commanders judged that the wetlands north of Nassiriya remained hostile because Marines had not rooted out Baath Party loyalists who were intimidating local people. The 3/1 was told to retrace its steps southward and enter some of the towns it had blasted through just days before.

At 4 a.m. on March 31, F-16 jets dropped precision-guided bombs on Baath Party headquarters and Fedayeen barracks in Shatra, a small town 20 miles north of Nassiriya. M1 tanks rumbled to the edge of town, and 3/1's APCs cordoned it off. At first light a Huey helicopter flew in, surveyed hotspots and destroyed an anti-aircraft position. Senior Iraqi leaders, including Ali Hassan al-Majid, or Chemical Ali, the cousin whom Saddam had put in charge of the southern front, were reported to have been in the town. Majid earned his nickname for overseeing the use of poison gas against Kurdish villagers in a 1988 attack that killed thousands. By midmorning it was quiet. Townspeople started coming past the ceremonial town gate with its bullet-pocked picture of Saddam and beckoned U.S. troops forward.

Craparotta, the battalion commander, ordered his men in. They kitted up nervously. Cpl. Antonio Talamantez, an indefatigably cheerful radio operator, heaved on his backpack with the sigh of a man whose heavy load would prevent him running if he needed to save his life. This was to be the first real urban patrol, and the Marines had little idea what awaited them. They trudged up the main avenue, stumbled over the rubble from the Baath building strewn over the street and got a round of applause. Cheering men lined the streets, clapping and hollering. "You are welcome in Iraq," shouted one youth in practiced but limited English.

Shatra was glad to see the Americans. Baath officials had fled, Majeed was nowhere to be seen. The town was the first of many I saw on the road to Baghdad where people enjoying the first flush of freedom from Saddam greeted U.S. troops enthusiastically. But a skeptical U.S. officer reminded me that Iraqis were used to telling men with guns what they wanted to hear.

We met two CIA agents in Shatra who were savoring what they regarded as liberty celebrations. "It's not every day you get to free people," one said. They were not pleased to meet the press. The two, who said their names were Andy and Darren, dressed in pick-and-mix desert casuals, carried guns across their chests and sported baseball caps with sepia Stars-and-Stripes badges on the front. They were with a Gulf Arab translator and a local informant hidden behind his keffiyeh. The CIA's intelligence gathering had been the basis for the combined air and ground raid. But their guidance brought mixed results. On a CIA cue, the Marines stormed a house looking for an Iraqi general who directed ambushes against U.S. convoys on Highway 7. The Iraqi had fled moments before. The troops searched a hospital for the corpse of a fellow Marine killed in the area. That was also unsuccessful. But the CIA men, who journeyed with us back to our staging position, were unambiguous about the merits of their mission. Targeting Baath Party leaders was key to winning the war, they said. When asked about his personal motives, Darren pointed at the American flag on his cap.

Picking Up the Pace

We moved back north again, but we never got to Kut, despite much tense preparation for the assault. The pause was over, the big offensive resumed and Kut was to be bypassed. In a coordinated move, the U.S. Army surged forward on the western flank, while Marines captured a key bridge over the Tigris, southeast of Baghdad, and poured tanks and men through the breach. Kut, pounded by air power and long-range artillery, was irrelevant. The Republican Guard's Baghdad division was judged so weakened that it could no longer reinforce the capital. I met the commander of the 1st Marine Regiment, Col. Joe Dowdy, on April 2. He was buoyant and gung-ho, telling me the Numaniya River crossing was "the last big bridge we needed for the advance on Baghdad." A day later, he was sacked.

It was never explained why Dowdy was relieved of his post, an almost unheard-of action to take at the height of a military campaign. Marine Corps commandant Gen. Michael Hagee said Dowdy's division commander "lost confidence in him" but would not be more specific.

Dowdy, a veteran Marine from Arkansas who resembled Marlon Brando in the film *Apocalypse Now*, appeared well-liked by his troops. But matters were awry in his sector. Officers complained of frequent changes in their mission and of confusion. The Marines are a hard-charging Corps and set high standards for their senior officers. I learned of Dowdy's removal after a long trek westward that was both farcical and uncomfortable. We spent hours searching in the darkness for a refueling point that was not where it was supposed to be. But the trip put us on the main road to Baghdad, and under the colonel's successor we were to make quick progress.

The Marines were glad to press on. The closer they were to Baghdad, the closer they were to going home. The temperature was rising and already sapping strength. There was neither water nor time for showers or laundry. We had been told to pack lightly, and the few clothes I possessed were stiff with sweat and smelled like a biology experiment. I had dropped jam inside my helmet while trying to make a sandwich in the darkness in a moving APC. My belt was already two notches tighter. "In the military you have to be comfortable with being uncomfortable," Lt. Bill Vaughan told me. Vaughan was a former enlisted man who had made the difficult leap to officer status. He had a wry sense of humor. "It's all good training," he would proclaim at each new hardship.

As we advanced, the sides of the highway were strewn with burned-out Iraqi tanks and ammunition trucks spilling cartons of bullets. Here the Iraqis had put up little resistance. Saddam persuaded his people to build fortifications, with linked trenches and bunkers, in the towns and villages. But the defenses were abandoned without a fight. Saddam could not convince ordinary Iraqis in the hinterlands of Baghdad to die tackling U.S. armor. Young Iraqi men streamed away from combat areas, having changed into civilian clothes, thrown away their guns and deserted their posts. Marines collected tons of unwanted rifles, RPGs and discarded ammunition. Trucks of mortar rounds and 120 mm artillery shells, still in their wooden crates, were left parked under palm trees. Compared to the technological wizardry of the U.S. military, Iraq's third-world weaponry was primitive. But it was plentiful and still deadly. What was missing was the will to use it.

"Thank you for coming. Now I don't have to serve in the army," said Taha Ahmed, 35, one of a group of cheering men who greeted the Marines as they swept through Aziziya, 50 miles southeast of Baghdad. "All of us have run away from our units. We don't want to fight; we are tired of war." They offered the Marines cheap cigarettes and bottles of soft drinks, which the troops gratefully accepted until a master sergeant said the local versions of U.S. colas were a health risk.

The Iraqis were eager to discover what U.S. occupation would mean for their daily lives. "Will we have new money, or will we have dollars?" asked Ali, gesturing with disgust at the local banknotes that prominently displayed the image of Saddam. "Will we have democracy and clean water soon?" quizzed Malek Farhan, who said

he was a local councilor. Others asked how long U.S. forces would
stay, when food aid would be handed out and if the Americans would
steal Iraq's oil, as the Baghdad government alleged frequently in the
run-up to the war. The Marines were bemused by the onslaught of
questions and sought shelter behind barbed wire.

U.S. forces squeezed Baghdad in a vise. Marines raced around
the city's eastern perimeter to join army counterparts moving in from
the west, sealing off all exits. Then they marched methodically
inward. The fields of rural Iraq gave way to the garden plots, grubby
industrial parks and well-appointed villas of Baghdad's suburbs.

The Marines faced their toughest resistance at the Diyala
River, a tributary of the Tigris that runs from north to south and
blocked their way to the city center. The 3/1 reached the river to
discover the bridge they were supposed to cross was only half built.
We waited for an engineering unit to build a pontoon bridge and
watched as U.S. artillery rounds whistled overhead and landed on the
opposite bank. A forward air controller spotted a surface-to-air
missile parked in distant trees and called for an F-16 strike.
Commanders vetoed the mission at the last minute when they realized
another Marine unit was advancing into the path of the bomb. A U.S.
tank fired at the missile, and it burned with a lurid, chemical flame.
Amid the artillery assault, a lone Iraqi gunman, hidden in the reeds,
fired on the U.S. bridge builders. An engineer ran across open space
to better cover, and bullets kicked up dust at his heels, a moment so
reminiscent of war movies that it appeared hardly real.

The Day of Flowers

The morning that Saddam fell from power, the Marines woke
up hungry beside an open sewer. They had bedded down in darkness
in an impoverished suburb amid reeking mounds of rubbish and
stagnant drains. Their advance had been so swift, food delivery trucks
could not keep up. They were to have their moment of glory on an
empty stomach.

The troops crept forward, knocking down doors to search for
weapons. They tramped across city parks where tanks were crushing
abandoned artillery pieces. They drove their APCs down narrow
alleyways, expecting grenade attacks. Instead, shy girls dropped

flowers through the hatches. Families came to their gates and shouted, "Welcome, welcome, welcome." Rose petals dripped from balconies onto the gun barrels and helmets. "Hallo, my guest, thank you for coming," shouted a well-dressed bystander as the tracks rumbled past his feet. A woman held up a baby, showing it a force that its mother hoped would change its life for the better. The troops picked up the flowers, smelled them and grinned. "Is it over?" yelled an Iraqi. "Almost," replied a Marine.

Dozens of surface-to-air missiles were scattered around residential areas, still on their launch trailers. Reports of sporadic sniper fire came over the APC radio. Trucks packed with grenades and mortar rounds were parked at the roadside. A U.S. M1 tank blasted a truck with its machine gun, and the trailer exploded furiously, its load of ammunition firing spontaneously in the flames.

The Marines came to a traffic intersection and were mobbed by a cheering crowd. I looked up and saw the twin blue clamshells of Iraq's Martyrs Monument. I had been in Baghdad during the 1991 Desert Storm campaign and knew the memorial was downtown. The penny dropped. Crowds welcoming U.S. forces this close to the city center meant Saddam's regime had collapsed. The war was over.

An old man made a kicking gesture with his foot, shouting "Goodbye, Saddam." The Marines of 3/1 battalion were astounded when I told them they were the lead unit in eastern Baghdad and had just witnessed the end of 25 years of Baath Party rule. "I'm just happy they are not going to fight. I was a little nervous when the crowd was so exuberant. We've heard so much about suicide bombings and drive-by shootings," said Capt. Dan Rose. I held up my shortwave radio so the Marines could listen to the toppling of Saddam's statue as it was transmitted live to the world.

The crowd's good humor deteriorated quickly into anarchic abandon. The sky was smudged with smoke from burning ministries, lit by rioters. The crowd felt the government owed them something in its death throes and stripped official buildings down to the last light fitting. Political vengeance turned to opportunistic theft. A warehouse with sports goods and children's toys was invaded close to a Marine strongpoint. I watched youths wearing stolen bright-red boxing helmets and gloves push a shopping trolley filled with old computer parts up the street. A car drove past with a life-sized Father Christmas figure strapped to the roof. Boys strolled past in stolen sneakers, fashionably unlaced. Outnumbered and uncertain, the Marines could do little to hold back the tide of crime.

I asked a Marine colonel how he felt about his welcome. "I'm not sure they are happy to see us—they are happy to be carrying away refrigerators and televisions," he said cynically. The warm reception the U.S. military received would quickly lose its gloss. Looters swept through streets, ripping the bars off shop fronts and driving stolen cars past unlit traffic lights. Baghdad was a lawless free-for-all where families were afraid to leave their homes for fear they would be stripped bare. At night unceasing volleys of small arms fire rippled around us, with the whiz of bullets coming alarmingly close as we lay in our sleeping bags on waste ground.

The Marines began to pull back from the city center to better protect themselves, and I realized my journey had ended. Someone else would write the story of Iraq's occupation and reconstruction. My last sight of Baghdad was through the open rear of a Marine Sea Knight helicopter as it sped low and fast over the roofs southward toward Kuwait. The chopper launched antirocket flares. I saw orange balls of flame fizzling toward the ground and took them for fireworks celebrating my safe departure.

Chapter 11

KURDISH REVENGE IN NORTHERN IRAQ

By Mike Collett-White

It was the moment we believed the war was over. A small convoy of press cars skirted carefully around a gaping hole in the bombed-out bridge over the Tigris River and through an impromptu checkpoint of U.S. armored personnel carriers. We were entering Tikrit, the last bastion of Saddam Hussein's brutal regime to fall. The troops were confident that the final battle had been won and were allowing a small group of reporters to see for themselves.

Within minutes we were in the center of the unremarkable town Saddam chose to call his birthplace—in fact, he was born in a humble village nearby. Low-level buildings lined a wide road, and most of the shops facing the sidewalk were shuttered up. Single-story houses were partly obscured by whitewashed walls, and a large building belonging to Saddam's Baath Party had been reduced to rubble by U.S. air strikes.

This was a very different experience from the fall of Kirkuk to the north days before, where relief at the end of fighting and joy among Kurds at Saddam's demise triggered wild scenes of jubilation. We witnessed none of the celebratory shooting and shouting, packed squares and toppling of Saddam effigies, nor the chaotic and violent looting that followed in Kirkuk and more seriously in Mosul.

Instead, there was an eerie calm punctuated by sporadic explosions, which we guessed were coming from U.S. artillery. Streets were empty except for a few men who sat outside a teahouse speaking calmly to reporters and U.S. soldiers about the events of the night before. A father and son held hands in front of their home, looking bewildered as U.S. armor rolled past. A towering statue of Saddam riding a horse was untouched, as were ceramic portraits of him that adorned the entrances to official buildings. The only visible activity on the ground was U.S Marines crouching low with rifles at the ready as they secured open spaces beside the main road. Suddenly, three Cobra attack helicopters swooped low over our heads, firing heavy machine guns at enemy positions a few hundred yards away. U.S. fighter jets circled high in the blue sky, one bomb sending a plume of black smoke into the air.

Soon we found the presidential palace complex, unmistakable for its dramatic entrance that looked like Iraq's answer to the Brandenburg Gate. The enormous, ornate sandstone structure would not have been out of place in the center of an old European capital except for the statues of Saddam at either end. We walked under its vast single arch and found a convoy of dozens of U.S. trucks and hundreds of soldiers lining the long approach to the palace itself. A small group stopped me and asked to use my satellite phone to call home, as most soldiers had not communicated with family and friends since the start of the war. "It's over," one relieved private told his wife. As far as major combat was concerned, he was right.

Just behind him stood the badly ruined presidential palace, a tribute to Saddam's garish and gargantuan tastes—and now a potent symbol of the demise of his power. We picked our way through the grandiose entrance blocked by huge lumps of concrete and twisted metal, and found what was left of the building covered in a layer of fine gray dust. Chandeliers still hung precariously from the small patches of ceiling left intact after heavy aerial bombardment. A dazzling mosaic adorned one wall, and an elegant staircase swept up toward the now collapsed second floor. In places, the sky peeped through large craters left by falling missiles. Polished marble floors were scattered with debris and shards of glass, while a bathroom still had its gold-plated tap fittings and a gaudy pink Jacuzzi. The palace is just one of 150 buildings making up the vast compound. Beyond the rose garden outside, the azure-blue Tigris snaked between sandy banks shaded by palm trees, and below us stretched a giant manmade lagoon where Saddam had allowed elderly locals to fish. At dusk, small groups of Tikritis wandered through the compound picking out vases, furniture and fittings left behind by fleeing occupants. One man dragging away a giant glass chandelier wrapped in a bed sheet could hardly believe his luck.

One question continued to bother me. Where were the Republican Guard and Saddam's feared Fedayeen militia? Some 2,500 die-hard Iraqi troops and fighters were believed to be in Tikrit preparing for a bloody last stand.

Speaking to Marines by the palace, the fighting of the day before had been sporadic, involving one or two serious skirmishes but nothing on the scale they had predicted. Capt. Joe, with the 1st Marine Expeditionary Force, said he expected more hit-and-run attacks of the kind his group had encountered the night before. He described how Iraqi fighters had hit U.S. positions with a hail of bullets from behind trees lining the street. Capt. Joe's men were forced to ground; as they crouched for cover, a lone man walked into the middle of the road and moved calmly toward the U.S. bunker before pulling out a gun from under his long black robe. Before he could shoot, a U.S. sniper cut him down. The man turned out to be a Syrian, supporting the view that some of the most dedicated fighters defending Iraq were foreign. According to locals, the bulk of Saddam's soldiers had fled, in some cases days before the fighting began. They had simply blended back into the communities around Tikrit, where support for the ousted leader was still strong. There seemed every chance that here, as elsewhere in Iraq, the invading forces were going to face a long, low-level guerrilla war that may never be won.

Photographer Nikola Solic, reporter Joseph Logan and I journeyed to Tikrit that morning from northern Iraq, where we had spent the best part of two months covering events in and around the Kurd-controlled enclave wrested from Saddam's control after the 1991 Gulf War. The original thinking was that U.S. forces would descend from neighboring Turkey in their tens of thousands to open up a northern front and divide Saddam's forces in two, split between the north and the south. To general surprise, the Turks refused the U.S. military permission to cross into Iraq by land, changing the dynamics of the war and the nature of our job. This was not to be the full-scale U.S. mobilization we had expected. But in the end we were glad of the freedom this twist gave us to race around northern Iraq unchecked and cover other stories we really wanted to cover.

One striking thing about Kurd-controlled Iraq is how much it differs from the rest of the country. While journalists embedded with troops in the south or working independently dealt with sandstorms and stifling heat, we in the north were driving through lush green valleys and coping with weather reminiscent of an English spring. And unlike the rest of the Islamic world, the Muslim Kurds fully supported the war, wanting above all else to see Saddam crushed and preferably killed.

No Ordinary Bombs

I decided to hear first-hand the accounts of some of Saddam's most infamous abuses against the Kurds and traveled south to Halabja near the Iranian border, where 15 years earlier Saddam's cousin, known as Chemical Ali, had unleashed a vicious attack using deadly nerve agents that killed more than 5,000 people. After a long search for someone willing to talk about what had happened, I found Fakhradeen Saleem, a soft-spoken schoolteacher whose story I will never forget.

The silver-haired 54-year-old quietly described how in March 1988 Iraqi warplanes had roared over Halabja and bombed the town. But these were no ordinary bombs; they contained nerve agents. People began to panic, seeing fellow residents collapse in the streets as they ran, writhing and gasping for air. Harrowing photographs of the aftermath show the bodies of parents and children hugging each other in final embraces and faces of infants etched with agony. The Kurds would never forget one of the most shocking atrocities of Saddam's rule. At the time, the United States, supporting Iraq in the war against Iran, remained silent about the chemical weapons attack and even suggested the Iranians were to blame. But by the time George W. Bush was seeking support to go to war against Saddam in 2003, Washington was only too happy to recall what really happened in Halabja.

Saleem was at home when the bombs fell. Realizing that this was no conventional attack, he quickly wrapped damp handkerchiefs and scarves around the mouths of his wife and children. The crude filters had little effect. His son of six, Sangar, and 8-year-old daughter Nigeen, died first. Saleem hastily buried them in a shallow grave before fleeing with the rest of his family. His 10-year-old daughter died during the flight, and in the panic sweeping the town two more of his seven children were lost, never to be seen or heard from again. Only daughters Tara, now 27, and Bafreen, 19, are known to have survived the attack, for which the Kurds will forever despise Saddam. "How can I feel happiness and sadness after what I have been through?" Saleem asked, holding up photographs of his dead and missing children. "To be honest, I can no longer feel the difference."

On a foggy, rainy afternoon I visited the main cemetery in the rundown town of Halabja and was shown the mass burial sites containing the remains of hundreds of people whose bodies were never identified. One small sign had a large bomb, painted on it in white, and beside it the names of 12 members of the same family who were wiped out in the attack. Many relatives still do not know where their loved ones are buried.

One of them is Zaki Saeed, a woman in her 50s who lost a daughter in Halabja. Tania died alone in a basement, choking on the gases that witnesses said smelt of rotten apples. Saeed seemed to me to be a mild-mannered woman as we talked at her home in Sulaimaniya. That was until she spoke of Saddam. "His death would bring me so much joy. I want him torn to pieces in front of my very eyes."

During the war, that bitterness was expressed time and again in northern Iraq. Millions of Kurds, traumatized by years of fear and brutality, dreamed of the day Saddam would answer for his actions. His regime was to fall, but if the fate of its chief architect remained unknown, Kurds would feel they had been denied their final justice.

Mass Exodus

The first real sign in the north that war was coming was the mass exodus of thousands of Kurds from villages and towns on the front line. Bush's ultimatum for Saddam to surrender had almost expired, and Kurds did not want to be anywhere near the trenches when the bombs started to fall. Long convoys of tractors, trucks and taxis packed with people and their belongings snaked along the roads. Kurdish fighters—*peshmerga* (or "those who face death")—took up bunker positions on hillsides along the main highways. Chamchamal, normally a bustling town overlooked by Iraqi soldiers from hilltops just a mile away, was virtually deserted by the time the deadline passed. The dusty, littered streets were silent and shop shutters firmly closed. Locals were well aware of the dangers of "friendly fire" from U.S. fighters and heavy bombers and the retaliation from Iraqi gun positions clearly visible on hilltops looking down on the town. But most terrifying of all was the possibility of chemical weapons being unleashed by a desperate army.

The war in Iraq began on March 20 with air strikes on specific targets in the capital Baghdad, and we did not have to wait long for things to start in the north. On March 21 the night sky above the key oil centers of Kirkuk and Mosul lit up as bombs fell.

For the next few days reporters Jon Hemming and Sebastian Alison, based in Arbil, and Joseph Logan and myself in Sulaimaniya raced to and from front-line positions with TV crews and photographers to record air strikes on Iraqi forces.

What we actually saw was as much to do with luck as judgment.

I spent one night on top of a TV tower overlooking Kirkuk, wrapped in a sleeping bag, scant protection against a howling, bitterly cold wind. With a radio, two cans of beer and Nikola for company, I took turns with the guards to watch over the city in case of a resumption of air strikes. None came.

On other occasions we saw much more. After traveling for hours along dirt tracks criss-crossing lush grass fields northeast of Kirkuk, we looked on as U.S. strike jets swooped overhead and pounded Buyuk Hassar, a military barracks just to the north of the city. Towering plumes of black smoke rose on the horizon, followed by powerful, deep rumbles that shook the earth. In Chamchamal the bombing was much closer, and more awesome, hitting Iraqi bunkers on the hilltops just outside town. In Kifri, a cameraman was close enough to the bombing to film Iraqi soldiers fleeing their positions just before a line of six or seven explosions formed a giant wave of black and brown behind them. The B-52s that had been so effective in Afghanistan were doing the same now in Iraq. Jon Hemming watched from hilltop positions as fighters pounded positions north of Mosul, and Sebastian Alison witnessed the slow, often difficult advance by Kurdish fighters from Kalak west toward Mosul, supported by small teams of U.S. troops.

Once the U.S. air assault on northern positions had begun, it took just a week for front lines to begin to buckle. The first breakthrough in the north was at Chamchamal on March 27. Commander Mam Rostam, a rotund veteran fighter with heavily lined features and gravelly voice, confirmed that it was his men, not the Iraqis, who now held the hilltop positions overlooking Chamchamal. Around 200 locals and Kurdish militia milled excitedly around a checkpoint controlled only hours before by the Iraqi army. Shots were fired in the air in celebration, and *peshmerga* back from forays into enemy territory reported no resistance. One fighter wearing the Kurds' trademark baggy green trousers and camouflage jacket shouted to colleagues as he casually waved about an antitank mine picked up from the road leading from Chamchamal 25 miles west to Kirkuk. Hundreds of mines had been scattered by retreating forces. At dusk, men returned from Iraqi bunker positions still wearing their gas masks but said they had found no evidence to suggest that chemical weapons would be used.

After a few hours we returned to our base in Chamchamal—a stone-floored house without beds where we whiled away the time sending e-mails to family and friends, playing solitaire on laptops, drinking beer and munching on pistachio nuts. It had become routine for Nikola to torture me by reading the daily menu he received via e-mail from a "friend" back home in Croatia who ran a restaurant. Tonight was no exception; the thought of Hungarian goulash washed down with a bottle of Spanish Rioja left us drooling.

At dawn the following morning, an imam calling the faithful to prayer over a loudspeaker mounted on the mosque next door ensured we did not oversleep. To our frustration, the Iraqi checkpoint where we had been the night before was swarming with Kurdish militia trying hard to stop inquisitive reporters getting past. At one point a pickup carrying several armed *peshmerga* raced through, waving at reporters to follow. We did so, only to be stopped two miles farther on. Heated negotiations between Kurds and journalists followed. Some turned around to look for smugglers' routes to the north and south. Others waited and were finally rewarded when the *peshmerga* allowed them to proceed. "Just watch out for friendly fire," a slightly nervous Rostam warned us. But with no U.S. fighters or bombers to be heard or seen in the clear skies above us, we decided it was time to move.

A convoy of nine or 10 cars sped across rolling green hills, their occupants peering nervously at abandoned bunker positions for signs of Iraqi stragglers. A few army helmets, a pair of boots and blankets were scattered by the sides of the road. The farther we went, the more eerie the stillness became, and it was with some relief that we arrived at Qarahanjir, an Iraqi barracks west of Chamchamal now controlled by Kurds. A portrait of Saddam Hussein dressed in Kurdish clothes greeted us. It had been daubed in yellow paint, and his face was riddled with bullet marks. On the other side of the same stone slab, the reviled leader wore a business suit. As we looked on, a group of young Kurds with scarves over their heads and faces began to fire at the portrait with Kalashnikov rifles, sending chips of concrete flying in all directions.

We visited abandoned Iraqi positions where Kurdish scavengers were sifting through trenches, huts and sandbag defenses for anything of value they could lay their hands on. One man found the old door to his house that had been taken by Iraqi troops many years before. "Jabar Salah," his name, was still written on it. Others were piling iron roofing, ammunition, backpacks and bricks onto the back of trucks. They were unapologetic when we approached them— they were merely taking back what was theirs. On one field the Iraqis had built a primitive firing range, at one end of which was an image of a kneeling, blindfolded man, hands tied behind his back, painted in black silhouette on a white wall. Latif Fatih Faraj, a Kurdish journalist who had collected evidence of Iraqi atrocities for years since being expelled from Kirkuk, told us this was where the army would execute people, including Kurdish rebels and deserters. He showed us an official letter found in an abandoned hilltop bunker confirming the death by firing squad of two young Iraqi deserters in June 1989. He had many more such documents.

From Qarahanjir we continued west, determined to get the clearest view yet of Kirkuk from the surrounding hills. We got to within 10 miles of the city and saw the "prize of the north" below us through the haze. But the Kurds had warned us of the risk of incoming artillery fire from Iraqi positions near the city as well as scattered mines, so we did not hang around. Returning to Qarahanjir, we waited long enough to watch Kurdish fighters shouting and cheering as they rammed a bulldozer into Saddam's portrait. "This is like being born again," beamed Baqir Faraj, the driver of the bulldozer.

The Ground Shook

I stayed behind in Chamchamal that evening to file a final update on the day's events from our house. It had been an exhilarating 24 hours, and I was looking forward to a good long sleep before the rigors of the next day. I had not banked on what was about to happen.

Just as I was putting the finishing touches to the day's story, two loud explosions shook the house and shattered windows not far from where I was sitting. I raced to the roof and was relieved to see two large black plumes of smoke on a hillside less than a mile away; this was probably mines being detonated by Kurds to clear areas recently abandoned by Iraqis. But as I returned to my laptop, perched on an old plank of wood that served as a desk, a third loud blast went off, this time much closer. I clambered back to the flat roof and saw brown smoke rising from the very center of town, three hundred yards from where I stood. It was clear that this was no mine-clearing exercise: Chamchamal was being shelled. At that point the driver, translator and I put on flak jackets, dashed to the car and drove towards the smoke. As we stood examining the damage—thankfully minimal, as the shell had landed on soft earth—a fourth explosion shook the ground beneath us. This was getting too close for comfort. I tried not to think the unthinkable: "Has one of these shells got my name on it?" I looked up into the clear evening sky and saw trails of white smoke left by the self-propelled shells. It was time to run for it. We sped out of town to a nearby hilltop, and while I phoned through a description of what was happening to editors in Dubai, we spotted a fresh trail in the sky and tried to guess where the shell would land. There was an agonizing gap of four to five seconds between the trail disappearing and the bomb exploding. This time it was close enough to send the translator diving for cover in a ditch, and we retreated further. Two more explosions went off in fields outside Chamchamal before the attack ended. In retrospect this had been a woefully inaccurate display from the Iraqi artillery, but it brought home clearly enough the dangers of what we were doing.

A week or so later we were covering an attack on Kirkuk from a hilltop with two other journalists in what had been Iraqi territory days before. While reporting on the heavy bombardment, we heard sporadic shots to our right and so took cover on the slope of a hill. Then a bullet fizzed over the head of a Spanish reporter with us and threw up dust in the ground between him and our translator. It was enough to have us scampering back to the cars.

Of course, others in the north were not so lucky.

- On March 22 a freelance cameraman for an Australian broadcaster was killed in a car bomb attack on a Kurdish checkpoint after covering the operation against the radical Muslim Ansar al-Islam near Halabja.

- A reporter for Britain's Channel 4 died in Sulaimaniya after falling from the roof of his hotel.

- On April 2 a mine at Kifri blew up a cameraman working for the BBC after heavy U.S. bombardment had forced Iraqi forces to flee. A BBC colleague suffered a foot injury when he stepped on a mine as the team attempted to film an abandoned Iraqi fortress.

- A BBC correspondent narrowly escaped with his life when U.S. aircraft attacked a convoy of Kurds near the front lines around Mosul. His translator was among some 18 people killed in the attack near the town of Kalak.

Whether involved in such incidents or just hearing about them from colleagues and friends, they were a sobering reminder of the reality of covering a war. Flak jackets emblazoned with media insignia, hard hats and all the "hostile environment" courses in the world could not protect us from massive U.S. bombs, Iraqi land mines, suicide squads, friendly fire or road accidents. I would try to call or send a text message to my wife, Gabrielle, and parents each time a journalist was reported killed or injured in Iraq, but inevitably the war was a huge stress for wives, children, family and friends trying to follow what was happening to loved ones in the field. It was with a huge sigh of relief that I eventually met Gabrielle off a plane at Amman airport after leaving Iraq for neighboring Jordan.

The retreat of the Iraqis from Chamchamal was followed by other breaches along the northern front line, in Kifri, Taq Taq and around Mosul. The bombing of key cities also intensified, with Khanaqin near the Iranian border, Kirkuk and Mosul bearing the brunt. Kurds built up forces close to the strategic targets but insisted that they would not launch an assault without a U.S. green light. Washington was desperate to prevent Kurds storming northern cities and carrying out reprisals against the Arabs.

Another important consideration was Turkey, which was eyeing events on its southern border with increasing alarm. It had built up a significant military presence of its own along the Turkey-Iraq frontier, ready to cross if it felt Iraqi Kurds were using the war to win control of key cities like Kirkuk. The government in Ankara was worried that events in Iraq might embolden its own Kurdish minority of several million people to demand greater autonomy.

Baghdad Falls

On April 9, Baghdad fell, and the streets of the main Kurdish cities in the north erupted in a din of rifle fire, car horns and shouting. Traffic ground to a halt in Sulaimaniya, and the Stars and Stripes was hoisted aloft wherever we looked. To be with thousands of ecstatic Kurds, probably the most hospitable people I have met, at this turning point in their history was a privilege. Young children approached us and tugged our sleeves saying "Thank you, mister!" treating anyone who looked even vaguely American or European as a liberator.

We could not witness the celebrations for long. The same evening, we traveled to Chamchamal in anticipation of a push for Kirkuk. Hundreds of *peshmerga* had gathered in the front-line town with the same thought in mind. Mam Rostam and other commanders, mindful of U.S. and Turkish pressure, insisted they would not storm Kirkuk, but their assurances seemed half-hearted. We decided to stay close, so it was back to the cold floor, warm beer and imaginary Croatian cuisine at our house in Chamchamal. In the early hours of the next day, Kurdish fighters carrying rifles and machine guns were piling on to the backs of pickup trucks and speeding west toward Qarahanjir and Kirkuk. Reporters again were blocked at old Iraqi checkpoints and forced to wait. A Reuters TV crew from Georgia managed to sneak through in an armored Land Rover, which was similar enough to vehicles being used by the U.S. military in the area to fool the guards. They got to the hills above Kirkuk and filmed as B-52 bombers struck defenses on the edge of the city, sending up huge waves of black smoke and debris. Gradually, Kurdish guards began to leave their posts until there were too few of them to stop reporters hungry to get to the action. Within minutes, we were on the edge of the city, watching as Kurdish fighters poured in, shooting in the air and whooping with delight—Iraqi resistance had collapsed. All the while, senior commanders were officially denying that forces from the Patriotic Union of Kurdistan (PUK) party had entered Kirkuk, knowing that the move would anger not only the Pentagon but also the PUK's former rivals, the Kurdistan Democratic Party (KDP). PUK commander Mam Rostam said later that the show of force after the collapse of Iraqi defenses had filled a potentially dangerous power vacuum in the ethnically diverse city of 700,000. But personal rivalries were also at play. When I found him amid the mayhem and asked him who had entered the city first, the PUK or the KDP, Rostam smiled: "The PUK, of course."

On the edge of the city I interviewed Kurdish families leaving in taxis to see relatives and friends desperate for news of loved ones after weeks of heavy bombardment. A painfully thin and visibly frightened Iraqi soldier, heading for Kurd-controlled country to surrender, said he and others had no idea that cities across the country were falling like dominoes, because his commanders had banned access to television and radio. Kurdish fighters were everywhere, firing into the air, singing and cheering, and pouring into Kirkuk in the hundreds. There they were greeted by thousands of people on the streets, relieved the siege was finally over. Like Khanaqin before it and Mosul after it, Kirkuk fell with barely a fight. Reporters saw the bodies of four dead Iraqi soldiers on one bridge and three more outside an Iraqi security office. One in the latter group had apparently been executed, a single bullet wound to his head, but Kurds denied this version. Traffic built up in the city center, and a large crowd gathered at the main square to deface and topple the statue of Saddam. In scenes reminiscent of Baghdad, a crane was brought in to finish the job, and a swarm of Kirkuk residents and *peshmerga* fighters clambered over the collapsed statue to beat it with metal pipes, shoes and bare hands. His portraits everywhere were shot at and daubed in paint or smothered in gasoline and set alight. But it did not take long to see the ugly side of the "liberation."

Looting and Killing

Arabs and the smaller Turkmen and Assyrian groups were clearly apprehensive at the arrival of so many armed Kurds. Some of them had scores to settle from the days of Saddam's brutal "Arabization" program, which displaced Kurds and replaced them with Arabs. The anxiety only increased when looting and burning of former government offices and security headquarters erupted in parts of the city and was to continue for several days. *Peshmerga* did nothing to stop the mayhem and in some cases joined in.

Entering Kirkuk once again the next morning, we found U.S. soldiers securing the two facilities they obviously deemed most important—oilfields and the airport. Kirkuk and surrounding areas were literally swimming in crude, and when driving south out of the city a few days later, we saw giant rusting refineries and storage facilities as well as acre upon acre of dry, dusty ground covered in a thin layer of oil that had risen to the surface. When I stumbled across Americans at the airport, a jumpy unit commander ordered us to stop, and a heavy machine gun mounted on a Humvee vehicle was pointed straight at our chests. The euphemistic Pentagon phrases "collateral damage" and "friendly fire" came briefly to mind, but the soldiers quickly realized I was a reporter who had got lost and impatiently waved me on. Only a few hundred yards away, the looting was becoming more chaotic. People were siphoning fuel from tankers and taking guns and ammunition from abandoned barracks by the airstrip; *peshmerga* fighters, again, were among them.

Even worse for the people of Kirkuk, hospitals were struggling to cope with the casualties from looting and fighting overnight, partly because Arab doctors had fled their workplace, fearing vigilante attacks once the Kurds arrived. We visited one ward where a young boy and his elder sister had just been told by doctors that their brother, whose body lay covered in a dirty blanket on a stretcher, had died. I wanted to be sick, not because of the blood or wounds but from the intensity of the disbelief, despair and anger on these people's faces. "We get rid of Saddam, and now this," the sister shouted, pulling at her hair, unable to comprehend that tragedy had struck when the battle for Kirkuk was supposedly over. Her younger brother, suffering from shock, looked on alternately whimpering and screaming. Doctors said the man had died of shrapnel wounds, probably from a mortar, but it was not clear who had fired it in the chaos that had gripped parts of the city. Close by, bloodied Kurdish fighters waited for treatment on chairs and tables in the packed waiting area.

The looting had clearly worsened since the previous evening, and more Baath Party buildings were ablaze. Whole families swarmed over rubble and down into giant craters left by the heavy U.S. bombardment. They took office furniture and fittings, rolled away barrels of gasoline and stripped abandoned cars for their parts. Taemin hospital had treated 50 to 60 Kurdish fighters in the last day or so, all of them hurt during clashes sparked by vandalism and looting. I saw two roughly made coffins being taken from Kirkuk on the back of a pickup truck, and more fatalities certainly went unreported.

To the northwest, about 120 miles, Mosul was falling, again with hardly a fight, and the war along the northern front was effectively won. As in Kirkuk, it was Kurdish fighters who moved first to the city center, and as in Kirkuk, the initial mood was one of celebration as crowds chanted anti-Saddam slogans and tore up thousands of banknotes bearing the ousted leader's portrait that had been looted from an abandoned branch of the Bank of Iraq. The lawlessness quickly spread, descending into a frenzy of arson and plunder made all the more dangerous by the city's deep ethnic divisions. The Reuters team covering the events fled from the city after a man clutching a hand grenade approached them and screamed at them to leave.

Anarchy in Mosul was to last several days and forced our reporters there to withdraw again. Kirkuk was quicker to stabilize with the arrival of more U.S. troops and tanks, but there too the tensions simmered. About a week later I returned to find dozens of Arab families outside the main administrative office, demanding Americans stop Kurdish threats and violence against them. Mithad Abdul Rahman Mohammad Amin, a 37-year-old taxi driver, took me to his home to tell his story. He and 10 other anxious family members gathered round and explained how Kurdish men in *peshmerga* fatigues had come to the house with Kalashnikov rifles and issued an ultimatum—leave or die. Amin begged me to intervene, thinking that a Western reporter surely had the power to influence such cases. But in the end all I could do was escort Amin through the U.S. security cordon blocking the entrance to the Kirkuk administration and point him to the relevant security official whom I had interviewed a few hours before. The standoff between Arabs and Kurds was to turn bloody—10 people were killed in similar disputes over resettlements in the city a few weeks later.

Destination Tikrit

The world's attention quickly turned to Tikrit, now the last major population center in Iraq still held by Saddam's forces. We knew that we could get there as fast as anyone by heading southwest from Kirkuk. But Joseph Logan, who got as far as Hawaija some 40 miles away, had run into angry Arab tribesmen who had fought gun battles with Kurdish fighters passing through their territory toward Tikrit. Clearly shaken by events in Kirkuk and Mosul, and having been robbed by Kurds in recent days, the turbaned gunmen were determined to defend themselves. At least eight people had been killed in the clashes.

On Sunday, April 13, U.S. forces backed by F-18 fighters and Cobra attack helicopters closed in on Tikrit, engaging Fedayeen fighters and Republican Guards on the outskirts of the town. Our mission for the following morning was clear. Try the road to Tikrit once again.

The drive to Tikrit via Hawaija was not one I would repeat in a hurry. Again we encountered a series of checkpoints set up by armed Arabs. These villagers were clearly nervous, especially when they saw our cars were being driven by Kurds. One group helpfully suggested we used whatever tape we had to stick the letters "T" and "V" all over the vehicles to avoid a nasty accident. This we did, using silver tape given to us as part of our chemical weapons kits at the beginning of the war. At first, that appeared to ease our passage southwest, but halfway between Kirkuk and Tikrit we were approaching another heavily manned checkpoint when an excitable Arab, his eyes hidden behind dark sunglasses, raised his rifle to the car windshield and signaled with his other hand for us to stop. The only Arabic speaker in our convoy had already passed safely through the barrier, and the third car behind us had wisely gone into reverse. There were too many men and too many weapons, including heavy machine guns, to contemplate making a dash for it, and I felt we had to do something quickly to defuse the hostility. I got out of the car wearing a flak jacket marked clearly with "PRESS," raised my hands in the air, walked straight toward the group of men and tried to communicate. After a brief, tense exchange of hand signals and smiles on my part, and shouting and waving on theirs, the guns were lowered and the danger had passed. The passage to Tikrit was clear, and soon we would be ushered into the town by jubilant American forces aware that victory was theirs.

My last week in Iraq I spent in Arbil covering Mosul after the teams there had left for home. Our assignment in the north was nearly over, and it was time to mop up a few stories we still wanted to do before a new team arrived to relieve us. It was also time to part with our drivers, translators and housekeepers, a sad moment after forging such close friendships in a matter of a few weeks. In the evenings I would sit on the roof with Nikola and Al Burke, our security adviser, and watch the setting sun throw a pink glow across the sky above the ancient citadel and towering minarets. We could talk and think of little else but home, fantasizing about the food we would eat, what wines we would drink and where we would go and spend our leave.

We made three trips to Mosul in all. On one we saw U.S. fighter planes swooping to within a few hundred feet of the ground with a deafening roar. "So this is Bush's freedom?" an Arab resident shouted at me as he looked on.

Daren Butler and Shamil Zhumatov, an old friend from Central Asia, finally arrived to replace us. Within two hours Nikola and I were on the road to Baghdad. The following day we crossed the border into Jordan, and by evening we were in the Jordanian capital of Amman, exhausted but halfway home.

Chapter 12

PILGRIMS' PROGRESS

By Christine Hauser

In times of war, battles are waged and won. Civilians bury their dead. And cities fall to victorious foreign invaders. But in the war that toppled Saddam Hussein, Iraqi Shi'ites broke these rules.

The victorious foreign army fought the battles, but in at least one Iraqi city—Kerbala—the people took over, organizing a tumultuous religious pilgrimage while U.S. forces kept to the outskirts.

In Najaf, Iraqi Shi'ites went to cemeteries, but it was not just to bury war casualties. They also dug up their dead, finally free to search mass graves for thousands executed by Saddam.

And they left their homes. But for many it was a fearless flight to sacred shrines in their first free pilgrimage for more than a quarter of a century. Some marched all the way from the city of Basra in a 10-day journey for which they could have been killed had the Iraqi president's forces still been in control. "We are all soldiers of Islam," read one banner carried by Shi'ites after U.S. forces took Baghdad.

If that is so, then one of the spoils of war for the soldiers of Islam was the freedom to perform their rituals openly in the pilgrimage called Arbaiin.

Hundreds of thousands of Shi'ites from all over Iraq surged along country roads by foot, bus, bicycle or car to Kerbala to mark one of the holiest events in their calendar. The pilgrimage to the shrines and tombs of Shi'ism's earliest leaders commemorates the end of the traditional 40-day mourning period after the death in 680 AD of Imam Hussein, grandson of the Prophet Muhammad.

Hussein is a symbol of martyrdom for pious Shi'ites, and his cause has been exploited in the past for political purposes in Iraq, the reason Saddam repressed the pilgrimage. The last time the Shi'ites marked the event in public was in 1977, when troops attacked pilgrims with tanks and machine guns. But in April 2003, it would be different for the Shi'ite pilgrims.

Just days before the pilgrimage started, Reuters photographer Yannis Behrakis, cameraman Sasa Kavic and I packed up our camp in an abandoned port in southern Iraq and loaded our armored car for the journey north to follow the pilgrims. Petrol and water were loaded on top. Cameras, laptops, camping stoves, sleeping bags, tents and medical kits were piled into the cramped interior. We stuffed tinned food and water bottles into any space that was left.

There was hardly room for Sasa in the back. I was in the front with Yannis at the wheel, wrestling the top-heavy, overloaded vehicle around. The journey was laborious, following U.S. military supply convoys on the main road north.

After hundreds of miles we passed through the town of al-Samawa. That is where we started to see the first pilgrims, carrying flags or marching in small groups. With hundreds more miles left to Kerbala, they had a long way to go.

South of al-Diwaniya, the numbers swelled into the thousands. We began to see posters of Shi'ite leaders on the sides of houses. We turned left toward Najaf, the road shrinking into a narrow lane that wound through villages and farmland.

It was here that we came upon a group of pilgrims—Ruda Diwan and his four companions. They had hitched their long robes through their belts so they could walk more easily, and they carried bits of bread in plastic bags.

For years, Diwan and his friends were secret pilgrims, sneaking through the palm trees. But not this time.

"We used to keep to the fields, staying far away from the roads to avoid being seen by security forces," he said.

Barefoot or wearing sandals, they had walked for five hours, with 100 miles to go before they reached Kerbala. Around them, other pilgrims strode along, forcing cars out of their path. They beat their chests and waved flags. Black was the color of mourning, green for Islam.

Youths rode bicycles with flags fluttering from handlebars.

Day after day, the pilgrims streamed along the roads to Kerbala. Some carried exhausted children on their shoulders or balanced parcels on their heads.

"The villages are emptying out!" said Jamil Halil, who lived in a small mud house along the pilgrimage route.

One group waved a bloody white flag to symbolize solidarity with Imam Hussein's martyrdom. "This flag has been dipped in the blood of men who have wounded themselves for Hussein," said Riad Diwan, toiling along the road in hot sun.

We drove slowly through the crowds. The pilgrims raised their hands in pride or flashed V-for-victory gestures, shouting as the car inched past.

Sasa and Yannis dragged their cameras out of the bags and stood up on the seats in the back, shooting through the rooftop trapdoor. I took the wheel, struggling to steer the heavy car around the potholes.

"Saddam is a dog!" yelled one man.

"We could never have done this in Saddam's time," said another.

Chanting adoration for Imam Hussein, each held an arm high in the air then slapped his hand across his chest.

Another group carried white flags, which they said symbolized surrender to show the American soldiers occupying their country that they marched in peace.

U.S. Army vehicles moved slowly through the throng, which parted defensively to let them pass.

The contradictions of celebrating their new freedom while being suspicious of the forces that brought it about were not lost on many of the pilgrims.

Jihan al-Abaydi was wrapped head to foot in a black *abbaya*, the enveloping robes and veils worn by many Shi'ite women. She stopped at the side of the road to drink, surrounded by other women.

We pulled the car over. I asked if I could speak to her, and she agreed, but with one condition.

"Only if I can talk to you like this," she said, screening her face with a black, mesh-like cloth. She answered my questions in perfect English.

"We are a civilized, educated people. Do the Americans really think we can't govern ourselves?" she asked, raising her finger and voice. "I thank them for getting rid of Saddam Hussein. Now they should get out."

A crowd gathered, attracted by the spectacle of foreign reporters.

"We don't want to see even one American soldier on our soil," Abaydi continued. "If the Americans do not leave, we will kick them out by force."

Food and Water

Islamic charities dispensed food and water from tents along the road. Pilgrims reclined in the shade on carpets and pillows, scooped water out of brimming oil drums or ate meats roasting on grills. Men laid down carpets on the ground and prayed, their prostrate forms partially obscured by a choking sandstorm.

We camped at night outside Najaf, changing our clothes in the car and throwing down sleeping bags in the sand. The air was cool, the black sky sparkled with stars. In the morning we washed with bottled water, boiled coffee on a camping stove and then set off.

We made slow progress, pulling into Kerbala for the pilgrimage. Our armored car, plastered with taped letters that read TV, attracted a lot of attention.

Iraqis had set up informal checkpoints with metal barriers, blocking our entrance deep into the city. Thousands of people, many of them dirty and tired from the road, milled around us.

"Stop, stop, you have to come with me!" A man in civilian clothes waved our car to a halt. It was quickly surrounded by dozens of men. They peered into the windows, staring at our equipment and at us. "You have to come inside with me and get permission," the man said.

Our car's bulletproof windows do not open, so I had to open the door to hear him. As an Arabic speaker, I was the one he dealt with. I climbed down from the car and followed him to a one-story, whitewashed house. The man had identified himself only as an "authority" in the city, but since his men were blocking our car, I had no choice but to follow him, trying to keep up the small talk until I could figure out what he wanted. Armed guards wore home-made badges that read "Guardians of Kerbala." I decided to wait outside. When the man returned, he had written our names and his own in Arabic on a slip of paper.

"If you have any trouble, just tell people my name and show them this paper," he said. He asked us our nationalities. As an American, the question made me cringe. I told him Yannis was Greek and Sasa Croatian, and then I quickly got into the car and we drove on.

The pilgrims had taken over the city. The streets were unsuitable for vehicles, so packed were they with exhausted, dirty straggling men, women and children who had walked for days and now rested on mats on the sidewalk.

As a pilgrimage city, Kerbala had no shortage of places to stay. We pulled up to the Anwar al-Huda hotel. I was dressed in a long-sleeved blouse and baggy trousers with a white scarf over my hair, but it was still not modest enough in this conservative Muslim city.

"Miss! Cover up your neck!" an old man shouted from a street corner.

We claimed a few rooms on the upper floors. My first action was to send one of the young workers at the hotel off to buy a black *abbaya* robe and headscarf. While it took some practice learning how to tie it on so wisps of hair did not escape, it was worth it.

When I went out alone, people occasionally cheered me or gave me the thumbs up sign and said "Good, good!"

One day, covered in black, I joined a group of Iraqis who climbed to the rooftop of our hotel for a view of the pilgrimage. In front of us was the Imam Abbas shrine, the sun reflecting off its golden minarets and elaborate arches clad in blue and green mosaics.

From the other side of the roof, the minarets and dome of the Imam Hussein shrine soared over the rooftops of Kerbala, enticing the eye upward to the heavens.

Into this gleaming skyline the men on the roof unfurled a banner calling the pilgrimage "A Scream in the Face of the Oppressors."

The slogan could have been directed at the oppressors of the past as well as at any future attempts to keep them down.

Alaa al-Sarraf, a resident from Kerbala, and I watched the streets below. Dozens of men in black tunics chanted and walked in unison, lashing their backs with chains, first across one shoulder and then the other, leaving a black residue and raising sweat on their brows from the exertion.

"Do you see all this? For years we could not express ourselves so openly and in such masses. We used to be executed or thrown in jail forever for doing this when Saddam Hussein was in power," said Sarraf.

The pilgrimage was an early indication of how the Shi'ites could govern themselves, as they took over a city once threatened by Iraqi security forces and which now had American occupation forces on the outskirts.

Flyers issued by clerical seminaries were taped to electricity poles and shrine walls, calling on the faithful to respect law and order, dress properly when entering shrines and refrain from looting or trading and bearing weapons.

They also told pilgrims not to allow anyone to exploit the event and to disregard wild rumors. Once, a loudspeaker mounted on an ambulance toured the streets, trying to dispel fears that food had been poisoned by saboteurs.

The pilgrims poured in from the countryside, camping out on the streets and dozing on rugs around the shrines. People maneuvered around the faithful, sitting cross-legged on mats and reading the Koran.

Boys ran through the crowds, spraying rosewater on exhausted pilgrims. The oily smoke from meat kebabs and tomatoes on skewers roasting on sidewalk barbeques wafted over the sleeping or worshipping forms.

I was offered sweet tea by street vendors balancing silvery trays loaded with clinking glasses. Threads of smoke rose from the glowing tips of incense sticks, and fruit sellers broke mounds of sticky dates into bite-sized chunks.

On the sweltering streets, volunteers gave ice water to marchers parched from hours of chanting as they walked around the two shrines. Other volunteers swept up garbage, and doctors circulated in ambulances, handing out medicines.

In a city with no official security, there was still crowd control.

At dusk, Iraqi men with laminated badges designating themselves as Guardians of Kerbala milled about, watching the crowd. Several carried machine guns.

Haidar Mohammad, a cleric, had just emerged from prayers at the Imam Abbas shrine. He spoke to me about the political implications of the pilgrimage.

"All of this careful organization shows that the Iraqi people can take care of themselves and must get rid of the American and British forces on our land," he said. "We have experimented with a variety of governments in our history, and what we now need are fair elections. I am sure they will endorse an Islamic one, which will respect Iraq's diversity of Kurds, Jews, Christians and Sunni Muslims,"

His words were nearly drowned out by marchers. "No, no, America! No, no, Israel!" they chanted. "Yes to Islam!"

Politics overlapped seamlessly with religion.

Volunteers formed human chains to keep an orderly flow of pilgrims into the shrines, dividing the traffic into queues for men and women. As they entered the Imam Hussein shrine to pray, women kissed its marble walls and great, wooden doors. As they left, men bowed deeply.

In the weak light of early morning, a chorus of chanting roused the residents of Kerbala. Men and women came to their windows, some still in their nightclothes.

In a ritual of solidarity with the blood shed in Imam Hussein's killing, groups of men were nicking their foreheads with blades. They were surging through the streets, slapping the shallow incision to keep the blood from clotting so that it flowed down their sweaty faces. Their eyes were vacant. Some collapsed and were helped to their feet or were supported by friends who wiped the blood from their eyes and fed them sweets.

Ali Mohammad carried his 9-month-old baby, Hussein, in his arms. The baby's head was smeared with blood.

"This is a blessing," said Mohammad, holding his child toward me proudly.

Women were overcome with emotion at the sight. Some wept as they watched.

Although dramatic, the bloodletting and self-flagellation were not the most common medical complaints during the pilgrimage. When they called at the makeshift clinic set up in a school in Kerbala, most people sought treatment for sore feet.

Limping pilgrims passed under an archway decorated with the words "We will not kneel to anyone but God."

Dr. Hussein Naama showed me to a seat next to his desk. "Some of them walk a long way, on their feet for 10 days or more," he said.

He said the blood and chains rituals were technically prohibited by clerics because they harm the body. "But they let them do it without stopping them by force."

Thair Naim, a young man who had spent three days on the road, wore a green bandanna tied commando-style around his head with picture postcards of leading Shi'ite clerics tucked into it. He propped his aching foot up and explained why the old regime had oppressed his people. "Saddam Hussein used to fear the influence of the clerics. He was afraid of a revolution."

In 1991, Shi'ites in Iraq, emboldened by the U.S. war that ended Iraq's occupation of Kuwait, launched an uprising against Saddam that was brutally crushed. Thousands were rounded up and killed or taken away, never to be seen again.

Outside of the clinic, a roster of loss was posted on the walls. Page after page listed names of people missing. A crowd gathered around the lists. There were 414 typed names of Shi'ites from Kerbala whose whereabouts were unknown. Other names were penciled in by hand.

"The people in Kerbala are still living in hope that they will find their loved ones," said Hussein Kazim, standing in the group scanning the names.

Abdullah Hadi, a 55-year-old man, listened as his compatriots told me about family members dead or missing. The onslaught of detail was like a tidal wave, impossible to hold back and seemingly endless.

Hadi's silence suggested he had his own story to tell but little heart to introduce it. Finally some in the crowd uneasily looked his way. He lifted his trouser cuffs to show two raised scars across his heels. "I was tortured for praying like a Shi'ite," he said, finally speaking with the authority that direct knowledge brings. "The regime used electricity torture on my fingertips."

Mass Graves

The same road that took us with jubilant pilgrims from Najaf to Kerbala later led me to join distraught Iraqis on their way to mass graves. I went with Shi'ite officials from the opposition Supreme Council of the Islamic Revolution in Iraq (SCIRI) about nine miles north of Najaf to where a dusty, unmarked road branches off the pilgrim's highway. We wound west across barren terrain to an area known as Khan al-Rubae, cultivated by Iraqi farmers who live in mud brick homes.

They told us they had seen Iraqi security forces drive up in cars with men who were blindfolded, their hands tied behind their backs. The men were shot in the back of the head. The bodies tumbled into ditches.

After the fall of Saddam, Iraqis were finally able to speak about the horrors they had seen. And that was how the gravediggers of Najaf uncovered the remains of human beings in the tilled soil where the land confessed its history.

"This is one, this is one, this is one," said a man helping with the digging.

He was standing in a ditch, pointing out bones still embedded in layers of sand. The way they were piled up, he suggested, indicated that corpses had fallen on top each other.

Working carefully, the diggers used small garden tools or their bare hands. They did not hesitate to touch the remains, prizing up any bones stubbornly clinging to the grave.

A bone jutted out. The soil was carefully brushed from around it to uncover the rest of a skeleton held together by rotting clothes.

The bones looked alike—brownish or bleached, slender, disjointed from their skeletons. But then it became apparent that although the land had hidden the bodies of men, it would still reveal their identities.

The gravediggers uncovered a pocket comb. One man had apparently carried it to his execution. Another still wore his wristwatch. There were coins and plastic-coated identity cards in trouser pockets.

And then we saw the calling cards of the executioners: spent bullet casings among the bones. Yellow twine coated with a coppery crust, which the gravediggers thought was blood, had been wound around wrists.

The workers tore up white sheets to wrap the remains, trying to rebuild skeletons from pieces of bone. One worker, Alwan Khudayr, dipped his hands into the dirt and then patted down the remains to cover them with earth. I asked him what he was doing.

"Muslims respect their dead, and whatever is salvaged must be given a decent burial," he said.

Anxious relatives who said family members were missing since 1991 stood watching. More than three dozen sets of remains would be displayed there that day.

Human rights groups say more than 250,000 people were murdered or taken away by Saddam Hussein's forces. Mass graves were unearthed in most other areas of Iraq—from Basra to Babylon to Baghdad.

Iraqis told my Reuters colleague Akram Salih about another site south of Baghdad not far from the town of Hilla, where local officials said about 3,000 sets of remains were uncovered at a farming area known as Mahawil. After turning off the main highway, we drove along a bumpy dirt road, deep into the countryside. The area appeared sparsely inhabited, but the fields were lush with crops. As I looked out the window, it occurred to me that the men and women whose remains were being uncovered at the end of this road might have watched the same landscape as they went to their executions.

It was very quiet in the car. None of us spoke.

Soon I could see groups of people in the distance. We approached on foot. Barbed wire ringed a digging site, where a man was operating an earthmover.

The farmland at Mahawil had been transformed into a field of death. Hundreds of piles of remains had been exhumed, stuffed into bags and placed in rows that stretched as far as the eye could see.

Workers tried to re-create human forms, filling the bags with bones and skulls and whatever identity cards were found next to them.

Distraught relatives wiped dirt from the cards and tried to decipher names in print faded from years in the grave. A familiar piece of rotting clothing could mean an end to years of uncertainty.

For a long time, I watched what was going on. I wanted to stay out of the way. But I knew I had to talk to someone. I told myself it was important to put a human face on the story, though I dreaded intruding.

I saw a man staring for a long time at the bag at his feet. Finally, he tied the ends of the bag, which was full of bones and dirty pieces of unidentifiable matter. Then he carried it off. I followed him, but he waved me away.

I left him alone but stood where he could see me so he would become accustomed to my presence. He sat on a small mound of dirt, watching the condensation form on the inside of the bag.

When he lit a cigarette, it seemed like a good moment to speak to him again. He said his name was Ali Mekki.

"I think this is my brother," said Mekki, picking up the bag. "This is my sweatshirt, which my brother Jaafar used to borrow from me all the time," he said, pulling out a maroon-colored garment.

Mekki last saw Jaafar in 1991. He was unable to read the faded identity card found in the grave, but he said he hoped to match the number with other records. He wanted to give Jaafar a proper burial.

Gathered at the Shrine

After Saddam fell, Shi'ite religious leaders returned from exile and competed with each other for influence, sometimes violently. In April 2003, the cleric Abdul Majid al Khoei was hacked to death outside the Iman Ali shrine in Najaf, the center of Shi'ite religious learning in Iraq.

Not long after Khoei's death, I went to the shrine, where hundreds of Shi'ites gathered to pray and sit in the shade of its courtyard. I was quickly surrounded by a crowd. One man, trembling with anger, berated me for not wearing an abbaya, even though I was dressed in long, loose clothing with a headscarf.

I explained that while I was not a Muslim, I respected the culture and had dressed conservatively. I turned to a woman and asked her where to buy an abbaya. Instead, someone ran to fetch one. I draped it over my head and it cascaded shapelessly around me. Now the interviews could start.

Their anger flowed at me all at once. They hated Saddam Hussein but they had no love for President Bush either.

A man said, "Where is the water and electricity and food that we need? Our city has been bombarded in a war by the Americans." People pulled at my clothes, impatient to speak.

Najaf's residents complained of looting and anarchy. There was a sense that the same old faces were back on the streets. Some of the men who were employed as police during Saddam Hussein's time returned to work with fresh laminated identity cards and the U.S. stamp of approval.

My hotel was next to Najaf's largest open-air souq, which was known as the Ali Baba market—a reference to the famous thief.

The area lived up to its reputation. Once, gunmen, angered at the arrest of a suspect in Khoei's killing, opened fire on the volunteer police station in front of my hotel. The lone guard inside ran across the street, taking cover in the hotel lobby. The gunmen escaped into a cemetery.

During the day, the market was back to work. Iraqi merchants barked out the prices of goods as hundreds of buyers wandered through a maze of shacks where everything from Arabic robes to aluminum pots to looted, blank Iraqi passports were for sale.

But suddenly the chaos of commerce was drowned out by machine gun fire. Women in black veils dropped the plastic buckets they were examining. Men picked up the edges of their robes so they could join the panicked stampede out of the market.

Like all other Iraqi cities as they emerged from the war, Najaf was struggling to survive the shaky peace.

Many of its people would not do so unscathed, like the children I saw with amputated limbs in the city's Saddam Hospital a month after the battle at Najaf.

I wanted to check hospital records of civilians who were killed during the fighting. Driving up to the hospital, I noticed the letters "Saddam" had been torn off the side of the building. In front of the hospital a mural of Saddam Hussein's face was vandalized and replaced by a poster of a Shi'ite cleric.

But in a sign that the legacy of the war would not be as easy to erase as Saddam's portraits, hundreds of civilian casualties were listed in hospital records, either killed in the war or by cluster bombs that still littered their neighborhoods.

Najaf was the scene of U.S. ground and air strikes to root out Iraqi paramilitaries and soldiers loyal to Saddam Hussein. The debris of war still lay near homes in the Hay Karama district, an indication of how fighting was conducted in residential areas. Multiple Launch Rocket System casings littered the road. Boys climbed onto anti-aircraft guns and mobile artillery, which stood crippled in their hiding places among the trees, a futile camouflage judging by the bombed and scorched wreckage.

Residents told how Iraqi fighters had fired with heavy weapons from around their homes and then fled. They described nights of terror during the U.S. strikes that followed, hearing their neighbors screaming and crying. Ambulance sirens shattered the darkness. Emergency units were set up in Najaf hospitals.

"We arrived during the night and found many victims lying on the ground or in their houses with severe injuries, fractures and amputated limbs," said ambulance man Ahmed Mazhar.

Dr. Safa al-Amaidi, director of the Najaf Teaching Hospital, said they recorded 256 civilians killed and 393 wounded in the fighting in Najaf, mostly in Hay Karama, and from subsequent cluster bomb explosions, from March 21 through April 17.

Najaf General Hospital records say seven were killed, six of them civilians, and 112 civilians wounded during fighting there.

Many more were buried in outlying areas by villagers unable to bring the bodies into the city because of the fighting.

"After the cessation of hostilities, most of the casualties were from cluster bombs. Families said people picked them up and played with them," Amaidi said.

I went with some professors from Najaf to the Kufa University, where they were meant to start holding classes again. What we found were looted classrooms with chairs and desks broken or covered with dust and rubble. Windows were shattered. The few students who showed up had joyful reunions with friends in the stairwells, but the institution was in no shape for lectures.

Faculty members said they looted their own books and hid them at home to save them from what was sure to be an orgy of postwar plunder.

It was a wise precaution, as they found out when they returned to survey the damage, although the looters apparently had no taste for Shakespeare's *Twelfth Night* or Samuel Beckett's *Waiting for Godot*, both left untouched in the English department.

Model sentences from last term's English exam were still on the blackboard: "His son's loss grieved him" was one.

Amar Ahmed, a student of English, wandered with his friends through the trashed classrooms. He told me that all he wanted out of life now was to find a way to practice English pronunciation. "I feel like we will grow old waiting for peace," said Ahmed, a thoughtful 23-year-old. "We may not have much, but we have brains."

Iron Doors Ajar

After it became clear that Saddam's rule had ended, Basra became a city where the iron doors of the jail stood ajar, and the men who were once imprisoned walked freely through them.

The upper parts of the Baath party's security intelligence headquarters had been flattened in an air strike and had collapsed onto the lower floors. Holes larger than a man were punched through the masonry.

I stumbled over the rubble, catching wisps of conversation from the hundreds of Iraqis who swarmed through the yard of the once feared security building, where some said they had been tortured or imprisoned. The building was now theirs. They scavenged through destroyed offices. They took over the upper floor, peering from scorched windows.

Iraqis had come to the site after they heard rumors there were prisoners still trapped in underground chambers. Women wept as men dug with shovels.

When people discovered I could speak Arabic, they expressed their anger.

"Where is the help from British and American forces?" an Iraqi man shouted at me. I quickly singled out an elderly man named Ahmed and asked him to show me around.

"Ask them to bring in some heavy equipment," someone else shouted. I went to a British armored fighting vehicle parked in front of the building.

"They asked me to tell you they need digging equipment," I said to the soldier.

But dozens of people had surrounded us. The soldier grew nervous and radioed to say he was evacuating. "It's getting really busy here," he shouted into his headpiece.

Ahmed and I walked away. We went to watch men hammering away at concrete or hard earth. They lowered small earpieces or microphones into holes they had dug.

"Did you hear any more voices?" said one man anxiously. "No. We haven't found anyone either," said another worker, drenched in sweat.

Standing against a wall watching were three old women, their foreheads dotted with black and blue tribal tattoos. They were sobbing.

"I haven't seen my son since 1991," said one woman, Badria Jassim. "The government of Saddam Hussein took him from my house to this very place where we are standing."

"And I have not seen my son Riad Hamed since then either!" said her companion, Fawzia Radi, her face flushed with emotion.

The people of Basra say many of their kin went missing in the 1991 rebellion and afterward.

Hussein Hamad Hussein was one of them. He showed me the one-story jail behind the security building. "They arrested me last year and interrogated me about my relationship with Muslim clerics," said Hussein, a 47-year-old Shi'ite. "They arrested men for having beards or for saying special Shi'ite prayers."

Hussein knew his way around the garbage-strewn jail and was only too eager to offer a tour. It was not an uncomfortable place when the doors were open. He could now come and go at will, and he took me with him.

Just inside the door, a metal bar ran along the floor the length of the corridor.

"They used to chain us to the floor like this," Hussein said. He squatted down, his back against the wall with his hands crossed behind him, to show how guards cuffed prisoners to the bar. "We would stay like this all day if they wanted."

Now there was graffiti along the wall of the corridor where Hussein said his hands had been chained: "Saddam the criminal has fallen."

Prisoners long gone had marked the walls, scrawling time served with chalk. One fearless soul had carved a prayer into the wall. The lettering was worn smooth, either by time or by men who had run their fingers along the cursive Arabic etching.

Outside, I joined people scavenging through the garbage. I picked up a water-stained 1992 letter to the local intelligence chief and wondered what had happened to a man named Abdullah Mohammad. His name was on the document I held. It was a formal request for an investigation into his behavior.

"Please investigate Abdullah Mohammad, a resident of Basra, for his stance with regard to incidents of treachery" the letter said.

"Victory to Great Iraq," was written across the top.

An Exile Returns

It was not the Iraqi regime, but the Shi'ites of Basra, who were triumphant on May 10, 2003. That was when one of Saddam Hussein's enemies came back from decades in exile to a hero's welcome.

I set out early from Basra, driving 12 miles to the frontier to see Ayatollah Mohammed Baqer al-Hakim, 63, an influential Shi'ite cleric, return from Iran.

Hakim was jailed and tortured in the 1970s for opposing Saddam, and members of his family were killed. He fled to Iran where he led the Iraqi opposition group SCIRI since 1980.

Thousands of Iraqis drove through remote and barren countryside east of Basra to greet Hakim. Old armored combat vehicles from the Iran-Iraq war of the 1980s were rusting in the fields.

Iraqis came with flowers, banners and posters of the man they called their leader. Iranian border guards with Kalashnikov rifles moved to the Iraqi side to hold back the crowds. The road flowed with sticky red blood from sheep slaughtered in his honor.

Men wept openly as they waited.

"It is the right of any of us to return after the fall of Saddam Hussein," said Mohammad Lamrayani, a 36-year-old Shi'ite man watching in the crowd, calling out Hakim's name.

Finally, Hakim's convoy appeared in the distance. The crowd roared and surged forward, held back by increasingly angry Iranian guards. I jumped on the roof of a parked car to avoid being crushed and to get a better view.

If Hakim had looked up, he would have seen a mosaic of Saddam Hussein on the arches marking the Iraqi side of the border crossing. But the portrait was now featureless and vandalized, the colored tiles torn from the face.

The convoy pressed through. Men beat their chests, threw flowers and tried to pile onto Hakim's vehicle, but were pushed off by bodyguards. Everyone then made a mad dash for buses and cars to follow the cleric to Basra.

Vehicles stuffed with people bounced along the narrow lane, horns blaring, some speeding along the shoulder of the road and sending up tornados of dust.

Inside Basra, Iraqis lined the streets or ran alongside the car, trying to press their faces to its window or holding up babies for Hakim to see. The cleric lowered his window a crack and waved.

We stopped our car to wait to cross a narrow pontoon bridge over the river. "This is a great day for Shi'ites. Today Hakim has returned," Majida Sajjad, watching from the sidewalk, told me. "For years I have been afraid to look behind me."

Hakim's convoy moved slowly through Basra, followed by hundreds of cars, past the defaced portraits of the Iraqi leader who had once oppressed him. His destination was the city's stadium, where he would address his people.

I fought my way into the stadium along with other journalists, and we climbed the stairs into the grandstand. We watched Hakim's convoy inch its way through an ocean of thousands of men, so tightly packed that they surged and swayed in one mass.

The roof of Hakim's car was dented as his supporters tried to climb onto it.

Hakim's bodyguards fought through the crowd. "Yes, yes to Islam!" the crowd yelled. "This is our leader, Hakim. Death to the Baathists!"

Men tried to scale the sides of the grandstand to be closer to Hakim, but were pushed off by guards and fell back into the crowd. Hakim climbed higher and took the podium. At that moment I turned around, wanting to see the expressions of the audience. Men were crying; elderly tribal leaders had raised their hands to the sky.

"We have gone such a long way and through such hard times. Now we are on a road to safety and stability," Hakim shouted into the microphone, struggling to be heard above the din.

"Hakim! We are your soldiers of liberation!" the crowd chanted.

Hakim spoke with his chin jutting defiantly, pointing his finger into the air. "I was with you through every minute of your fighting and your struggle. And I swear to God—I will be with you every minute from here on."

Hakim was killed in Najaf on Aug. 29, 2003, in postwar Iraq's deadliest car bomb attack, which claimed the lives of more than 80 people.

Loneliness of Death

Abed Hamoodi told me what happened to him and his family at about 2:45 a.m. on April 5. It is a moment he will never forget.

Hamoodi is a 74-year-old oil executive who lives in the Tuwaisa suburb of Basra, where the streets are quiet and the houses have spare rooms and walled gardens. His neighbor was "Chemical Ali," or Ali Hassan al-Majid, who had ordered a chemical bomb attack against 5,000 Kurds in the Iraqi village of Halabja in 1988, when Iraq was an ally of the United States.

Now British and American forces wanted Chemical Ali dead, and the air raid that targeted him in his Basra home on April 5, 2003, killed 10 members of Hamoodi's family as well as other neighbors.

On May 11, I met Hamoodi quite by accident. In search of something to write about, I told my driver Saeed to "just drive around Basra." He took me through the city. Shops were open, schoolchildren with book bags crossed the street, life appeared normal.

I saw something out of the corner of my eye. It was a man on his knees, sobbing at a dirt mound in an empty lot. Nearby, a worker was whitewashing other mounds. It was a temporary graveyard. "Stop the car," I said.

I approached Hamoodi's daughter, who was standing to one side as she watched her father crying over the grave of his wife, killed along with nine other members of the family in the air raid.

They took me to their home. Hamoodi told how 70-year-old Khairiya and relatives, including a 5-month-old granddaughter, died when the roof fell in during the air strike.

The family had all moved into the house because it was far from the front line on the outskirts of the city. Most of them had slept in a small back room. "We thought that room was safest because it had no windows," Hamoodi said, his hands clenched into fists.

Hamoodi asked questions no one in the room could answer. Like this one: If they were so sure Chemical Ali was in the house, then why didn't they send someone to arrest him instead? His face flickered between rage and tears.

It was not until Aug. 21 that the U.S. military confirmed that Chemical Ali had finally been arrested. But Hamoodi knew the fate of his wife and the children, because he remembered how they looked when he tried to dig them from the rubble with his hands. He could hear voices calling "father, father." He tried to resuscitate his 18-year-old granddaughter, Zeinab, but she died.

Khairiya died with the Koran open on her chest. She had apparently been reading it after the bombing started at about 2:45 a.m.

Hamoodi's son, Sudad, went to fetch the Koran. Its cover is scratched, dusty and damaged, but they kept a ribbon in the place where Khairiya had been reading. One verse says not to fear death, for believers are taken care of in the afterlife.

One of the sons had made a home video of the family just hours before the air strike. It shows some of them watching White House spokesman Ari Fleischer on television. The grandchildren are laughing and clowning. Hamoodi's son Wissam, who was killed, smiled at the camera before throwing the dice in a game of backgammon.

Then the video showed them settling into bedding in the small room to sleep. The clock on the wall showed 2:20 a.m.

"I have been waiting 22 years for Saddam to fall," said Hamoodi. "At first, we were so delighted that the coalition troops had come to protect us from the regime."

The family was buried temporarily in the lot in Basra because the roads were not safe to travel hundreds of miles to the main Shi'ite cemetery in Najaf. Hamoodi said they plan to exhume the bodies and take them to permanent graves in the holy city. Then the remaining family members might leave Iraq.

"Everything has changed now," said Sudad, who lives in England. "No one wants to stay."

Chapter 13

SOUTHERN DISCOMFORT

By Michael Georgy

Riding in an armored vehicle wearing a flak jacket as explosions rocked the southern countryside, I expected Iraqis to be running for cover. But staring out of the thick, bulletproof windows, I noticed a strange scene that would define the Iraqi psyche for me in the early days of the war.

British troops were crawling slowly through the scrub, burdened by their weapons and baked by the desert sun. As they inched forward, their rifles were trained on a cluster of mud huts. I thought it must have been a training exercise. But it wasn't. They were looking for the enemy in those huts.

Just a few feet away, women in black shawls and elderly men in headdresses were carrying on with daily life—washing clothes in old plastic buckets filled with dirty water or sitting around chatting with village elders.

Where British soldiers feared for their lives, defenseless Iraqis hardly noticed they were in danger. Decades of danger, terror, and persecution had left these Iraqi Shi'ites numb.

The stakes were higher than ever for Saddam Hussein—whose tanks had wiped out Shi'ite villages like these during years of repression. The Shi'ites had wondered for years why the United States did not get rid of Saddam in the last Gulf War, but now his survival was finally on the line, so Iraqis feared he would do anything to survive. The tanks could come back and destroy their villages. The chemical weapons that the whole world was talking about could be used here, where small boys and girls caked in dirt played in bare feet on the burning desert floor. Yet the children chatted and smiled, glancing at the soldiers from time to time, as if watching the dull second half of a bad soccer game.

And there I was, watching them, feeling distinctly uneasy in my flak jacket and helmet, with a five-star hotel room waiting for me in Kuwait when this was all over.

The Iraqis, meanwhile, had watched their mothers, fathers, brothers or sisters disappear into Saddam's torture chambers and prisons for nearly a quarter of a century. Now they were caught up in another war, barely able to provide themselves with food and water, let alone any means of protection from bullets or bombs.

Whenever we stopped for gas, or just for a break, I stared at the ravaged countryside and imagined being an Iraqi here, living in a mud hut village. You spend your life struggling to grow a crop to support your family. One of your sons cracks a joke about Saddam, and he ends up in prison. Then you are blacklisted for the rest of your life, and your son may never come home.

Then my thoughts turned to my own position. My colleagues and I had arrived in Iraq having been sent on survival courses and kitted out with the latest safety equipment designed to spare us from any nasty surprises while we were here.

The Iraqis, however, had been living in fear for years—Saddam's spy in the house next door, the soldier at the checkpoint down the street who demanded bribes, or the neighbor who would make up stories and report you just because he didn't like you.

Now, emotions that had been bottled for decades were spilling over, as if a 24-year secret was finally being told. But amid bombing raids and shortages of water and electricity, Iraqis had to suffer yet more hardships as they were releasing all the pain of the past.

The way Iraqis described it, the south of the country had been a playground for Saddam's henchmen. When they showed up, Iraqis believed the dictator's troops had a license to kill, rape and rampage. Many of the victims ended up in mass graves.

So, why weren't the Shi'ites of the south celebrating the prospect of American and British troops removing Saddam and his Baath Party? Many had bitter memories of 1991, when then-U.S. President George Bush urged them to topple their dictator, and the United States stood by and watched Saddam's tanks crush the Shi'ite revolt.

Getting Iraqis to tell their stories was difficult. They were poised uneasily between high hopes of a new era and deep fears that Saddam's troops could return if he somehow managed to stay in power, destroying villages that were seen to be siding with the Americans. It was a situation that became unbearable for many Iraqis, especially as the hardships of life in wartime multiplied.

As an Arabic speaker, I was overwhelmed. Scores of Iraqis asked me questions that the Americans or British could not seem to answer. Why do I have no water? Where is the electricity? My child is sick and I have no gasoline to drive him to the hospital.

Many people tried to contact relatives abroad, waving crumpled pieces of paper with faded phone numbers at foreign reporters and begging to use their satellite telephones.

All I could do was watch them go past, with the fear of Saddam's wrath always in the back of their minds, obscuring hopes for freedom. Their early encounters with invasion forces usually brought disappointment.

At one intersection, where British troops had detained Iraqi soldiers and corralled them with barbed wire, a white pickup truck pulled up. Inside, a father held a son whose robe was drenched with blood from a shrapnel wound to the leg. He asked for help. But the answer was one that would become all too familiar to Iraqis whether they needed morphine or bread—it's not my job, I am a soldier.

"All I can do is change the bandage," said a British soldier, wrapping a white dressing around the wound.

Hungry, Thirsty and Ingenious

Iraqis had become resourceful during the 13 years of United Nations sanctions that followed Saddam's 1990 invasion of Kuwait—for example, keeping their cars moving by cannibalizing spare parts from other types of machinery.

This time, the thirsty and hungry were just as ingenious. They dug dirty wells to find water, or they posed as surrendering Iraqi soldiers to try to get food at military checkpoints.

At a hospital in Safwan, a usually sleepy town on the Kuwait border, patients and doctors were angry. "We try to move the wounded to bigger hospitals and we find American forces pointing guns at us at checkpoints," said Fadil Abbas, the exhausted director of the Safwan Hospital, standing by a stretcher covered in blood stains.

It was a society in which children grew up quickly. Children such as Majid, 15, who like countless others roamed the streets, trying to hustle a cigarette or a bottle of water, or just to win some attention. He had come to his own conclusions about what was happening.

"The Americans and British said it was going to be a liberation, but this is an occupation," said Majid.

Many Iraqis in the south soon began to say they were better off under Saddam. The thought was shocking after hearing the horror stories about electrocution, fingernails ripped out, ears sliced off and summary executions.

Policymakers in Washington were probably dismayed to hear of this nostalgia for the days of Saddam so early in the war just because there were shortages of food, water and electricity. But Iraqis explained it in a very simple way that led me to believe that President Bush's campaign to win their hearts and minds would fail if his troops did not quickly improve matters.

A system of state rations under Saddam gave Iraqis a steady monthly supply of bread, cooking oil and detergent, which kept them afloat under sanctions. Now they faced chaos, and the armies controlling their country were not even satisfying their basic needs. During the three weeks it took to depose Saddam, Iraqis wanted something more basic than talk of democracy from Washington.

"We need water. All we can do is dig for water in wells. It is water that even animals would not drink," said 30-year-old Muhammed Ali, who was unemployed.

When the water finally did come, it was delivered with added humiliation thrown in. In the narrow alleyways of the town of Umm Qasr, British soldiers tossed bottles of water from the back of a truck at a throng of thirsty people.

"They treat us like dogs," said an Iraqi teenager.

Desperation made Iraqis act in strange ways. In most wars, rockets, shells, mortars and mines usually force people to flee. Not in

Iraq. They defied the logic of conflict, refusing to take themselves out of harm's way.

On foot, bicycles or in cars if they were lucky, Iraqis traveled the countryside on roads ripped up by American tanks. Old women in black shawls loitered on the edge of battles, picking up artillery boxes to burn on their cooking fires.

Some entrepreneurial Iraqis even discovered ways to make money from the misery. Minibus driver Salim Wuhayib started a shuttle service between Basra and Nassiriya, two cities caught up in the fighting.

"I am going to Nassiriya to drop these people off, and then I am turning around and coming back," he said as his 12 passengers sat calmly, shrugging their shoulders when reminded of the artillery fire and bombs in their city.

Kneeling at the Roadside

Others, who couldn't afford a ride, waited at the Basra Bridge, hoping for a chance to enter the city. British troops, trying to maintain order, made them kneel on the roadside as a mortar landed nearby. I worried that another one would land closer, but the Iraqis didn't flinch—and none got up to get out of the way.

Two young men I met on their way to a fishing trip, of all things, made me realize just what Iraqis had gone through. They were heading for a town that had been hit by air strikes a few hours earlier, but that didn't seem to worry them.

"We are used to this. It is nothing new," said 25-year-old Kazim Abdullah. He was wearing a grubby patch over one eye, which he said had been damaged by shrapnel.

I asked if it was the result of the latest war in his country.

"No. The explosion was from the war in 1991, not this war," he said with a smile.

Iraqis wanted this war to end quickly not because they couldn't take the pain but because they thought that if Saddam didn't fall swiftly, he would never fall at all. And if Saddam did fall or was killed, they needed to see his prison cell or his corpse.

Baath Party officials usually modeled themselves on Saddam, sporting the mustaches that are seen as a sign of manliness in Iraq and trying to look fierce in their military uniforms. So, I was amazed to hear people say that the Baath Party official who terrorized Umm Qasr was a woman.

Everybody knew Om Omar but nobody dared to talk to her on the street. Described as a big, intimidating woman with frizzy hair, she was on everyone's mind. The head of the hospital, the barber, the ice seller—they all knew her movements. One night she slept in one house, the next night she had moved, to avoid capture. Her whereabouts were important to the townspeople because her departure would signal the first defeat for the Baathists in a town in the south, a symbolic victory in the drive to crush Saddam loyalists.

Even the bombing of the Baath Party headquarters was not enough to give Iraqis hope. As the building blazed, a man picked through the few remaining documents and posters that were used to brainwash people for three decades. Beneath his feet, hundreds of ballots asking Iraqis to vote for another term for Saddam were a chilling reminder of the old days, when people had to vote yes or risk imprisonment, or worse. A classroom with blackboards and chalk would no longer be used to indoctrinate Iraqis with the socialist Baath Party's pan-Arab ideology.

But that was not enough to ease the fear in Umm Qasr.

"Om Omar is still around," said the man, who declined to give his name.

Evidence suggested otherwise.

Saddam Hussein posters lay scattered beside heaps of abandoned clothes and Baath Party documents. A crowd gathered. I asked everyone about Om Omar. They just kept saying that her house, a separate building from the Baath Party headquarters, had also been looted, refusing to admit they lived right next door and knew exactly who she was. As I opened my car door, a man stepped up and whispered in my ear. "This was Om Omar's house. She was the Baath leader. These people are just too afraid to say it. She ruled Umm Qasr," he said.

The Fall of Basra

It became clear that only the fall of Basra would reassure Iraqis, who were wondering why it was taking British forces so long to topple Saddam's terror network in the country's second largest city.

As the battle for Basra wore on, onlookers gathered at the

bridge into the city. They watched the fighting, and they watched thick clouds of black smoke rise from oil pits that were set ablaze in an attempt to confuse British pilots.

Fedayeen guerrillas were putting up unexpected resistance to British troops. They slipped into civilian areas and fired their rocket-propelled grenades at British tanks, holding off the advance for a while.

But the arrival of the British appeared to embolden Sattar Jabber to speak out. He had no ears, and he finally had a chance to tell the world why. Standing near a small cement hut with the helmet of a dead Iraqi soldier on the floor, he explained justice, Saddam style. Like many other Iraqis, he dreaded military service, which could last three years or more, depending on whether Iraq was at war. But he paid a heavy price for deserting.

As he spoke, his friend kept a close watch for the secret police.

"They caught me and took me to a hospital. When I woke up I realized they had cut off my ears. Then they took me to prison and beat me with a cable and broke my arms."

What was more shocking was his decision to desert from the army for a second time.

As the Baath fighters came under fire from U.S. and British troops, much of their rage was still directed at their own people.

Word began spreading that the Baath Party was waging a terror campaign to force people to fight on. The Party headquarters in Basra had been bombed, but fighters had picked up their AK-47 rifles and rocket-propelled grenades and regrouped around the city.

"The Party says fight, fight, fight or face the consequences once they all return after the war. It blares out on loudspeakers around Basra. They are trying to scare the whole city," said an Iraqi man who did not want to give his name.

"It is not food we are worried about. It is the terror in Basra, state terror."

Diehard Baathists showed up at people's homes late at night and forced them to join the war. They threatened to rape women in front of husbands and fathers.

Some managed to escape the terror. Their faces were always blank, as if they had been emotionally anesthetized after decades of brutality.

Sitting in the dirt and puffing on a cigarette after surrendering at a British checkpoint, Iraqi soldier Saad Kassem said the pressure from Saddam loyalists was unbearable, so he risked his life and fled.

The calm look on his face suggested that he could take anything now after escaping Saddam's thugs.

"They have been arresting many people over the last few days. They have also killed some," he said, showing a bruise on his head. "My two brothers were forced to go to the front, and they were killed in this war. I can't afford to feed the rest of my family, so I surrendered to the British."

At first I wondered why people like him seemed so calm about their suffering. Then I realized that so many Iraqi families had lost at least one loved one that it all sounded the same. Repetition removed the element of shock.

Saddam Hussein's Reach

Saddam Hussein's reach was extraordinary. It seemed he could find anyone at any time, even as his troops were being crushed by the United States and Britain.

A 15-year-old boy rode a donkey across the Basra Bridge. He was a poor child with ragged clothes who rented out his donkey for pennies. But as the war started, Saddam's police knew exactly who he was and what he thought.

"They came to my home and took me to the police station. Then they hung me upside down and beat the soles of my feet with a club," he said. "They were punishing me because I refused to fight the Americans and British."

The terror was spreading across Basra, where people like Waleed Ja'awil learned just how far the Baath Party was willing to go to stay in power. He and his three cousins were driving out of the city after visiting an automobile repair shop when three gunmen in Baath uniforms ordered them to stay in Basra to fight. When they refused, their vehicle was riddled with bullets.

Ja'awil lay in the back of their truck with a bullet in his thigh when it pulled up to a British military post at Basra Bridge. His robe drenched in blood, he groaned in pain.

"As we turned on the road out of Basra, three Baath Party militiamen with AK-47s started shouting, 'Come back, you must fight,' and then shot at us," said his cousin, Saachid Aber, as a British medic administered morphine to the wounded man.

I could not make sense of this. It was almost as if Saddam loyalists were trying to inflict one last act of cruelty on their compatriots before they were deposed.

As a reporter I felt I was not supposed to judge events. Nearby, an elderly man named Muhammed Saeed provided some perspective. He stood holding a piece of shrapnel as British tanks rumbled along the highway, skirting antitank mines intended to slow the advance.

"God never meant any of this to happen," he said, shaking his head. Two dead Iraqi soldiers lay face down in a patch of grass 20 feet away. A towering poster of Saddam Hussein proclaimed him a "great leader for a great people."

The fog of war gave rise to a wave of conspiracy theories. As an Arab who grew up in the United States, I never really understood why these wild ideas were so popular and influential in the Arab world. Iraq made me understand.

Iraqis had suffered in silence for three decades under Saddam, and the only way they could express themselves was in their thoughts. It was a confusing process that delivered no answers—just more fears.

The Iraqi psyche could not believe that Saddam could lose or that the invading troops really wanted to remove him. They had been betrayed by everyone before, including Saddam and George Bush, Sr. Why should they believe that Bush's son would rescue them from Saddam, a former U.S. ally?

At least for a while, the Baath Party fighters were holding off the world's most powerful armies, and there were plenty of Iraqi conspiracy theories to explain why:

- Saddam Hussein is an American agent, and they will take him to Washington after Iraq is destroyed.
- The United States and Britain are going to hand Iraq to Israel when the war is over.
- Saddam has cut a deal with the West to crush the Shi'ites in southern Iraq.
- Saddam is Jewish.

"Saddam is an American agent. We have known that for a while. He works for the United States. That means this whole war is useless. All of this destruction will not lead to Saddam's end. It is all make-believe," said Ibrahim, who was standing with a group of friends watching from the Basra Bridge.

Conspiracy Theories

Conspiracy theories were the lighter side of Iraq's culture of paranoia. More importantly, people had developed a sort of mental radar that could transmit warnings when Saddam's Mukhabarat intelligence agents showed up.

At one hospital, Iraqis were trying to get treatment. One man just stood and observed, detached from the jostling.

"He is a spy for Saddam. I know who he is," said an elderly man. When the alleged agent moved closer, the man suddenly began saying life was perfect in Umm Qasr, the kind of cautious talk that journalists heard when they were forced to work with official Iraqi minders at their side.

A few minutes later, as I was getting water from the car, I noticed the suspected spy was looking inside our vehicle, trying to figure out what we were doing in Umm Qasr.

Relief came when British troops pushed deep into Basra for the first time, cutting down Iraqi soldiers and Fedayeen fighters and taking control of key points in the city. My colleagues and I were told not to go too deep into Basra. But I didn't need to move far to understand some of its history of terror.

At a neat white building that seemed like the town hall, a tall man grabbed my hand and led me inside, pushing away young boys who wanted to sell pieces of looted wood. Wearing a long-sleeved, stained white shirt, Adnan Shakir gave me a tour of what turned out to be the British-built Basra prison. He walked past the execution chamber, where prisoners with nooses around their necks were dropped to their deaths into a crude wooden box dug below floor level.

He finally reached the room where he had paid a heavy price for just stealing a piece of bread. He stood for a moment before walking into the tiny, stuffy chamber where he had been tortured. It took a few minutes for him to take his eyes off the wires dangling from the ceiling that fired electric current into his arms, face and testicles. Shakir mustered the courage to grab the wires to show how they worked.

"One Baath Party member blindfolded me and tied these cables to my ears, and another electrocuted me. They said 'Why did you steal bread?' and I said I could not afford it," he said. Then he paused to lift up his shirt to show dozens of scars on his chest. They were inflicted at another prison, at another time in a history of pain.

"At a prison near Baghdad they crushed my fingers with a rifle butt and lashed me with cables," he added, displaying his deformed hands.

It was almost as if his words had to stay in the chamber. It was a personal affair, no matter how tragic.

Outside, excited teenage boys who had not yet learned about terror the hard way ran down the street after British tanks. They were fascinated, as if they were watching a war movie unfold in the streets of Basra, where all the shooting and killing had been real enough over the years.

In the city center, Iraqis were still cautious, even after British tanks took up positions.

A 29-year-old jobless man looked around carefully before describing life under Saddam, whose supporters were still telling Iraqis he would be back.

"Nobody can really talk because they are scared. People like Saddam come to power by secretly killing people and buying others. This is our life," he said. "I don't even trust you."

Seconds later, a bulky man walked across the street and told him, "I am going to report you." It was a brief encounter that said a lot about Iraqi fear.

Saddam, the ultimate survivor in many Iraqi eyes, was finally toppled on April 9. But Iraqis soon found a new enemy. Armed with the same AK-47 assault rifles used by the Baath Party men, thousands of looters became the new terror in the streets of Basra. It seemed every building was gutted. Nobody was safe. People stole kerosene, ceiling fans, toilet bowls, chalk, blackboards and Iraqi military helmets.

"They are terrorizing our neighborhoods. At night, during the day, they steal everything," said Hussein Akil, standing with an angry crowd on Basra's main street. "What kind of liberation is this?"

Some of his angry friends accused British soldiers of turning a blind eye as Basra was stripped of everything, including its remaining pride. Were the culprits just thieves, or was looting a way of rebelling against one of the world's most brutal dictatorships? It was impossible to tell, but the anger led some Iraqis to long for the days when Saddam was in charge, when the punishment for looters would have been torture, and in some cases death.

Small-time looters roamed Basra with wheelbarrows full of stolen property. Others used donkeys to haul stuff across the city as shells landed. Looting became so rampant that British troops punished thieves by crushing the fronts of their cars with tanks and setting free donkeys after seizing stolen goods from their owners.

A man grabbed me by the hand and took me to a bridge manned by British troops to show me "how insane" life had become. "Look, these British are just standing around their tanks, and down there near the river bank there are hand grenades that were looted, just sitting there," he said.

There were other forms of anger that the Americans and British didn't understand either. A group of men came up to a British tank to protest what they called disrespect for Muslims.

"These soldiers take their shirts off and stand around on their tanks. What about our women when they see this? They are humiliating us," said an Iraqi man. A barber nearby said the soldiers should "get out."

When the looting subsided because there was nothing left to steal, Iraqis began to consider how the country might be run now that Saddam was gone. But democracy may not be so easy for Iraqis as they try to form a government from the country's volatile mix of Sunnis, Shi'ites and Kurds.

One morning, a few weeks after Saddam fell, a store of abandoned Iraqi weapons exploded, flattening three houses and killing at least 14 people. A man who had lost his family wept and held his one-month-old daughter in his trembling arms. Old women were screaming in shock.

Suddenly two men started arguing. One threw a large rock at the other and then beat him with his fists. I wondered how they could be fighting while their dead still lay trapped under rubble.

"Don't worry, it's nothing," said a man watching the fight and smiling. "They are relatives."

Chapter 14

FROM CAMBRIDGE CAPPUCCINOS TO RESOLVE FOR REVENGE

By Saul Hudson

Laleh Tarighi, 22, spoke to me with a southern English accent—long vowels and sentences punctuated with "you know?"—a lazy affectation that was fashionable at her high-school hangouts but which now jarred against the seriousness of her convictions.

She was brought up in the British university town of Cambridge and, remarkably, we both used to go to the same café: Clowns, a trendy Italian-run place where the cappuccinos stretched a student's budget. I lived in an apartment directly above it for two years and liked to talk soccer with the owner.

Now, here I was in the desert plains of northeastern Iraq under wide blue skies, nostalgically chatting about a favorite watering hole in cold Cambridge with a fighter from the People's Mujahideen, the largest Iranian rebel group.

After my tour of duty covering the Iraq war and its chaotic aftermath, I would return to lattes in stylish cafés. She had given all that up. Why?

Wondering why rebels choose to dedicate themselves to a cause, and often a seemingly lost one, is inevitable. In Latin America, I had spent time with guerrillas and understood that they were angry peasants fighting in their own neglected countryside to claw their way out of poverty.

But the Iranian fighters were different. Many had moved halfway around the world, leaving behind easy lives for the discipline of the Iraqi desert and the rigor of a group that many considered an authoritarian personality cult rather than a rebel force against the Islamic clerical leadership in neighboring Iran.

I should have understood Tarighi. It was not difficult to picture her former life. She went to high school in Cambridge, taking English literature, sociology and media studies. At Clowns, where her light brown eyes and wide smile must have turned boys' heads, she used to ask her friends what she should do with her life and wonder what girls did in the place where she was born—Iran.

Headed for university in Manchester, she was about to take a year off to find herself in Paris. "I had a good life, but I had no purpose," she said.

When she was one year old, her father was tortured and executed for trying to overthrow the Iranian government. Her mother joined the Mujahideen, also known by its Farsi name, Mujahideen-e Khalq, based in neighboring Iraq. Tarighi was sent to England to be brought up by her aunt in a comfortable middle-class home.

Seventeen years later, Tarighi's mother made contact. For the first time, Tarighi learned of her father's execution and was also told that the People's Mujahideen had taken revenge.

"When I heard about the brave man who killed my dad's torturer, I knew every second I stayed in England was a waste of time," she said. "From that moment, I have had something to live and fight for."

Dressed in khaki military uniform and head-scarf, Tarighi was now a tank gunner in an all-women unit training at Ashraf, the Mujahideen headquarters in Iraq. Her Clowns friends had failed to dissuade her from joining the rebels—a group classified as terrorists by the United States, the European Union and Iran. She said she misses the Cambridge cappuccinos but has no regrets about the choice she made four years ago because women like her could not expect men to overthrow the Iranian government alone.

"I decided I could not leave the fight up to others," she said. "If we all left it up to somebody else, then none of us would be here."

She showed me around her Brazilian-made wheeled tank, tightened some bolts, swung the turret about and said goodbye.

When I offered to shake her hand, the young woman from Cambridge's trendy social spots stretched out her hand—only to jerk it back and hide it behind her back like the Iranian rebel she had become. The rest of the tank crew giggled because Tarighi had almost touched a Westerner.

"We don't do that here," she said.

Eyes of Revenge

Women, mainly young and many brought up outside Iran, swell the ranks of the Mujahideen, a decades-old rebel group that has its roots in Islam and Marxism. Despite rock-bottom support at home, the group was a well-disciplined, heavily armed force of up to 9,000 fighters that had been hosted by Saddam Hussein.

Sixty or 18, from Tehran or Toronto, the female fighters have common bonds—a shared anger at perceived restrictions on the freedom of women in Iran, and above all, the loss of family members for whose deaths they blame the government.

Mahboubeh Jahani was 60, and it was hot. She trotted, her head up, back straight and knees lifting like an elegant show horse. It was midday, it was Iraq's unrelenting summer, and she did not break into a sweat or appear to tire in an hour of artillery gun drills.

High-pitched female voices sang out commands—"Take up your positions, load ammunition, fire"—and Jahani ran back and forth to the cannon, simulating firing shells in her third decade of preparing for a war that never comes.

When she broke away from the exercise, her weather-beaten face was cheerful—she enjoyed her star role in a show put on by another of the Mujahideen's all-women units. "These youngsters have to keep up with me," she joked.

When she told the story of what brought her to the 16-square-mile training base, she stood stiff, hands behind her back. Her body and voice had a toughness rooted in a resolve for revenge.

Jahani had lost three sons—all killed fighting to overthrow Iran's fundamentalist clerical leaders. Before that, Iranian authorities had also executed a brother and her husband.

"Losing a child is the most painful thing. But if you want to achieve something as valuable as freedom, you have to pay a high price," said Jahani, who has four children still alive. "I am proud to have lost my sons, to have made that sacrifice for my people."

"I think we will see a free Iran soon," she said. "But for me, personally, even if it is another 30 years fighting for freedom, I have no problem with that."

I was skeptical. After all, the Mujahideen's presentation of Jahani and the 100-odd women fighters at Ashraf, about 55 miles northeast of Baghdad, seemed more of a public relations exercise for the visiting Reuters crew than real military drills. And did all the women really need to be tightening every bolt on the wheels of their tanks—rather clean vehicles that did not look as if they had moved much recently let alone seen military action?

Would Jahani spend 30 more years waiting to fight a vastly superior enemy? It seemed unbelievable—until I looked in her eyes.

If you want to make someone your enemy for life, kill their relatives.

Across Iraq, I had seen the hatred in the eyes of Iraqis who vowed to take revenge on American soldiers for killing their loved ones. Mothers swore to strap explosives to their chests, and boys pledged to run away and join guerrilla groups such as al Qaeda. Men launched grenade attacks.

In Jahani, was I perhaps looking at those Iraqis' resolve decades on? The 60-year-old's small, dark-brown eyes no longer flashed hate. But they had a depth that showed how anger can turn into an unflinching determination. The Ashraf tour may have been stage-managed, but her look was real—she would have her revenge. The youngsters called her their inspiration.

Women make up a quarter of the Mujahideen army. They generally stayed at the base for fear of offending the Iraqi Muslims' sensitivities, but still rose through the ranks to leadership positions.

The Ashraf base commander, Pari Bakhshai, an unmarried 42-year-old whose bookcase includes titles such as *Misogyny in Power* and *The Subjection of Women*, said the Mujahideen were a natural magnet for women.

"The Iranian regime has cut 50 percent of the population out of the economy and politics, but our resistance holds out hope for women that they will fully participate in society," the soft-spoken commander said.

Men serving under female commanders drove tanks displaying portraits of the leader's third and current wife, Maryam Rajavi, who is also the group's nominee to be Iran's president.

The men dismissed charges that the group has evolved into a personality cult around Rajavi, saying women won command posts on merit because they cared about their subordinates more than a male commander would.

Mohammed Reza Torabi, 22, grew up in Canada, wore grenades around his waist and asked after soccer scores. He said he was happy to be led by women. "As leaders, they are more humane. You can talk to them about problems more openly than with men," he said.

The base was named after the first wife of founder Massoud Rajavi, Ashraf, who died fighting for the Mujahideen. A monument of her running with a rifle and dressed all in black dominates its central square.

Marriage for Mujahideen rebels was forbidden, but none of them saw any irony in their leader being married. Massoud Rajavi married his latest wife after she and her then-husband, another senior Mujahideen fighter, were ordered to divorce.

American Ambivalence

Just as that felt odd, so the Mujahideen's general presence in Iraq seemed incongruous. This was post-invasion Iraq, where the U.S. military had blasted to Baghdad, and now—three weeks later—its convoys of tanks, armored vehicles and gun-topped Humvees appeared everywhere.

Yet here was a group of "terrorists"—bombed by U.S. warplanes at the outset of the war—entrenched at their 17-year-old headquarters as if the shift of power meant nothing. The rebels pretended as much and trotted out stock replies if asked how they thought the removal of their longtime sponsor, Saddam, would affect the group or even threaten its existence.

"We have no worries about the future because our resistance was not born in Iraq. Our destiny is not tied to Iraq and never has been," Bakhshai, said. "Our destiny will be decided in Iran."

While Americans had overrun most of Iraq, visitors who arrived at Ashraf were in no doubt they were in rebel-held territory as they passed guard posts protected by concrete blocks.

At its imposing entrance, a large green, white and red Iranian flag and the Mujahideen banner of a fist holding a rifle and a sickle fluttered above a tall, chain-link perimeter fence.

Outside Ashraf, the rebels responded to Saddam's downfall by taking control of roads close to the Iranian border and setting up checkpoints with tanks and barbed wire. As their soldiers patrolled the highways with guns mounted on pickup trucks, shepherds and children playing soccer in the dusty streets stopped to wave.

Weren't the Americans supposed to be the occupying force?

The Mujahideen's show of strength was even bolder at the border. Jeeps drove around loaded with fighters carrying rifles and grenades, tanks rumbled through the hills, and rocket launchers were directed at the Iranian peaks.

The United States agreed to a cease-fire with the rebels shortly after toppling Saddam, and the Mujahideen were supposed to withdraw their weapons into noncombat positions. Instead, here they were flexing their military muscles and filling a power vacuum east of Baghdad.

"We are obviously in combat positions here, but we are not against the U.S. forces," said Mitrah Bagherzadeh, the commander of several border area bases.

That may have been her interpretation of the accord, but it was only a matter of time before the U.S. military would turn up and put the rebels back in their box. For now, they were allowed to roam around with their heavy weaponry.

The American willingness to tolerate the rebel bravado continued to resonate in Washington politics long after the invasion. Many conservative hawks were happy to use the Mujahideen as a pawn against Iran—a country President Bush bracketed in an "axis of evil" with Iraq and North Korea.

The Mujahideen cast themselves as a powerful and democratic force providing a shield against what they—and some in the Bush administration—called Iranian agents' meddling in the emerging postwar Iraqi leadership.

The United States and the Mujahideen certainly had a common interest in stopping Iraqi fighters of the Tehran-based Supreme

Council for Islamic Revolution in Iraq from returning to their homeland.

The Mujahideen's spokesman, Hussein Madani, a slick product of the group's formidable public relations machine, made his pitch to be regarded as a partner against Iran. "The reality of this region is that the greatest threat of destabilization comes from the Iranian regime," said Madani, whose English matched his impeccable dress. "If the United States' goal is democracy, then it is not in anybody's interest to take away our forces. It is only logical that if they want democracy, they will find themselves allies of the Mujahideen."

The rebels deny they are terrorists and claim Washington gave them that label only to appease Iran during the Clinton administration.

The rebels, who killed Americans in the 1970s and supported the takeover in 1979 of the U.S. Embassy in Tehran, would make strange partners for a United States that has focused its foreign policy since Sept. 11, 2001, on its war on terrorism.

The Mujahideen joined the 1979 Islamic revolution that toppled the Shah of Iran but later broke ranks with the new clerical leadership. They have been based in Iraq since the early 1980s, with offices of their political wing in major cities around the world, including Washington.

From Iraq, they coordinated bombings in Tehran and against Iranian embassies abroad. But since siding with Iraq in the 1980–88 war against Iran, the Mujahideen's popularity has plummeted at home, and they have been accused of helping Saddam suppress ethnic groups in Iraq.

After the Iraq war, France rounded up more than 100 of the rebels in exile there, saying the group was planning attacks in Europe.

In cities across Europe, faithful followers of Maryam Rajavi, who was detained and later released, set themselves on fire—an extreme response sure to alienate them from many Americans and add weight to arguments that the group is a personality cult.

The French arrests were welcomed by Tehran and dismayed Washington hawks hoping to use the Mujahideen against Iran. Iran said Washington's lenient treatment of the Mujahideen in Iraq showed it had double standards in its war on terrorism, while some in the Bush administration said the rebels should be treated as they are formally labeled—as terrorists.

But with Iraq's government overthrown, the United States is increasingly turning its sights on Iran and debating how best to thwart its apparent nuclear ambitions. Some conservatives argued the Mujahideen could be the answer. The Mujahideen could become like the Northern Alliance—the proxy force the United States used in Afghanistan to help remove the ruling Taliban. Or at least, the rebels' network of spies, which has spectacularly exposed some Iranian nuclear programs, could collect intelligence on Tehran.

Discipline and Dogma

The Mujahideen would certainly make for a well-organized ally. While postwar Iraq was mired in chaos, bombed-out and looted, with no electricity, little gasoline and even less patience for security to be restored, Ashraf was an oasis of quiet and order. Its numbered streets were palm-lined and paved, spreading out past barracks, training fields and factories producing soft drinks and ice cream.

American soldiers who came across the rebels on nearby highways praised them as courteous and, above all, disciplined.

"They are real clean, and they keep their weapons better than we do," said 1st Lt. Kyle Ford of the 4th Infantry Division.

Their well-established organization contrasted with the floundering U.S.-led civilian administration charged with rebuilding Iraq. While the occupying authority could barely muster a working telephone to call a news conference in Baghdad or provide an Arabic translator at their press events, the multilingual Mujahideen seemed masters of the media. They had a rigidly scheduled program, including staged shows of field drills, tank maintenance and computerized war games. For a finale, there was a trip to the border. There, the same handful of tanks appeared in various locations, creating the impression that rebel firepower was somewhat greater than it probably was.

They provided a ready supply of tea and cookies and professional translators for English, French, Arabic and Farsi. Still, behind the charm offensive lurked an unsettling need for control. Most interviews were conducted through a Mujahideen-provided translator, and all conversations with rank-and-file members were observed—and sometimes clarified—by spokesmen or senior commanders.

The rebels also took pains to direct the message broadcast by the media. The day I traveled to the border, I felt trapped inside spokesman Madani's vehicle as he critiqued my previous day's article about the Mujahideen.

Spotty communications meant I had not seen the final version, but the spokesman clutched a faxed copy and picked it apart, upset I had cited Iraqis calling the rebels unwelcome neighbors. He also complained to Reuters photographer Petr Josek that a caption illustrating his picture noted that Washington branded the Mujahideen terrorists.

For one event, we were running late after our armor-plated car had been caught in crossfire between police and looters en route to the camp. Madani berated me: "You are not very organized, Mr. Hudson."

And after a day of interviews—full of tea and cookies, not to mention Coca-Cola and chocolate ice cream—we felt unable to decline an invitation to a hearty Iranian meal, even though we insisted deadlines were passing.

"It is a suggestion that you stay and eat," translator Massoud Farshchi said. In fact, we had little choice.

Dining on the lamb and rice, I recalled how so many times the Mujahideen members emphasized they had "made a free choice" to commit to the group. That contrasted with the Americans in Iraq. None of the soldiers from the "land of the free" bothered to articulate that they made a free choice to sign up. They were fighting "to kick Saddam's butt," avenge Sept. 11 or in most cases just to get the war over and get home.

I began to wonder about Tarighi's decision to join the Mujahideen.

Was the moment when she learned of her father's death staged for maximum impact on an impressionable teen-ager searching for a goal in life? She said it was her free choice to join. Every woman on the Ashraf base had also made her own free choice to wear a head-scarf to cover her hair and, of course, never to marry.

For years, media reports have cited former Mujahideen members complaining that the group's cultlike style created an intolerance of dissent, including imprisonment and beating of anybody who asked to leave.

While the rebels I met claimed they exercised free choice, there was little evidence of freethinking among them. Bakhshai carried a folder of Mujahideen press releases from which she read aloud when asked about the group. And schooled to deliver stock replies, rank-and-file rebels parroted word-for-word statements from the leadership or cited the same sometimes obscure sources.

The Mujahideen had 30,000 fighters—according to an article by a Jordanian journalist—or the Mujahideen were forbidden from marrying "so that they can dedicate all their energies to the resistance," they all said.

Endgame

A week after I first visited the Mujahideen at Ashraf and saw their display of strength at the border, the Americans showed up—in force. On Friday, May 9, after a tip from a U.S. officer that the Americans were making the Mujahideen surrender, I raced with my Iraqi translator back to the rebel strongholds to see what was happening.

It was a typical display of overwhelming force by the United States. Where once the rebels had proudly manned checkpoints and deployed heavy weapons, the U.S. forces had suddenly set up roadblock after roadblock. This was not five tanks scurrying about in an attempt to look like 20—the occupying power was around every bend and over every hill.

"We sent them home," said Staff Sgt. Christopher Gill, standing in front of a tank. "Now we have established a presence."

For me, it was inevitable. The United States could not allow "terrorists" to cruise around in tanks after a war the Bush administration had linked to its war on terrorism.

For my translator, it was my fault. Waleed Ibrahim, who had become my companion on stories throughout Iraq, was convinced I was in league with the U.S. military. I had started the war as an embedded journalist with the 3rd Armored Cavalry Division, I still ate the military's MREs, and he suspected it was more than my smooth talk that got us through many a U.S. checkpoint.

While he would drive us back to Baghdad each day, I would bang out stories on my laptop and send them to my editors by e-mail. He accused me of copying the U.S. Central Command in on the articles, arguing the military only took action after I had covered a story.

Ibrahim had blamed me when the Americans ousted the self-appointed mayor of the southern city of Kut after I interviewed him in the city hall, where he had taken up residence. And now, despite our growing friendship and trust, he was sure the Mujahideen were back in their barracks only because I had exposed their military maneuvers on the border. Ibrahim reminded me that the Mujahideen had said I was the only writer to visit their border bases, so it must have been me, he argued, who tipped off the Americans.

While it was flattering that he thought my stories could have such influence, sadly, it also revealed how Iraqis just assumed the media was a tool of the state.

Whether the Mujahideen's border publicity blitz had indeed backfired and provoked the U.S. Army or the military had been waiting for a signal from a divided Washington to take over, the result was that the Iranian rebels were nowhere to be seen. It was all done under a surrender agreement hashed out at a meeting in the border area where the rebels were told to withdraw to Ashraf under U.S. guard and leave their heavy weaponry at another base.

Back at Ashraf, two U.S. tanks blocked the entrance, while a handful of Mujahideen men hung around forlornly in the rear. The American ambivalence remained. These "terrorists" were not prisoners of war, nor were they headed for Guantanamo Bay, the U.S. Naval base in Cuba housing Taliban and al Qaeda fighters caught in the Afghanistan war. They were even allowed to keep their rifles—for self-defense—and who knows, maybe one day as a reconstituted army.

Still, they were no longer the fighting force that showed off tanks and rocket launchers so proudly at the border. They did not invite us in for tea and cookies. "No media events today," Farshchi said with an apologetic shrug.

I looked toward the calm base from its perimeter fence. I imagined Madani waiting by the fax for his copies of the "rebel capitulation" stories in the press and Bakhshai preparing a statement for her folder of rebel spin that began "Our destiny will be decided in Iran."

I imagined the 60-year-old Jahani, deprived of her Belgian-made cannon but still trotting back and forth training for the fight in Iran that seemed yet further away.

And, finally, I thought of Tarighi. Now she had no bolts to tighten, no turret to swivel, no tank. Was she missing her cappuccinos? Would she go back to Cambridge? It was, after all, her "free choice."

J

Chapter 15

INMATES TAKE OVER THE ASYLUM

By Rosalind Russell

We ended up at the al-Rashad Psychiatric Hospital by mistake, lost on the edge of Baghdad as a dust storm gathered pace. We climbed out of the car to ask directions and saw someone approaching through the gritty haze. He wore a suit and addressed us in perfect English. Was he the director? "No," said Hagop Ouzorian, elegantly gesturing us through a hole in the hospital wall where the door used to be. "I am one of the patients here." It was little more than a week since Saddam Hussein's administration had collapsed, unleashing a wave of looting, which for many Iraqis proved as destructive and frightening as weeks of American bombing raids. In the capital, smoke drifted from the smashed windows of government ministries where fires lit by looters burned for days. Shops, banks and offices were stripped bare. Door frames were hammered out of their housings and electrical wires ripped from the walls. Nothing was too much trouble for the looters, and nowhere, not even the mental asylum, was out of bounds.

Ouzorian was a trained draughtsman and long-term resident of al-Rashad. He said he had an "obsessive-compulsive disorder," but his behavior revealed nothing but complete sanity. He was impeccably polite and brushed over his troubled life story as if he didn't want to inconvenience me with the details. An Armenian Christian, he came from Mosul in the north of Iraq where his family owned a winery. He had trained in California and had returned home in the early 1980s to begin his career when things began to go wrong. His sister had a good job at the oil ministry, but when she fell out of favor with Saddam's Baath Party, the family was collectively punished. Ouzorian was imprisoned, a time he did not wish to talk about, and sometime after his release ended up in al-Rashad. He had two good friends in the hospital; one was a poet. They enjoyed reading and painting, they drank tea and smoked cigarettes. The asylum was their home, it was where they felt safe.

As U.S. forces entered Baghdad in early April, there was a day and night of fighting around the hospital on the city's southwestern edge. The soldiers moved on, and the looters moved in. The small number of medical staff who had remained in the hospital took their cue to flee, leaving Ouzorian and his two friends as possibly the only rational witnesses to the scene that followed. The raiders were armed and frenzied, screaming abuse at the inmates. Some patients tried to lock themselves into holding cells, others cowered in corners, moaning, rocking themselves back and forth. The mob smashed windows with the butts of their rifles, battered down doors and ripped mattresses from beneath bedridden patients. Several of the female inmates were raped. Looters took medical equipment, air conditioners, fans, furniture and books. The pharmacy was emptied and trashed; drugs that kept most of the hundreds of patients just the right side of psychosis were stolen. Many of them ran away; madmen let loose in an anarchic city.

Ouzorian and his friends left too, heading for the center of Baghdad. Perhaps they thought they were going to start a new life, but the dream did not last long. American tanks cruised the streets, militiamen and looters prowled the alleyways. There was no electricity; shops and cafes were shuttered. They soon returned to the sanctuary of their devastated asylum. "It was a bad time," said Ouzorian, with characteristic understatement, as we crunched over bits of glass and examined the damage to the men's wing. In the absence of any real authority, Shi'ite clerics from the local mosque had taken over the running of the hospital, providing food each day and volunteers to clean up the mess. Ouzorian and his little faction were not entirely happy with this state of affairs. "We are not religious people," whispered the poet. But he picked up a broom to show willingness. They had seen what was on the outside, and they didn't want to go there again.

Back in town, the looting spree reached heights of frenzy that almost defied belief. Rampaging through an amusement park on the edge of one of Saddam's palaces, a group of thieves, not content with the generator from the model railway or plastic seats from the merry-go-round, broke into the Baghdad zoo. They smashed the padlocks on the cages and made off with the animals. Monkeys, chimpanzees, bears, dogs, horses, birds and camels all went, more than 300 animals in all. But the zoo's seven lions and two tigers remained, apparently too fearsome for the robbers. The trouble was they had not been fed. As U.S. forces approached Baghdad, the Iraqi military dug in around the zoo, and the animals were not spared the fighting. A burnt-out armored vehicle at the gate and a crater on the edge of one of the enclosures showed just how close it was. The looting ensured zoo staff kept away for another week. On the day we went there, the big cats had not been fed for 10 days. Like us, the zoo's veterinarian had decided to run the gauntlet of armed gangs to see what had happened.

"I was frightened to come here," said Hasham Mohamed Hussein. "But I needed to see it for myself. Now I am in shock." Hasham had no time to grieve for the lost animals. He was more concerned about the ones that remained, starving in their enclosures. Mandor, a 20-year-old Siberian tiger and the personal property of Saddam's elder son Uday, was slumped against the green bars of his cage, his beautifully marked coat hanging off his bones. He looked up briefly as Hasham approached, only to hang his head again when he realized his keeper was empty-handed. Next door, Sudqa, a 9-year-old lioness, stumbled to her feet and let out a low moan. The remnants of her last meal lay in the corner, a white bone chewed over and over. The zoo was funded by a government that no longer existed. Hasham said it would cost $30 a day to feed each of the nine animals, that each usually consumed 10 pounds of meat a day. "I have nothing like this kind of money," he said. "We are alone here, and without help our animals will die."

His plea was heard. The Kuwaiti government learned of their plight and sent volunteers and money for food. Within a week, a South African conservationist had also turned up to help, and international animal charities sent more donations. When I next went back to the zoo, there was a unit of American soldiers detailed to protect it. They had parked armored vehicles by the gates and had chased off the looters. Sgt. Matthew Oliver of the 3rd Infantry Division was friendly, but he had bad news to tell me. The night they arrived, four lions, still crazed with hunger, clawed their way out through a crumbling wall on the edge of their enclosure and made a charge for the soldiers. They were shot dead in a hail of automatic fire. "They charged two of our guys," explained Oliver. "We had to take them down."

The looting in Baghdad and cities across Iraq should not have come as a surprise. In war, norms of behavior are often forgotten. At first, it seemed the collapse of Saddam's choking administration had triggered a wave of euphoria, evidenced by the scramble to pull down the dictator's statue, which, conveniently for the world's media, happened right outside their base in the Palestine Hotel. But the war also pumped a vein of aggression and opportunism that exploded onto the streets when the fighting stopped. In that respect, the Iraq war was no different from any other, but the painstaking planning that had gone into fighting the war was conspicuously absent in its aftermath. Once U.S. forces had lost their grip on security, it was hard for them to get it back. Eventually, they appealed for help, calling on Iraqi police officers to return to their posts to start joint patrols with U.S. forces, but by doing so they invited back to work some of the most despised enforcers of Saddam's oppression. It was a lose-lose situation that only seemed to get worse when the first patrols took to the streets.

Driving through downtown Baghdad one morning, we came across a robbery in progress at a branch of the Rasheed Bank. It should have presented the perfect opportunity for the new U.S.-Iraqi teams to display some of their muscle, and within minutes a patrol, alerted by local residents, was on the scene. They were too late to catch more than a dozen thieves who had already made their getaway, firing a victory shot from an AK-47 rifle. But three, including one who looked barely in his teens, were snared and thrown to the ground by Marines, who taped their arms behind their backs and wondered what to do next. "We can't understand the language, so it's hard for us to communicate with the Iraqi police or the people," puffed Cpl.

Shane Weeks, standing over his captives. "I haven't got a clue what's going on here."

Passing motorists offered advice from car windows. "Shoot them!" shouted one. Weeks looked bewildered. An Iraqi policeman, dressed in a dark green uniform and armed with a truncheon, offered more advice that Weeks didn't understand. A crowd was gathering, and farther down the street, a scuffle broke out as a bag of Iraqi dinars was found discarded on the roadside. Jumping into his unmarked car and leaving his new American colleagues behind, the policeman went racing after the opportunists to the next junction. Five minutes later he returned, defeated, minus his truncheon and his car. "That's great, that's just great," sighed Weeks. It wasn't a good start.

Disillusioned by U.S. efforts to prevent the looting, some Iraqis decided to take matters into their own hands. Saddam City, an impoverished, disaffected Shi'ite slum on the capital's northern edge, was awash with guns and a near no-go zone for U.S. forces. The area was quickly renamed Sadr City, after the country's most revered cleric who was killed by Saddam in 1999, and order was restored from within. Mosques organized volunteers to take on the looters, protect hospitals and businesses and even to direct traffic. Where security was lacking, the gap was filled by Shi'ite Islam, the sect that claimed the allegiance of 60 percent of Iraqis and whose leaders had called for an immediate withdrawal of U.S. forces. Hundreds of Islamic students descended on the capital from al-Hawza University in the Shi'ite holy city of Najaf, sent by their tutors to act as vigilantes. In the wealthy Mansour district, Sheikh Nadhum al-Baradeli, a prominent local businessman, marshaled more young men to collect garbage and to start repairing public buildings. "Why am I doing this? I am doing this because I am an Iraqi, to protect my family and my neighborhood," said Baradeli. "We don't need the Americans to help. We are Iraqis and we can look after ourselves."

National Pride

The strong sense of national pride felt by many Iraqis meant that the theft of archeological treasures from the Iraqi National Museum was one of the most painful blows to residents of postwar Baghdad, particularly to the city's large, educated middle class. Iraq sits on the land of ancient Mesopotamia, the "land between two rivers," home to prehistoric man and the cradle of civilization. On the banks of the Tigris and Euphrates, the Mesopotamians were the first people on earth to study the stars, enforce laws and develop a written language, cuneiform—marks incised on clay tablets. They built the first cities, and their trade routes reached east to the Indus Valley and west to the Mediterranean. The museum contained artifacts from the kingdoms of Sumer, Akkad, Assyria and Babylonia, priceless objects that bore witness to mankind's development. After the war, it seemed the worst had happened. Thousands of precious antiquities, which had survived wars and invasions by Cyrus of Persia, Alexander the Great and the Mongols, were gone.

Archeologists around the world said it was the most catastrophic theft of antiquities in modern times. Two cultural advisers to the Bush administration resigned to protest the U.S. military's failure to stop it from happening. Standing outside the museum less than a week after the city had fallen, Moayad Damerji, a professor of archeology at Baghdad University, was on the verge of tears, having inspected the damage inside the museum. "They were savage and furious in their deeds," he said of the looters. "They used iron bars and different kinds of tools to go through the doors. They went through every single room, every place. They took what they could and broke down the rest into pieces to show that they were here."

The looters used the cover of fighting between the U.S. army and Iraqi forces to break into the museum. On April 7, a tank battalion of the 3rd Infantry Division took control of an intersection less than 500 yards away. They tried to advance but met fierce resistance from Saddam's Fedayeen militia and members of the Republican Guard. As bullets, grenades and shells flew around the building, Donny George, the museum's research director, and two members of his staff remained inside, determined not to leave its treasures unattended. But when looters poured in through the back door, there was nothing they could do. In a remarkable act of courage, one of the staff members ran up to a U.S. tank to tell the soldiers what was happening inside, only to be told "it is not our responsibility." Lt. Col. Eric Schwartz, the battalion commander, said afterwards that his first priority had been to protect his men. "You can't just charge into a city straight to the museum. You have to secure the zone first, and we were taking some pretty heavy casualties," he told me. "There were 30 to 50 Fedayeen defending the compound. Once it was defended, it lost its protected status."

Museum officials could not disguise their fury with the U.S. military. The fact that Iraq's oil ministry but not one of the world's greatest archeological museums had survived the war intact made them question the Pentagon's motivations and priorities. "The question asked of American forces by everyone in Iraq is, 'Why did they protect the oil ministry and not this place?'" George said at a news conference under the frescoed dome of the museum's entrance hall, with Schwartz standing stony faced in the corner. As time went on, relations between the two sides grew more strained. The Marine Corps task force leading the hunt for the missing antiquities complained of a lack of cooperation by Iraqi officials, saying they had failed to provide an inventory of museum contents.

It became apparent that museum officials had been less than candid about the true extent of the plunder. It was true that the museum had been sacked and almost everything inside it stolen or destroyed. But the world was led to believe that this meant that the museum's entire collection, as many as 170,000 objects, was lost. In fact, this wasn't the case. In early June, museum workers led American investigators to secret vaults in Baghdad, some in the flooded depths of the gutted central bank, where they had hidden most of the museum's main collection in the months before the war. The only exhibited pieces that remained had been too fragile or too heavy to move. The Treasure of Nimrud, a set of gem-studded gold Assyrian jewelry, had been placed for safekeeping in the central bank before the 1991 Gulf War and had remained there even after the museum reopened in 2000. George called another news conference and told reporters that in all, 33 items from the main collection were missing, plus thousands of recently excavated items from the museum's storerooms.

The number was far smaller than initially feared. Amid their relief, some of the world's leading archeologists who had led the outcry after the war admitted they felt duped. It is not clear why senior museum staff appeared to make exaggerated claims. One explanation could be that they wanted to embarrass the Americans for what they saw as a callous disregard for Iraq's cultural heritage. Another is that they did not want to reveal that items were hidden in the city while security was still so precarious. In the end, it perhaps only served to distract attention from the priceless items that were really missing, including the 5,500-year-old marble face of a

Sumerian woman and the Akkadian bronze statue of Basitki from
2300 BC. The sacred Vase of Warka, an intricately carved Sumerian
piece from 3200 BC, was returned in the trunk of a car in pieces two
months after it was stolen.

A Scorched Shell

Cultural losses were not confined to the museum. A week after
the war ended, the National Library still smoldered from a fire that
reduced it to a scorched shell. Inside, the air was still warm and the
floor covered in flimsy pieces of black charred paper. Its prized
collection had included royal court records and thousands of
documents from the earliest Islamic periods, along with thousands of
books on Islamic law and practice. The Awqaf Library, attached to the
Ministry of Endowments and Religious Affairs, was also looted and
torched. Its losses included a rare collection of handwritten Korans,
religious manuscripts and calligraphy. At the Saddam Arts Center, I
found artist Moayad al-Haidari picking through lumps of plaster,
glass and discarded picture frames scattered on the floor, searching
for his paintings. "My work was here. Before the war my work was
here," he said, gazing at the empty white walls of the exhibition space
on the ground floor. "We painted our dreams, our ideas, our future.
It's a complete disaster." Upstairs, the works of the Iraqi Pioneers, a
group of early 20th century painters and sculptors who laid the
foundation for the modern Iraqi art movement, had also disappeared.
Haidari did not dwell on the thieves and vandals who had caused the
destruction. "Garbage people," he said. "Not educated people. Every
city has this scum." His anger was directed toward America, the
superpower with a short history and a consumer culture. "The
Americans used guns and tanks like it was a video game, a
PlayStation," he said. "Do they understand this? I respect their
civilization. But where is their feeling for this?"

On the streets, anger toward the U.S. occupation grew. Iraqis
warmed quickly to their newfound freedom to demonstrate and turned
out in the thousands each day to shout and chant in front of the
Palestine Hotel. New political parties sprang up within days, and
some long suppressed under Baath Party rule were revived. Islamic
groups, Kurdish parties, communists, monarchists, intellectuals and
jobless civil servants all jostled for their turn to wave banners and yell

at U.S. soldiers who stood unmoved behind a ring of razor wire. For the most part, the demands were the same: They wanted security, water, electricity, jobs and a new Iraqi government.

Restoring the city's essential services was proving to be a major headache. War damage and sabotage had left most of Baghdad without electricity, and as a consequence some districts had no water, as there was no power to run the pumps. The Americans appealed for help, calling engineers and utility managers for meetings at the Palestine. But their efforts were undermined by mistrust and misunderstanding. Some officials came to the meetings, others boycotted them, preferring instead to work with Mohammed Mohsen al-Zubaidi, an Iraqi exile who had returned home to declare himself mayor of Baghdad. Zubaidi, always in the same gray suit and silver tie, tried to increase his popularity by promising civil servants, unpaid for two months, their jobs back. He printed out application forms that were snatched up and completed outside his headquarters in the Sheraton Hotel. Zubaidi said he had the support of the Americans; the Americans said he did not. For two weeks, two administrations ran side by side, and little got done. Eventually, the Americans put an end to the confusion by arresting him.

As the power struggles went on, others got on with the job. The International Committee of the Red Cross had stayed in Baghdad throughout the war. They had the forethought to install generators at hospitals and water treatment plants. They repaired the bombed Qanat water station, which fed the north of the city, and began work on local electricity substations, working with Iraqi engineers with whom they had long-established contacts. UNICEF, the U.N. Children's Fund, had evacuated its foreign staff before the war, but its Iraqi workers, operating from a looted office, were sending tankers of water to areas without a main supply and organizing garbage collections, hoping to prevent epidemics as the temperatures soared toward summer. But they could not do everything alone. Iraqis awaited the arrival of Jay Garner, a blunt-talking retired U.S. general whose job was to oversee their country's reconstruction. He arrived on April 21, urged Iraqis to work with him and promised quick improvements in security and basic services. He said the core of an Iraqi government, selected by Iraqis, could be in place within weeks. But after an initial tour of the country, Garner disappeared from view. He was holed up in one of Saddam's palaces. Key Iraqi officials couldn't get access to him; most Iraqis never saw him and saw little improvement in their daily lives.

They sensed their country was rudderless, and Washington agreed. Within weeks, Garner was replaced.

It would have been easy to have mistaken anti-American sentiment for some kind of loyalty to Saddam Hussein. But almost universally, Iraqis hated Saddam. The U.S. occupation was a humiliating reminder that they had failed to get rid of Saddam themselves. To them, he seemed invincible, and they were ultimately disappointed by his weakness and betrayal. As they saw it, letting the Americans take over was the final blow Saddam dealt to his people. Most were convinced he was alive and in hiding, but as the days went by, they were more reassured that he wasn't coming back. Some began telling tentative jokes about Saddam and his playboy sons Uday and Qusay, words they would have not dared utter before, even among family and friends. Others had more serious things to say, finally unburdening themselves of the horror they had kept bottled up for years. They spoke of informants and fear, murdered brothers and cousins, night-time visits by the secret police. The hunt for the missing became an obsession. Saddam's palaces, the headquarters of the intelligence service, prisons and police stations were scoured for secret tunnels and underground cells. After years, sometimes decades, with no word from their loved ones, the tens of thousands of Iraqis with missing relatives still held out hope they would find them alive.

A Thousand Graves

The cemetery at Abu Ghraib revealed the grim reality. In a thousand graves, each marked with a number on a yellow metal plate, were the bodies of political prisoners executed at the jail nearby. Monday and Wednesday were execution days, said gravedigger Mohammed Alaa. "Most weeks they would come with bodies, sometimes one, sometimes 10," said the old man. "The security men would bring them, no one else was allowed to come near." Qassim al-Temimi wandered among the mounds of earth, clutching a piece of paper bearing the name of his nephew Abas and the date of his arrest in September 1982. "I don't know if anyone can help me. I wish someone could help me," he said. "We want to know, we want to find him." It took another week before the records were found that matched numbers to names, and grieving relatives began to exhume bodies with their own hands.

Abu Ghraib prison, Iraq's largest, was empty when I got there. The jailers had fled in the early days of the war, leaving inmates to go free. The metal doors of tiny, windowless cells lay open, watchtowers on the top of 30-foot walls deserted. Along the paved internal roads of the huge complex were portraits of Saddam, smiling, waving, holding a gun and receiving a kiss from a small girl. One road led to the gallows. Inside a dank, dark building, two trapdoors were cut into a metal platform with the executioner's lever between them. On the floor lay a discarded rope noose. Under the orders of U.S. troops, some of the jailers had started to return. A police colonel with gold-rimmed sunglasses pulled up in a Toyota Land Cruiser, reluctant to give his name or answer questions. "I worked here as a policeman, just a policeman, checking names and identities," he said. "What can I say? I feel sadness about the treatment of prisoners here. I was only following orders."

There were many more ordinary stories in Baghdad, of families whose lives were turned upside down by war. I met Yasim Abas Jabir outside the Red Cross. He, along with hundreds of others, had gone there in the hope that he would be able to use the phone to call relatives abroad, to let them know he was safe. Bombing raids had destroyed the city's telephone exchanges and all landlines were down. With no cellphone system, the only means of communication with the outside world was through Thurayas, small pocket-sized satellite phones owned by journalists, and a few sharp-thinking entrepreneurs who were charging $10 a minute for roadside calls. That was beyond the means of most Baghdadis, and every time we left the hotel we were besieged by people desperate to use our phones. Mostly we resisted, not just because of the expense but because of the near riots that broke out when we took out our Thurayas. But Yasim was charming and chatty, and I promised to call his nephew in Abu Dhabi when I got back to my room.

He was inordinately grateful. On several mornings I found him in the lobby of the Palestine, waiting to take me to visit his family. It was a busy time, and I kept having to put him off, but when he discovered I was about to leave Baghdad, he wouldn't take no for an answer. On my last night he picked me up in a taxi, and we went to his comfortable home in an eastern suburb. Yasim was a physiotherapist, and his wife Suhad was an engineer at the oil ministry. Their three teenage sons, Mohamed, Ahmed and Ali, spoke English and were mad about computers and Jennifer Lopez. Yasim told long, rambling stories about his time spent training in England, about his landlady in Manchester and how he had visited Prime Minister Harold Wilson at 10 Downing Street as part of a Palestinian lobby group. The boys smirked and rolled their eyes—they had heard the stories a thousand times. Suhad brought me cups of tea, English-style, and kept apologizing for the power cut that had struck just as I arrived, leaving us sitting in the pleasant glow of a gas lamp.

The boys should have been studying for their end-of-year examinations, but schools were closed and Mohamed's computer college had been stripped bare of all its equipment. They had a computer at home, but no phone lines meant no Internet. Under Saddam, access to the Internet was strictly controlled, but young Iraqis like them knew all the tricks to get around the restrictions. Their free time had been spent downloading the latest pop songs and Hollywood movies to share among their friends. Now they were bored. Suhad had gone back to work but had no idea when she would next get paid. Yasim said security was too bad for him to reopen his practice. Food prices had doubled in the market, and they were worried about how they would get by. "You have chosen the worst time to visit Baghdad," said Yasim. "Usually, it is really a very nice city."

Time ticked by. I knew I would have to leave at least half an hour before the 10 o'clock curfew, but there was no sign of us moving to the heavily laden table in the next room. Yasim saw my concern but waited for his wife to take the teacups to the kitchen. "She feels ashamed, because there is no light," he said. "She thinks it might come on again. She's waiting." It was my turn to feel ashamed, of how the war, even in small ways, had dented the pride of this kind and very ordinary family. I persuaded them we should eat and we dined in style by candlelight.

IRAQ'S TROUBLED MODERN HISTORY

July 16, 1979: Saddam Hussein takes power after President Ahmed Hassan al-Bakr resigns as chairman of Iraq's Revolutionary Command Council.

September 22-23, 1980: Following border skirmishes, Iraqi troops invade Iran. The war lasts eight years, killing hundreds of thousands of people on both sides.

March 16, 1988: Iraq attacks northern Kurdish town of Halabja, which had been seized by Iran. Tehran says Iraq used chemical weapons to punish inhabitants for not resisting. About 5,000 people are killed.

August 20, 1988: U.N.-sponsored cease-fire effectively ends Iran-Iraq war. Iraq keeps up attacks on Iraqi Kurds.

August 2, 1990: Iraq launches invasion of Kuwait, prompting U.N. Security Council to impose sanctions on Iraq.

January 17, 1991: U.S.-led forces start Gulf War with air attacks on Iraq and occupied Kuwait.

February 28, 1991: Hostilities end after 100-hour ground war in which U.S.-led coalition drives Iraqi forces from Kuwait. Revolts erupt in Kurdish north and mainly Shi'ite south.

March 1991: Republican Guards crush uprisings, prompting hundreds of thousands of Kurds to flee to Iran and Turkey.

April-May 1991: U.S., British and French troops create safe haven in north to protect returning refugees. Iraqi troops withdraw. Allied planes patrol "no-fly" zones.

April 1991: United Nations declares Gulf War cease-fire after Iraq accepts terms of Security Council resolution 687, which demands dismantling of Iraqi weapons of mass destruction and payment of war reparations from Iraqi oil revenue.

June 1991: U.N. arms inspectors begin work. Disputes over Iraq's compliance with U.N. demands for the scrapping of its chemical, biological, nuclear and ballistic arms programs lead to successive crises and keep sanctions in place for years.

May 20, 1996: Iraq accepts "oil-for-food" deal with United Nations, under which it is allowed to buy food and humanitarian goods with oil revenue under U.N. supervision.

December 16, 1998: U.N. inspectors withdraw from Baghdad a day after reporting that Iraq is not cooperating with their work.

December 17, 1998: United States and Britain launch four days of air strikes.

January 30, 2002: President Bush brands Iraq, along with Iran and North Korea, part of an "axis of evil" armed with weapons of mass destruction and supporting terrorism.

September 12, 2002: Bush urges United Nations to force Iraq to disarm.

November 8, 2002: Security Council unanimously approves resolution 1441, giving Iraq a last chance to scrap its weapons of mass destruction or face "serious consequences."

November 13, 2002: Iraq accepts resolution 1441 unconditionally.

November 27, 2002: U.N. inspectors resume work after four-year break.

March 17, 2003: United States, Britain and Spain abandon efforts to get international endorsement for war against Saddam. Bush later gives him 48 hours to leave the country.

March 20, 2003: United States launches war against Iraq with selective strikes on Baghdad targeting "very senior" leadership.

April 9, 2003: U.S. forces sweep into the heart of Baghdad to an ecstatic welcome as Saddam Hussein's 24-year rule crumbles into chaos and looting.

May 1, 2003: Bush says the major fighting in Iraq is over.

May 6, 2003: Bush names former State Department counter-terrorism chief L. Paul Bremer as the top civil administrator for Iraq, supplanting Jay Garner.

May 11, 2003: The U.S. commander of coalition forces in Iraq tells Iraqis that Saddam Hussein's Baath Party is dissolved and asks them to surrender all of the group's possessions.

July 13, 2003: A 25-member U.S.-backed Iraqi Governing Council holds its inaugural meeting in Baghdad.

July 22, 2003: U.S. military confirms that Saddam's two sons, Uday and Qusay, were killed in gunbattle in Mosul.

August 19, 2003: A Massive truck bomb devastates U.N. headquarters in Baghdad, in the worst attack on a U.N. civilian complex in the U.N.'s history. Twenty-two people are killed including Sergio Vieira de Mello, the top U.N. envoy to Iraq.

August 29, 2003: A car bomb kills at least 83 people, including top Shi'ite Muslim leader Ayatollah Mohammed Baqer al-Hakim, and wounds some 175, at the Imam Ali mosque in Najaf.

GLOSSARY

A-10 Thunderbolt	Highly maneuverable U.S. plane designed to support ground forces; nicknamed "tank buster" or "warthog."
AAV	Amphibious assault vehicle.
AK-47	Soviet-designed assault rifle.
Al Arabiya	Arabic satellite television channel.
Al Jazeera	Arabic satellite television channel.
APC	Armored personnel carrier.
Arty	Military slang for artillery.
AV-8B Harrier	British-designed jump jet developed in the 1960s. Its ability to take off vertically like a helicopter still makes it unique among warplanes.
AWACS	U.S. Airborne Warning and Control System aircraft.
Beans and Bullets	U.S. military slang for supplies.
Black Hawk	UH-60 main U.S. utility troop and cargo helicopter.
Bradley fighting vehicle	U.S. Army's primary armored fighting vehicle.
C-130 Hercules	Most widely used light transport aircraft in the world.
Cobra	Assault helicopter.
Dismounts	U.S. military slang for armed soldiers on foot.
Embedded journalists	Officially assigned to military units.
F-16	Workhorse of the world fighter fleet, versatile and agile multirole fighter.
Fedayeen	Iraqi paramilitary group known as the Saddam Fedayeen, or men of sacrifice. Founded in 1995, the Fedayeen were recruited from areas loyal to Saddam.
Global Hawk	Unmanned aerial vehicle used to monitor situation on ground and relay enemy positions.
GPS	Global Positioning System.

GROM (Thunder)	Polish elite commando unit.
Grunts	U.S. military slang for infantry/Marines.
Heavy Metal Warriors	Combat engineers.
Hogs	U.S. military slang for AAVs.
Huey	Bell UH-1 combat helicopter gunship.
Humvee	U.S. military vehicle.
JDAM	Joint Direct Attack Munition.
Kaffiyeh	Traditional Arab headdress.
Kevlar	Protective material used in helmets and other protective gear.
Kiowa	Reconnaissance helicopters.
Lion of Babylon	Iraq's homegrown version of the old Soviet T-72 tank.
M-16	Standard U.S. rifle.
M1-A2 ABRAMS	U.S. Army's most advanced battle tank.
MA	Mortuary Affairs.
MEU	Marine Expeditionary Unit.
MK-19	40 mm grenade launcher.
MOPP	Mission-Oriented Protective Posture. MOPP1, MOPP2, MOPP3 and MOPP4 are the four levels of protection needed in case of attack by weapons of mass destruction.
MOUT	Military Operations in Urban Terrain.
MRE	Meals, Ready to Eat.
Mujahideen-e-Khalq	Iranian opposition movement listed by the United States and the European Union as a terrorist organization.
Mukhabarat	Iraqi intelligence service.
NBC	Nuclear, Biological and Chemical protection suits.
Predator	Unmanned aerial vehicle, sometimes equipped with missiles but used to collect intelligence.
PUK	Patriotic Union of Kurdistan.
Remains pouches	Black, zip-up body bags.
Republican Guard	Iraq's elite troops.
RPG	Rocket-propelled grenade.

Sabot rounds	Uranium-tipped tank shells fired from the U.S. Abrams tank.
Sagger	Iraqi missile fired from Soviet-designed antitank weapons.
SAW	Squad Automatic Weapon.
Scud	Iraqi missile.
Sea Knight	CH-46 "Sea Knight" helicopter used by the Marine Corps for all-weather day-or-night transport of troops.
SEALs	Sea, Air, Land elite force.
Slimed	U.S. military slang for being under chemical attack.
Thuraya	Satellite telephone.
UNICEF	The United Nations Children's Fund.
Unilaterals	Independent teams of journalists in the field, as opposed to embedded journalists with military units.
WMD	Weapons of mass destruction.

WRITERS

Luke Baker

Luke Baker was born in 1972 and was educated in Britain and the United States. He joined Reuters as a correspondent in South Africa in 1998, from where he helped cover the country's second post-apartheid elections, civil war in Angola, flooding in Mozambique and stories from Gabon to Malawi. He was posted to Rome as a correspondent in July 2000. During the war in Iraq, he was embedded with combat engineering units of the 3rd Infantry Division.

John Chalmers

John Chalmers reported on the war from U.S. Central Command's forward headquarters at Doha, Qatar. He is a senior correspondent in Brussels covering NATO and European security and foreign policy. He was previously chief correspondent in India, where he reported on the Kargil conflict in Kashmir, the devastating earthquake in Gujarat and a giant Hindu pilgrimage on the banks of the Ganges. As a correspondent in Hanoi, he chronicled the hesitant opening up of one of the last bastions of communism and, elsewhere in the region, reported on the financial meltdown of Southeast Asia's tiger economies and the Taiwan Straits crisis.

Mike Collett-White

Mike Collett-White has been with Reuters for eight years. He worked in London before going to Moscow for two years and then to Central Asia, where he was senior correspondent for two more years. After a stint back in London, he is now deputy bureau chief of Pakistan and Afghanistan. He has worked in Kosovo and Macedonia, and in 2001 was on the front lines with the Northern Alliance during the war to topple the Taliban in Afghanistan. He was in northern Iraq for nearly two months during the 2003 war, where he covered the fall of Kirkuk and of Tikrit, the last bastion of Saddam Hussein's regime to fall.

Adrian Croft

Adrian Croft is Reuters deputy bureau chief, Iberia, based in Madrid. A Reuters reporter since 1982, Croft reported on the end of apartheid in South Africa from 1985 to 1989 before moving to Nicaragua, where he covered the Sandinistas' 1990 election defeat. From 1990 to 1992, he wrote about the drug war in Colombia before moving to San Francisco, where he covered the Oklahoma City bombing. He reported from Panama following the 1989 U.S. invasion and from Kuwait and southern Iraq after the 1991 Gulf War. From 1997 to 2002 he was based in Brussels. In March and April 2003, Croft traveled with the 15th U.S. Marine Expeditionary Unit as it captured the Iraqi port of Umm Qasr and later tightened the U.S. grip on the southern city of Nassiriya.

Caroline Drees

Caroline Drees is Reuters bureau chief for Egypt and Sudan, and has been based in Cairo for the past three years. A U.S. citizen, she has worked for Reuters since 1994, covering political and economic news throughout the Arab world and Israel as well as in several European and African countries. Since Sept. 11, she has written extensively on Islam, militant violence and Arab responses to the aftermath of the attacks, including the challenge of political reform.

David Fox

David Fox joined Reuters in 1990 and has covered conflict in Africa, Asia, the Middle East and Europe. He was bureau chief in East Africa—reporting on war in Somalia, Ethiopia, Eritrea, Sudan, Rwanda, Burundi and the Democratic Republic of Congo, formerly Zaire. Since then he has covered stories in Afghanistan, Pakistan and Iraq. Fox crossed into Iraq as coalition forces invaded and was one of the first independent reporters into Basra and Baghdad.

Michael Georgy

Michael Georgy, an Egyptian American, joined Reuters in 1995. Since moving to the Arab world from the United States in 1991, he has reported from Egypt, Sudan, Saudi Arabia, Kuwait, Lebanon, Israel and Iraq. Georgy covered Iraq several times while Saddam Hussein was still in power but never traveled to the south before the war.

Andrew Gray

Andrew Gray is Reuters' Chief Correspondent for the Balkans. He joined the company in 1994 as a graduate trainee and worked in London, Bonn and Geneva before spending a year reporting from Kosovo after the end of the war there. He has been based in Belgrade since October 2000. In the Iraq war he traveled from the Kuwaiti desert to Baghdad with a tank unit, the 2nd battalion, 70th armored regiment of the U.S. Army.

Matthew Green

Green joined Reuters as a graduate trainee in September 1998, spending a year in London, 18 months in Paris and then moved to Nairobi in April 2001. Green was embedded with the Marines during the Iraq conflict. He returned to Kuwait on May 1.

Christine Hauser

Christine Hauser has worked for Reuters since 1992 throughout the Middle East and in Chad, Sudan and Afghanistan. She has covered the Israeli-Palestinian conflict since 1999, based in Jerusalem. She reported for UPI during the 1991 Gulf War and in April 2003 wrote stories from the major cities south of Baghdad as well as in the Iraqi capital itself. She has a Master's Degree in Middle Eastern languages and cultures from Columbia University.

Saul Hudson

Saul Hudson, who started with Reuters in 1996, has reported from across Latin America on guerrilla wars, natural disasters and political crises. He worked in Washington for the last three years and covered the 2000 presidential election, the Sept. 11 attacks and the buildup to the Iraq war. Acting as a unilateral, he spent a month inside Iraq reporting on postwar politics emerging around the country and on the hardships for residents in the chaotic capital. He wrote a series of reports from the northeast of Iraq on Iranian rebels.

Nadim Ladki

Nadim Ladki joined Reuters in Beirut in 1989, where he covered the end of the Lebanese civil war and the Western hostage crisis. He moved to the Middle East and Africa desk in Nicosia in 1994 before moving to London to work on the World Desk and Energy reporting unit. Ladki went on reporting trips to Algeria, Lebanon, Saudi Arabia, Syria and Iraq, where he covered the 1998 U.S. and British bombing campaign. In 1999 Ladki became Amman bureau chief with responsibility for Iraq. He spent most of his time since August 2002 in Baghdad. He ran the Reuters operation during the war in the Iraqi capital until he was expelled three days before the fall of Saddam Hussein.

Sean Maguire

Sean Maguire watched the first missiles strike Baghdad during the Desert Storm campaign in 1991 and 12 years later accompanied the U.S. Marines on their advance into Iraq. He was embedded with an infantry unit that was one of the first to reach the Iraqi capital. Maguire, who joined Reuters in 1990, has spent much of his career in Eastern Europe, reporting on the bloody collapse of former Yugoslavia and the economic and political development of former communist states. He is currently based in Warsaw, Poland.

Samia Nakhoul

Nakhoul joined Reuters in Beirut in 1987. She covered the Lebanese civil war, hijackings, the Western hostage crisis, political assassinations, Israeli incursions and the Gulf War in 1991. In her four-year posting in Egypt, she covered the Islamist insurgency and the land-mark Palestinian-Israeli peace talks. She was bureau chief for Lebanon and Syria and is currently bureau chief, Gulf. She was in Baghdad reporting the Iraqi side of the war.

Rosalind Russell

Ros Russell has worked as a correspondent with Reuters for seven years with postings in East Africa, the former Soviet Union and New York. She covered the U.S.-led war in Afghanistan and the fall of Kabul in November 2001. She reported on the Iraq war as a unilateral, cross-ing the border from Kuwait with a Reuters multimedia team. She covered the fall of Umm Qasr and Basra before heading to Baghdad to report on the aftermath of the war.

Other Contributors

David Cutler

Cutler is senior researcher at Reuters Editorial Reference Unit in London. Born in Glasgow, Cutler started his career at London's Imperial War Museum. He later joined the BBC and then, in 1987, Reuters. Cutler now leads the unit that provides research and infor-mation for Reuters journalists around the world.

Faleh Kheiber

Kheiber is Reuters chief photographer in Iraq. During the Iraq conflict, Kheiber was based in Baghdad.

Jason Pickersgill

Pickersgill qualified in newspaper design and information graphics at Newcastle College and has worked with Reuters as a freelancer since 2001. He has worked for Britain's *Independent* and *Observer* newspapers, as well as the BBC.

Oleg Popov

Popov has been a photographer for the Bulgarian Telegraph Agency and Bulgarian newspapers and magazines. He began working for Reuters in 1990 and has covered wars in the Balkans and Chechnya as well as Iraq. During this latest conflict, he was embedded with U.S. Marines.

Damir Sagolj

Sagolj was born in Sarajevo in 1971 and worked with the Paris-based Sipa press agency for several years before joining Reuters as a photographer based in Bosnia. Sagolj was embedded with U.S. Marines.

Goran Tomasevic

Tomasevic started working for Reuters as a freelance photographer in 1996 and cites covering the conflict in Kosovo as one of his greatest professional challenges. During the Iraq conflict, Tomasevic was with the Reuters team in Baghdad.

Mike Tyler

Tyler, a freelancer for Reuters News Graphics in London since 1997, studied graphic design at John Moores University, Liverpool, and worked on a range of corporate identity projects before establishing Mapstyle, a custom map design service, in 1994.